Lenses on Blindness

ALSO BY SHARON PACKER, M.D.,
AND FROM MCFARLAND

Welcome to Arkham Asylum: Essays on Psychiatry and the Gotham City Institution (edited by Sharon Packer, M.D., and Daniel R. Fredrick, 2020)

Neuroscience in Science Fiction Films (2015)

Cinema's Sinister Psychiatrists: From Caligari to Hannibal (2012)

Lenses on Blindness
Essays on Vision Loss in Media, Culture, Religion and Experience

Edited by SHARON PACKER, M.D.

McFarland & Company, Inc., Publishers
Jefferson, North Carolina

ISBN (print) 978-1-4766-8230-3
ISBN (ebook) 978-1-4766-4731-9

Library of Congress and British Library
cataloguing data are available

Library of Congress Control Number 2022059888

© 2023 Sharon Packer. All rights reserved

No part of this book may be reproduced or transmitted in any form or by any means, electronic or mechanical, including photocopying or recording, or by any information storage and retrieval system, without permission in writing from the publisher.

On the cover: Denzel Washington in
The Book of Eli, 2010 (Warner Bros./Photofest)

Printed in the United States of America

*McFarland & Company, Inc., Publishers
Box 611, Jefferson, North Carolina 28640
www.mcfarlandpub.com*

In honor of Jim Carlson, whose unwavering assistance with our technological challenges has continued, even when faced with his own vision challenges.

Table of Contents

Preface
    SHARON PACKER   1

Introduction
    SHARON PACKER   5

Sound Over Sight: Depicting Blindness in Horror Films
(From a Sound Specialist's Perspective)
    JEFFREY BULLINS   33

A Blind Boyhood: Reflections by a Poetry Professor
    REJA-E BUSAILAH   44

Blindness in Science Fiction: From Mary Shelley's *Frankenstein*
to *Star Trek*'s La Forge—and Much More
    JASON W. ELLIS   55

Looking at the Unseeing: Blindness in the History of Art
    CARLOS ESPÍ FORCÉN   66

Visual Loss in Cinema: A Psychiatrist's Viewpoint
    FERNANDO ESPÍ FORCÉN   74

Unsighted Superheroes: Insights from Comics, Films and TV
    JAQ GREENSPON   83

Pastoral Counseling and Impending Blindness: Vision Loss
and a Quest for Meaning
    CURTIS W. HART   93

Blinded on the Battlefield: True Superhero Stories
of Mikhail Margolin and Al Schmid
    GEORGE HIGHAM   98

Blindness in the Jewish Tradition: From Written Text
  to Oral Law to Contemporary Medical Practice
    Jerome M. Karp *and* Howard L. Forman   111

Native Stories About Vision and Impairment: Western
  Medicine Meets Aboriginal Mythos
    Andrew J. McLean   119

Blind African American Musicians: Insights
  from a Social Psychiatrist
    H. Steven Moffic   130

Idioms and Ideas: Meanings and Metaphors
    Sharon Packer   144

Through the Eye(s) of Tiresias: From Thebes and Beyond
    Caleb Puckett   154

"Close your eyes and see": Blindness and Literature
    Eric Sandberg   161

Blindness as Holocaust Metaphor: Elie Wiesel's
  A Beggar in Jerusalem and *The Forgotten*
    Eric J. Sterling   168

In Darkness and Light: The Meanings of Blindness in the West
    Brenda S. Gardenour Walter   179

Out of Sight: Body and Building from Medical Architecture
  to Post-Modern Haptic Space
    Brenda S. Gardenour Walter   188

Filmography   199
Bibliography   201
About the Contributors   205
Index   209

Preface

SHARON PACKER

Some projects steam ahead, pushing forcefully toward a singular destination, as if on a superhighway, undistracted by sights and sounds of the surrounding landscape—if only because that alluring landscape that lies outside of paved roads and yellow lines is out of sight. Yet sometimes that straightforward path is blocked, and detours are necessary—and that roundabout route actually augments the itinerary in unintended and unexpected ways.

As a result, those projects travel down a winding path, akin to a country road that winds around and around and moves up and down, as hills and valleys punctuate unpaved paths. During that journey, we find ourselves admiring wildflowers, growing naturally, unplanted by human hands. Sometimes we pick a few of those blooms. We traverse rickety bridges and cross small streams, discovering unexpected sights and smells that would have gone unappreciated had we stayed on the express lanes, stopping only occasionally and grabbing snacks at fast food franchises housed in expansive look-alike buildings that are indistinguishable, one from the next. When a tire blows out, or is punctured by jagged stone roads, we do not necessarily welcome the delay, yet we are not surprised and are willing to find replacements. Eventually, we reach our intended destination, having accrued small town trinkets and freshly farmed fruits from roadside stands that are so different from standardized products sold at state highway rest stops.

Which approach sounds more interesting? Hopefully, you will agree with me and concur that the country road is more appealing than the more straightforward superhighway—because that is how we accrued essays for this collection about visual loss. Rather than producing a text about psychiatric medicine, as originally intended, this book veered in a direction that is better categorized as "medical humanities." Because we collected so many unique and intriguing essays on topics that are far afield from clinical practice, we saved the original academic medical articles for a different collection.

We focused instead on articles from artists and academicians from far flung fields, each of whom sees visual loss through a different lens. In the introduction that follows, we explain this approach and its evolution in greater detail.

For now, let me backtrack a bit, to thank Dr. Michael Asher for his early enthusiasm and for co-chairing a workshop presented to the American Psychiatric Association, titled "Finding Light in the Darkness: Treating Patients with Visual Loss." Of course, I must acknowledge the American Psychiatric Association itself for hosting such a workshop, as well as the attendees, who added their own insights during the discussion that followed. I also owe a debt to *Psychiatric Times* for publishing excerpts from that original workshop and to *Psychiatric Times* and to its current editor, Heidi Anne Duerr M.P.H., for permitting publication of redacted or expanded versions of those articles in this essay collection. I am also grateful to the unnamed visually challenged patients whom I have treated, and whose accomplishments have served as sources of inspiration in more ways than one.

I must also thank George Higham profusely for his extra efforts in proofing this manuscript. Tanya Busailah deserves credit for carrying the torch in spite of her grief after losing her late husband, Professor Reja-e Busailah, before this book made it to print. The information she forwarded about her husband's tips to enhance anyone's sensory perceptions, blind or sighted, was as unexpected as it was enlightening. Laurie Martin, then Digital Editor of *Psychiatric Times*, deserves special mention. Her encouraging (written) words rang loud and clear when she wrote that she was especially interested in this topic because of her own sister's lifelong experiences with hearing loss. Her essay on this topic was especially educational.

At the time, I naively assumed that the deaf community received more targeted attention from health care professionals than the visually challenged persons on whom we focused. After all, the renowned writer and neurologist Oliver Sacks himself championed the deaf community. Dr. Sacks wrote extensively about their condition and their culture, devoting an entire book to the topic of neurology, audiology, language and learning: *Seeing Voices: A Journey into the World of the Deaf* (1989). A much later book about *Musicophilia: Tales of Music and the Brain* (2007) took the opposite approach, and focused on auditory perceptions, real or unreal. Another short story by Dr. Sacks turned into a film: *At First Sight* (1999). A best-selling author as well as a practicing physician, his books inspired other movies such as *Awakenings* (1990), which starred Robin Williams and Robert De Niro. That film increased his visibility in American pop culture and expanded his allure well beyond his many admirers in the literary world. (Dr. Sacks' eloquent essay collections, esteemed for his story-telling abilities and for his impressive wordsmithing, typically attracted far more readers outside of mainstream medicine, although his medical source material has not been called into question by physicians.)

There were other reasons for my apparently inaccurate assumptions about resources for hearing-impaired patients—as compared to those who are visually-impaired. For one thing, I had met sign interpreters meandering around hospital premises, which to me meant that such interpreters were available when and where they were needed. Sign interpreters are visible on many television programs, and one very animated interpreter attracted a cult following. Sign interpreters are also mandated by law for job interviews and in hotels. Adding ammunition to that argument, articles comparing ASL (American Sign Language) to other forms of non-aural/non-oral communication appeared in leading newspapers. Heated debates about the advantages or disadvantages of these various signing modalities made news in mainstream media, leading me to believe that these issues were on everyone's radar.

Moreover, the deaf community had a university, Gallaudet, exclusively devoted to educating hearing impaired persons. In addition to offering a standard range of college classes, Gallaudet presumably provided camaraderie on that campus and set the stage for self-sufficiency and self-respect among deaf students—or did it? Some disagreed. In 1988, when yet another non-hearing-impaired person was appointed president of this unique university, the students struck. They publicly expressed their dismay that one of their own was once again displaced by someone who did not share their life experiences and never faced the same medical or social challenges. The public took note and the university reacted. The newly appointed non-hearing challenged president stepped aside in response to the outcry. The *New York Times* chronicled the events that followed the protests, once again encouraging readers to believe that the deaf community could care for its own, and that it had found its own "voice" via those demonstrations ("Gallaudet University Installs Deaf President," October 23, 1988, 45).

Laurie Martin's essay about her hearing-impaired sister's experiences with the "medical establishment" made me aware of the parallels with the experiences of "Fred," the visually impaired patient whose near miss via a medication error inspired our initial project. It is to my regret that we cannot publish that essay in this collection, but it is my hope that her experiences will make it to print in another collection devoted to that important topic.

For now, it is my hope that these essays will encourage more medical/psychiatric progress in these directions. It may also become clear why this essay collection veered in the direction of medical humanities, with essays expressing many different perspectives, and why it strayed from the path of a pure medical or psychiatric textbook compiled exclusively from medical journals, as it was originally intended.

Introduction

SHARON PACKER

The Oedipus myth about an errant king's self-inflicted blindness was once central to psychiatry, back in the days when Freudian psychoanalysis reigned supreme. One could not speak about psychiatry, much less study psychiatry, without recollecting Oedipus' vision loss, and the events that propelled it, and the even worse events that followed. Suicide, murder, and incest add to the tragedy, augmenting Oedipus' auto-enucleation, as if that were not enough.

The Oedipus tale and psychoanalytic psychiatry were so interconnected that the (supposedly) conservative and controversial cultural critic Allen Bloom addressed this issue in his best-selling book about *The Closing of the American Mind: How Higher Education Has Failed Democracy and Impoverished the Souls of Today's Students* (1987).

The late professor lambasted American education and lamented that Americans knew next-to-nothing nothing about the classics (his own academic specialty) and largely learned about Sophocles through Freudian filters only. Were it not for the fame of the Freudian Oedipus Complex, and presumably the American infatuation with Freud, American students might not know of Greek theater or Greek philosophy, which were once emblematic of a liberal education.

Psychiatry has evolved dramatically since mid-century, when Freudianism was at its peak, and when psychodynamic explanations for behavior revolved around so-called "family romances," and their psychosexual connotations, whether they be on the surface, as in *Oedipus Rex,* or more subtly implied. For the last few decades, psychoanalysis has been supplanted by evidence-based medicine. Biological approaches to behavior have become the norm.[1] By the mid–1980s, psychiatrists were not enrolling in American psychoanalytic institutions as they once did, and psychologists and social workers were filling vacancies that had previously been restricted to psychiatrists only (at least in the U.S., but not in Europe, where the tradition of non-medically trained "lay analysts" persisted long after Freud perished).

At a time when medical treatments of mental illness command center stage and when the medical model has supplanted the previously predominant metapsychology that prevailed until the last decade or two of the 20th century (and that remained in place even longer in psychoanalytic training bastions), one might expect that a medical condition—such as vision loss—would merit more attention. Yet 21st-century psychiatry in general has been strangely silent on this subject, perhaps because generalists expect persons suffering from vision loss to seek treatment from practitioners who subspecialize in this domain, or who are employed by specialty clinics. Or perhaps the very phenomenon of vision loss frightens off too many practitioners, just as it frightens the general public.

Mythology aside, vision loss is obviously essential to those who endure it, and to their families, and to all varieties of eye specialists, be they ophthalmologists, optometrists, opticians, or visual rehabilitation specialists. One could not practice family or internal medicine or emergency medicine, much less neurology, endocrinology, or infectious disease, without awareness of potential vision loss, its causes and its cures. This issue is also secondarily important to psychiatrists, psychologists and other mental health professionals, because visually impaired people have twice the rate of depression as the general population, making mental health consultation more likely. Moreover, several commonly used psychotropic medications carry risks for vision-impairing side effects, putting more persons at risk.

Historically, infectious causes of blindness have had important public health implications. Trachoma remains the most common infectious cause of blindness worldwide, followed by onchocerciasis (river blindness). Although the World Health Organization (WHO) has long been concerned with these conditions, which remain endemic in impoverished rural enclaves of several continents, the Bill and Melinda Gates Foundation also turned their attention to their elimination. Public recognition of these conditions and their routes of transmission increased in turn. As Dr. McLean relates in his essay on Native stories, at the turn of the 20th century, up to one fourth of all Native Americans had the so-called "Indian Sore Eyes," which was due to trachoma.

Infectious causes of eye disease, and the risk of blindness, were once the concern of American immigration officials as well, who sought to protect public health by examining the eyes of itinerant immigrants before permitting their entry at Ellis Island. Great waves of immigrants arrived around the same time as the prevalence of "Indian Sore Eyes" peaked.

Sholem Aleichem (1859–1916), the acclaimed Russian-born Yiddish storyteller whose American fame skyrocketed through the *Fiddler on the*

Roof stage and screen adaptation of his stories, highlights immigrants' fears of such dreaded diseases, and their equally important fears of being refused entry at "Castle Garden." Speaking through his youthful protagonist, Motl, Sholem Aleichem captures the trepidations of aspiring Americans (read, Eastern European Jewish émigrés) through dialogues between the childish Motl, the orphaned cantor's son, with his brash older brother Eliyah, and their weeping widowed mother. Mother's eyes are incessantly red from crying. She wipes them constantly, just as she has done since the start of the story, even before her bedridden husband with a hacking cough succumbed to an unnamed illness.

Young Motl recounts rumors about mass inspections of naked immigrants at Ellis Island. The older son, in turn, chastises the tearful mother, warning her that immigration officials may turn away their entire entourage from those coveted American ports, once they see her swollen eyelids and mistake them for communicable eye diseases.[2]

While Sholem Aleichem's accounts about the travails of immigrants' health inspections may be dated, and young Motl's reports about public disrobing may have been hyperbolic, concerns about blindness are not relics of the past. Rather, realistic concerns about vision loss are ever-present, and are not limited to out-of-the-way locales or other continents, as addressed by the Gates Foundation or WHO. However, the main causes of vision loss have changed over time.

This subject will soon become relevant to more people, both in the U.S. and abroad. Right now, 285+ million people worldwide have significant vision loss. Worldwide, 2.2 billion people have near or distance vision impairment, but almost half—or one billion—of such cases could have been prevented, as per WHO data from February 26, 2021. In America, those numbers are expected to explode as our population ages and as escalating obesity puts more people at risk of diabetes (DM), which is one of the four leading causes of blindness. We can speculate about the potential contribution of specific psychotropic meds to this impending diabetes epidemic and the visual sequela of diabetes, but right now we can only speculate. However, the data linking diabetes to common contributors to vision loss is definitive.

Far more people are affected by vision loss than meets the eye (if you will forgive the pun). We typically associate white canes or seeing eye dogs with blindness and may expect to identify any visually impaired person through these aids. When we do not see many white canes on the street or see even fewer dogs with their characteristic leather harness, we may incorrectly infer that the prevalence of vision impairment is far less than it actually is. Why? Because only 35 percent—roughly a third—of visually impaired persons use canes, and only 3 percent of legally blind persons have dogs. Our usual signifiers do not signify very much about the prevalence at all.

These issues concerning vision loss carry extra importance for the psychiatric community, since persons treated with "second generation" or "atypical" antipsychotic medications face extra risk for diabetes as well. Yet so-called antipsychotic meds are not reserved for persons with psychosis. They are commonly prescribed as adjunctive treatments for depression and are among the most profitable medications on the market. More recently, data confirming an association between cataracts and treatment with SGAs (second generation antipsychotics) was released. Previously, studies confirmed associations between cataracts and quetiapine in beagles only. In the distant past, when the anti-psychotic medication, thioridazine (Mellaril), was commonly used, persons with hereditary predispositions to retinitis pigmentosa developed visual loss when treated with doses above 800 mg per day. So this previously popular medication fell out of favor, so much so that most younger psychiatrists have never prescribed it and are often unaware that this particular adverse effect is not universal but is dose related.

We can identify subpopulations that face extra risk of vision loss, for whatever reasons, but we cannot lose sight of the risks faced by "average" persons, especially older persons. Worldwide, 82 percent of persons with vision loss are over age 50. About a third of Americans over 65 have some sort of vision impairment. Southerners as well as African Americans have even greater risks for vision loss. Sometimes, especially talented persons have turned this disability into an "ability" and have produced memorable music, and achieved worldwide fame, as psychiatrist Steve Moffic, M.D., describes in his discussions of Stevie Wonder or Ray Charles or the Blind Boys of Alabama or Mississippi. Alternatively, one of the most recognizable SF characters of all times—Lieutenant-Commander Geordi La Forge of *Star Trek*—is portrayed as African American, possibly intentionally referencing the disproportionate impact of blindness on the Black American population, as proposed by science fiction expert Jason Ellis. In his essay, Professor Ellis cites extra examples of vision-impaired SF persons of color.

Aboriginal populations worldwide also have higher prevalence of vision loss, although some have invented ingenious ways to offset snow-blindness experienced in their Northern habitats, as illustrated in the essay by Andrew McLean, M.D., M.P.H. How and why this interfaces with "vision quests" pursued by some Amerindians is also addressed in his essay.

From Medical Text to Medical Humanities Essays

By now, it may be self-evident to readers that this book project began as a medical project, with a special focus on psychiatric interfaces with vision loss. (More details appear in the preface.) And, indeed, this essay collection evolved from a workshop conducted for the American Psychiatric Association, which itself was inspired by two particular patients (whose identities have been disguised in this text, for confidentiality's sake). The project itself, and the thrust of the book, underwent many gyrations since its start, having moved from being a specialized "medical" text, directed toward medical audiences, before expanding into collection of essays on medical humanities, with some chapters by psychiatrists, and even more essays by academicians and artists of different bents. More medically oriented essays appear in the appendix.

To explain how this book took shape, and how it evolved from a workshop on "Finding Light in the Darkness: Treating Patients with Visual Loss," let me "introduce" you to "Fred," whose abridged life story first appeared in *Psychiatric Times* and was a lead presentation at the annual American Psychiatric Association conference. "Fred's" history is semi-fictionalized to obscure his identity, in keeping with standards of practice. It was "Fred" who unofficially and unwittingly launched this study and the essay collection that follows.

Fred's Story[3]

There are good cases, there are great cases, and there are "there for the grace of G-d go I" cases. Our workshop on treating patients with visual impairments was inspired by one of those "there for the grace of G-d" cases that revolved around a youngish man whom we call "Fred."

Fred was a 30-something-year-old man who was slowly but surely losing his vision to an uncommon variant of retinitis pigmentosa. His symptoms began with night blindness. His family had found him stumbling around the hallway late at night, when all the lights were out. In hindsight, it became apparent that this was an early sign of what was to follow. Definitive diagnosis was delayed for decades. His family was in turmoil because one side blamed the other for their "bad genes"—even though half of such cases occur spontaneously, without any identifiable genetic transmission. When not pointing accusatory fingers at other relatives, everyone in the clan blamed the patient for his "eccentricities"—which extended far beyond his vision problems. They banded together, and achieved an otherwise unattainable sense of social cohesion, by ostracizing Fred and casting him as "the other." Not surprisingly, Fred sought psychiatric treatment, not so much for his visual difficulties, but because of the scars incurred by such family strife.

Schoolteachers had noticed that something amiss with Fred from the start, but for other reasons. They shared their concerns with the family in private meetings and at parents' night, but Fred's father refused to believe that his son had both Autism Spectrum Disorder (ASD) and ADHD (which sometimes go hand-in-hand). As far as the father was concerned, Fred simply did not try hard. Fred's serious vision problem was still brewing and had not yet begun in grade school, although he did break a metatarsal a few years later, after he tripped in a stairwell as the sun was setting on an already a dark winter day.

A one-time military man who expected everyone—his son included—to march in place and to follow the same stride, his father made it clear that he disapproved of white canes and Braille, because they "made men look weak." He sneered at the innovations introduced at the VA. Luckily, Fred was already literate before his vision symptoms worsened and interfered with his ability to read. So he never learned Braille, which had been the key to literacy for the visually impaired, before talking books and internet-based artificial intelligence (AI) dramatically increased sightless access to the written word.

Fred's family life was never easy, not even as he grew older, and his life in general might have been easier had his household shown more support, of both his education and his treatment. While vision-impaired people overall have twice the rate of depression as the general population, family support mitigates that risk. Statistics show that strong family support can be as effective at offsetting depression as professional psychotherapeutic interventions. Unfortunately, Fred did not have a supportive family.

That aside, in a strange way, Fred's Asperger traits made it easier to cope with his progressive visual deficits. He loved dinosaurs, even as an adult, and was thrilled to land a job at the local science museum, while he could still see somewhat. He felt fortunate that he was a full-time paid employee (albeit a poorly paid one), and hoped to avoid becoming a part-time volunteer, as were many of the people he encountered at his programs for the visually impaired. He knew that only half of legally blind Americans were gainfully-employed and he appreciated being part of that "lucky" half. He felt especially grateful that he received a discount at the adjacent planetarium store, where he bought a transportable toy telescope that helped him see better. Carrying the tiny telescope around added to his "eccentricities," but at least it was not a white cane that his father disdained.

Over time, Fred was promoted to a permanent position in the gift shop, where his limited vision was less of a hindrance. He could feel the tails and the horns, the humps and the bumps, of the plastic dinosaur models sold in the store. Fred knew brontosaurus from T-Rex by touch. He could tell stories about each prehistoric beast. He spoke non-stop about these extinct animals to every child who passed his way, impressing parents, teachers and tourists alike. His supervisor, on the other hand, found his tirades tedious.

Someone else might have grown bored, talking about the same subject day after day, year after year, without a promotion in sight, but Fred was in his element. He had long since accepted that he would never become the vet he once wanted to be. That is not to say that Fred did not grow depressed from the loneliness and the family strife, or from the scolding he endured from his supervisor at the shop. He benefited from antidepressants and a listening ear. His attention stayed in check because he was careful about his ADHD medications. He always arrived early for doctors' appointments. He visited the center for the blind biweekly, to hear volunteers read picture books about dinosaurs aloud. He sensed that his assigned volunteer preferred to discuss current events chronicled in newspapers, instead of describing details of dinosaur illustrations—so he was happy when technology advanced and talking video viewing terminals took over where his reader left off.

It came as a surprise when Fred emailed me mid-month, saying that he needed an early refill on his ADHD prescription. As usual, his email arrived in a huge font—far larger than the 140-point maximum supported by my PC. However, requests for early refills were *not* the norm for Fred, for he was not one to misuse medications. As a policy, I did not reissue refills for controlled medications—but this out-of-character request surely warranted an early appointment, and an emergency one at that.

Fred sounded more agitated than usual when he arrived at the office and explained that he confused his ADHD medications with new ones prescribed by his primary care provider. They were the same size and shape, so he assumed that they were the same pills. He knew them by touch, just like his dinosaur toys. His PCP told him to take two pills per day, so he reached into his usual bottle, taking two pills each morning, until his psychotropic medications disappeared in two weeks' time. Then he realized something was wrong and he emailed immediately.

Fred did fine with routine—as is typical of persons on the spectrum—but his routine had changed. Routine also helps persons with visual limitations, as we shall see. I called the pharmacy, to ask how this could happen. The answer was easy: yes, the pills were strikingly similar. I asked the pharmacist if they explain new pills to persons with low vision. The supervising pharmacist said that "there is no mechanism in place" (at a major chain!). I knew times had changed, and that my own vision of a "friendly family pharmacist" was a throwback to a bygone era, when pharmacists stepped out from behind the counter to counsel patients. Norman Rockwell's images on magazine covers were nice as recollections, and probably even nicer as collectibles, but such homespun scenes were no longer the norm in the big city.

At my urging, the pharmacist promised to review Fred's next refill with him personally—but she reminded me that she worked limited hours on rotating shifts. When I asked her to alert her staff to this situation, again she said that "there is no mechanism in place." No yellow stickies on the counter, no bulletin board on the wall, nothing to pass on information from one shift to the next. How different that was from a hospital.

Horrific visions of what could have happened passed through my mind. What if his new prescription had been anti-hypertensives—and Fred doubled the dose of a medication that potentially increases blood pressure (BP) when he needed meds to lower his blood pressure? Fortunately, his new medication lowered cholesterol, but the gravity of this near miss struck me just the same. I later learned that VA training programs that rehabilitate the visually impaired teach techniques to label and identify medications early on and justifiably so. Unfortunately, Fred's psychiatric symptoms made it difficult for him to understand the need for vision rehabilitation clinics, and his long-standing "eccentricities" interfered with his comfort in a group setting where others in similar situations confided their problems with daily living. It was just him and me, at the start. Then, with the help of an understanding research-oriented ophthalmologist, who also had a son on the spectrum, and who was willing to provide more personalized attention than is generally available, we were able to cobble together a plan that could, at the very least, keep him out of harm's way—until nature itself took its course, or until research advances or even gene therapy could thwart the progression of Fred's genetic disorder.

It was clear to me that this situation deserved further study, and seemed extra important, because advocacy groups for persons with visual impairments are not as "vocal" as groups for hearing-impaired persons. Deaf persons who use American Sign Language (ASL) develop group cohesion by sharing the same "language"—but even they have stumbling blocks within the healthcare system, as I later learned from a journal editor whose sister had been born deaf.[4] In contrast, vision-impaired persons are often socially isolated, afraid to venture outside to unfamiliar terrain, where they fear for their safety. Apart from some veterans' groups, their social networks are nowhere near as involved—at least not yet—as deaf persons' networks.

Importantly, at the time of Fred's near-catastrophe, I was supervising a resident whose patient lost most of his vision to diabetic retinopathy. Before starting psychiatric treatment, the patient had been too depressed to follow up with medical appointments. By the time he began treatment with the resident, he was barely able to attend to his own ADL (activities of daily living). He had difficulty walking from his home to the hospital clinic, even though the clinic was only a few short city blocks away. He was still too proud to use a white cane, which itself requires special training, and the likelihood of acquiring a seeing-eye dog was small, given how hard they are to come by, and the fact that they are typically trained to respond to English (in America), rather than in his native Cantonese. Those highly trained dogs are carefully paired with their humans, and humans are carefully culled before receiving their dogs, and an unwillingness to care for the animal would make someone ineligible from the start, even if dogs were available.

The resident was almost as sad as the patient himself after he saw his patient stumble on the hospital steps, because of diabetes-associated vision loss, which was accentuated by diabetic neuropathy that compromised sensation in his feet. The resident and the patient were close in age, albeit not in life experience, making the situation even sadder. The resident became sadder still, once he realized that once-promising opportunities to offset his patient's tragic outcome were permanently lost because his patient's untreated depression precluded pursuit of potentially preventive medical care.

Sadly, 98 percent of serious diabetes-related vision loss can be prevented with early diagnosis and good glucose control. In theory, one would not expect to encounter such complications in the developed world, much less in a major metropolitan area, where medical care is more available, but persons who suffer from serious mental illness typically suffer from more medical illnesses than average, and have significantly shorter life expectancies, partly because their compromised mental functioning interferes with their ability to obtain quality and timely medical care, and also interferes with their ability to appreciate the gravity of their situations. They may not follow up on medical recommendations or prescriptions as assiduously as needed. Sometimes, their physicians are put off by psychiatric symptoms and even the best of them may not know how to communicate effectively under the circumstances, as documented in Dr. Brody's essay.

Yet diabetes contributes to a high proportion of visual loss in the developed world, because of its direct effects on the retina, and also because of its association with three of the four major causes of vision loss, which include diabetic retinopathy, cataracts, and glaucoma. Age-related macular degeneration is another major cause of vision loss. It is associated with smoking, and, as the name states, with age as well. And there may be other secondary contributors, as we alluded to in our earlier discussion of "secondary generation antipsychotics" (SGAs).

Diabetes potentially impacts both young and old, although the prevalence of "adult-onset" or type II diabetes is far greater than type I, which was previously known as "juvenile onset" or "insulin-dependent" diabetes. As such, geriatric patients bear most of the burden of visual loss overall. Age-related macular degeneration is, by definition, related to age. Children who are born blind represent a small percentage of today's vision-impaired population and are likely to have other disabilities. There was a time when "retinopathy of prematurity" (ROP), also known as retrolental fibroplasia (RLF), was much more common and was unwittingly exacerbated by excessive exposure to oxygen in neonatal nurseries, in attempt to compensate for limited oxygen-carrying capacities of inadequately developed lungs in premature babies. Such is what happened to Little Stevie Wonder, as Dr. Moffic tells us in his essay on musicians.

From the get-go, it was clear that cultural preconceptions impact the way society as well as health care providers approach persons with low vision and subsequently influence the ways those persons view themselves. Some societies revere the blind, some blame them or marginalize them, and some insist on showing care and compassion, sometimes to the point of offending visually impaired individuals, as noted in a www.catapult.co article by M. Leona Godwin, written with Okezie Nwoka under the title, "When People See Your Blindness, They Stop Seeing You as Human."[5]

Fred's demanding and psychologically insensitive career military father was far removed from the officers who participated in the forward-thinking programs created by the VA (which did not evolve spontaneously and came into existence only in response to an outcry by veterans who felt that they were underserved by VA resources). Fred's father was surely distinct from the combat-blinded marine who was glorified in the 1945 John Garfield film, *Pride of the Marines*, as discussed in George Higham's essay. In that case, which was based on a true-to-life story, the blinded and wounded but unrelenting marine hero Al Schmidt was literally deemed to be the "pride of the marines" and was venerated for his unwavering valor, in spite of extreme circumstances.

Because culture is so critical to this topic, most of the essays in this book are devoted to cultural issues in the broader sense of the term. The literature or art or music produced in response to blindness, or by persons who are themselves visually challenged, is just as revealing as overt religious or mythological explanations for vision loss, as we shall see in the essays below. Our everyday speech attests to the value we place on vision and highlights how this specific sense is interjected into colloquial American English. My own essay on "idioms and ideas" illustrates the ways that language shapes our ideas or reflects otherwise unconscious attitudes, as it points out our many reflexive references to sight, vision, blindness, insight, eyes, etc., in our daily speech.

Summary of the Essays Included, and Explanations About What Could Not Be Included

In the introduction above, I have alluded to some of the essays that follow. Because so many of our essays cross boundaries, and fall into more than one category, confining those essays to a single subsection would be misleading at best, and undermining at worst. Moreover, because each essay is unique in its own right, and because the qualifications of each author are equally unique, it quickly became apparent that it was impossible to prioritize the essays in order of importance or relevance. And so I chose the easy way out: the essays are arranged in alphabetical order of the authors' names. The essay titles give a quick glimpse at the content so as to allow readers to choose those topics that interest them most.

In the first essay, Professor Jeffrey Bullins taps into his unusual expertise as a sound engineer for horror films, and as a media studies professor. Writing from far upstate in New York, near the Canadian border, he explains how a film's musical scores and sounds create the special atmosphere and emotive experiences that characterize horror films—even in the absence of visual imagery. This approach offers audiences a "glimpse" of the sightless world of the visually impaired, and how it is amplified by auditory cues that might not carry as much meaning for others. Curiously, those "audiences" are called "spectators" in film parlance, even though movies are multi-media productions that include sound as much as sight. Professor Bullins summarizes the function of horror films, and their crossover with blindness, stating that "the fear of what we cannot see is at the core of one of humankind's strongest and primal emotions. Horror films are defined by the emotion that they seek to produce in their audience." In addition to his primer on the philosophy of horror, he examines films such as *Wait Until Dark, See No Evil, Red Dragon/Manhunter, Jennifer 8, Blink* and more.

An interesting albeit tangential addition to this impressive list of horror movies might be *Cauldron of Blood* (1970), directed by Santo Alcocer and Edward Mann and starring Boris Karloff. As detailed in George Higham's *Wax Museum Movies: A Comprehensive Filmography* (2020), horror icon Karloff plays a sculptor who gains his greatest artistic fame after being blinded in an automobile accident. It turns out that the crash was a failed murder attempt by his wife, who then takes advantage of his disability and newfound success by manipulating him while continuing her evil plans.

From there, we proceed to a essay written by the award-winning poet and literature professor, Reja-e Busailah. The recently deceased Professor

Busailah poignantly describes his recollected experiences as a blind child who left his homeland, and his later incarnation as a poet and a Ph.D.-level professor who taught literature at major universities, both in America and abroad.

His unfiltered first-person perspective showcases the world of a completely blind person (which is relatively uncommon, compared to the much larger population of "legally blind" people in the world). His story is arguably more "colorful" than a similar story that might have been, had it been written by a sighted individual, for the youthful Reja-e recollects many different sensory experiences inundating him in the absence of sight. He talks about gustatory perceptions, tactile sensations, and sounds of all sorts, adding details that distract readers from awareness of the obvious—that his narrative was forged without allusions to sight. He tells us so many details about the weight of coins strung around his belt that we readers can also feel the tug.

Using dialogue and other literary devices as befitting a published poet, Professor Busailah simultaneously alludes to local folkloric beliefs about the demonic or diabolical source of a child's blindness. Bystanders credit the evil eye as the likely source of his vision loss, linking it to sinfulness of the parents—even though the infectious origin of Reja-e's blindness was already known. The superstitious ideas referenced by the late professor contrast with equally unscientific beliefs expressed in essays about the blind beggar at the gates to Jerusalem (in Eli Wiesel's novel) or Tiresias of Thebes. Those blind persons were revered as prophets, seers or visionaries and deemed to be gifted, not cursed. We see how such "folk religion" (sometimes dismissed as "superstition") overrides the authority of more formal religious ideology, and overshadows Islam's sophisticated medical legacy that dates to medieval times. Islamic medicine was much more advanced than contemporaneous Christian sources because it incorporated insights from the Greek medical legacy that Christians repudiated because it had pagan origins.

Professor Jason W. Ellis' essay on blindness in science fiction returns to the text and goes far beyond the iconic images of Geordi La Forge's *Star Trek* VISOR. Professor Ellis implies that casting black actors as blind characters in *Star Trek*, *The Matrix*, and more may have been intended to highlight the higher prevalence of blindness among African Americans, as compared to white persons, as noted earlier in this introduction.

As an expert in science fiction literature, who heads City Tech's Science Fiction department, with its extensive SF library collection, Professor Ellis' expansive study begins with a discussion of Mary Shelley's *Frankenstein, or the Modern Prometheus* (1818), which is arguably the first work of SF, and which, by synchronicity, features a blind character in a pivotal scene. He introduces us to the four-time Hugo Award winner, Robert A. Heinlein, whose "The Green Hills of Earth" (1947) recounts the life of "Rhysling, the Blind Singer of the Spaceways." He includes yet another luminary of the genre, José Saramago, the Nobel Prize-winning writer whose apocalyptic novel *Blindness* (1995, trans. 1997) imagines the effects of a highly contagious disease resulting in blindness—and also makes us consider parallels with our current state of contagion, death and disease. He explores lesser-known SF creations as well as several that are nearly household names, such as *The Matrix Trilogy*, *The Day of the Triffids*, and H.G. Wells' "The Country of the Blind."

Interestingly, Professor Ellis reminds us that Science Fiction (SF) emerged from discourses rooted in the Enlightenment, Scientific Revolution, and Industrial Revolution, when discourses about blindness "shifted from ideas of curse and gift to those of medical and scientific study." As we shall see from other essays included in this collection, many societies—and even more individuals—never fully abandoned beliefs that blindness is something other than a medical or scientific concern—and thus many myths persist, some of them endearing and others offending.

In the following essay, art history professor Carlos Espí Forcén provides a panoramic view of the artistic approaches to blind subjects in his essay on "Looking at the Unseeing: Blindness in the History of Art." Although the visual arts superficially seem far removed from the topic of vision impairment (save for sculpture, which employs tactile sensation rather than sight per se), Professor Carlos Espí Forcén informs us otherwise, explaining why portraiture of blind persons held a paradoxical attraction for painters of the past. Yet such concerns about vision and the visual arts are not relegated to history and even intrigued a premiere financial publication. Specifically, *Wall Street Journal*'s weekend edition on August 24, 2019, devoted substantial space to a contemporary documentary about vision-impaired artists, who are far fewer in absolute number when compared to visually challenged musicians.

As a native of Spain, Professor Carlos Espí Forcén understandably emphasizes Spanish luminaries who depicted the blind, such as Goya, Ribera, and Picasso. Yet he also delves into the ancient world, addressing a much-discussed image of the so-called "Blind Homer," a 2nd-century-BCE bust portrait of the allegedly blind poet, who was presumed to be the writer of the *Odyssey* and the *Iliad* but whose actual existence has been called into question.

Professor Espí Forcén's discussion of depictions of blindness in both the Old Testament (Hebrew Bible) and the New Testament, along with the Apocrypha, introduces the reader not just to the visual image itself but to the Western World's religious history, offering a much-needed discussion about the evolution of religious beliefs at a critical juncture in the Roman Empire. He reminds us that physical blindness was metaphorically referred to as spiritual blindness, directed at those who did not recognize Jesus as the Messiah, such as Jews who remained faithful to the Mosaic law. Miracle cures were common in Christian-influenced iconography, and Jesus' imputed ability to make the blind see (and the lame walk) were attractive subjects for artists.

In discussing Rembrandt's painting of Samson, he obviously alludes to a story with a religious origin, but Rembrandt's stature in art history pushes this example beyond the particularistic and into the universal. Professor Espí Forcén's expansive essay covers more secular artists such as Caravaggio, Jacques-Louis David, and Otto Dix, giving Dix special consideration, and explaining the social milieu in which Dix worked, and why Dix chose his specific, and disturbing, subjects. Otto Dix's "The Match Seller" (Staatsgalerie, Stuttgart) taps into a realistic style—"The New Objectivity"—which became popular among German artists who sought to denounce social injustices that peaked during and after the Great War. Blind men and amputees were common subjects in German painting, intended to highlight the catastrophic consequences of the war and to call attention to the miserable conditions of war veterans.

Physician, psychiatrist, and historian of psychiatry Fernando Espí Forcén explores another variant of visual art, focusing on filmic renditions of blindness but emphasizing the psychiatric aspects of such themes. He includes an iconic film about colorblindness, starring Sidney Poitier, who was arguably the best regarded African American actor of his time, and who continued to act into his 90s. Released as the civil rights movement peaked, *A Patch of Blue* (1965) tells the story of a young white blind woman who was born into an emotionally abusive multigenerational family, replete with alcohol abuse, repeated verbal degradation, and even threats to prostitute her. Unknowingly, she falls in love with a kindly African American man (Poitier) who provides a clear contrast to her family of origin.

This essay also covers *At First Sight* (1999), a Irvin Wilker film that tells the story of blind man who works as a masseur. The movie version is based on an Oliver Sacks essay, "To See and Not See," which is included in Sacks' 1995 book about *An Anthropologist on Mars*. It recounts the true story of a man who was born with congenital cataracts but who gains his sight after a surgical intervention. Rather than rejoicing in this medical miracle, he feels overwhelmed when confronted with the task of learning how to see. This film complements Sacks' other stories about *The Island of the Colorblind* (1996), which highlights how a disability can turn into an ability because the congenitally colorblind Micronesian fishermen can see fish clearly at night, whereas others cannot—and so they proliferated because their inheritable "disability" had a survival advantage. Here, we are reminded of Sacks' book about *Seeing Voices* (1989), where he valorizes other peoples' adaptations to disability and primes us to think about Professor Walter's discussion of post-modernist approaches, which will be mentioned later in this essay.

In contrast, Espí Forcén briefly broaches the blind samurai genre, a subject that merits a essay of its own. He mentions the Japanese film *Zatoichi* (2003), by Takeshi Kitano, where Kitano himself plays the titular blind samurai. Rather than being restricted to the single film mentioned in that essay, the 2003 film was Zatoichi's 28th appearance on the big screen. Zatoichi is actually a phenomenally successful franchise that dates to 1962, with a small screen television series that ran from 1974 to 1979, and dozens of different films featuring this character. As such, Zatoichi is as memorable in Japan as the diabolical Dr. Mabuse is in Europe (although not in America).

Samurai films spanned the globe at a point in time, with the blind samurai as a specific subgenre. These films capitalized on the Kung Fu craze of the 1970s, which did not distinguish one East Asian culture from another. The iconic "blind swordsman" of Japanese lore—incorrectly called the "blind samurai"—inspired countless knockoffs and homages, with Zatoichi himself appearing in some.

We can wonder if Japan's technological advances in the 1960s and 1970s, which dwarfed American and European endeavors, also stimulated the interest in this subject matter in the West, and reminded Americans that even visually-disabled samurai warriors (as symbolic stand-ins for Japanese persons in general) were a formidable force that had to be reckoned with and that could not be easily overpowered, in spite of superficial infirmities (in contrast to the U.S. victory over Japan in World War II, which culminated with the bombing of Hiroshima and Nagasaki).

Espí Forcén contrasts that time-honored blind samurai genre with the American *Daredevil*. In some *Daredevil* versions, a blind warrior teaches hand-to-hand combat techniques to the blinded American attorney Matt Murdoch. Murdoch in turn leads a second life, incognito, as a vigilante, known as "Daredevil." Curiously, the Daredevil character had an earlier life in a made-for-TV movie, *The Trial of the Incredible Hulk* (1989), when attorney Matt Murdoch defends Bruce Banner a.k.a. The Hulk in a court battle when Banner stands accused of damaging the NYC subway system while in the guise of his alter-ego, "The Hulk," as played by Lou Ferrigno.

Fernando Espí Forcén speculates about the reasons for the uptick in superhero films in the post–9/11 era, suggesting that this trend followed financial and political instability in America. Yet the trend began before the towers tumbled, when the dot-com frenzy was still in full force. In fact, a "Spider-Man" movie was made before 9/11, but had to be redacted, more for the sake of sensitivity than for the sake of accuracy, because it showed Spider-Man straddling the Twin Towers when they were still standing. Some say that it was Spider-Man who spearheaded the resurgence of this genre, while the more technologically minded credit CGI and the invention of better fabrics for improving the appearance of superheroes in their signature spandex. Others claim that generational issues came into play, and that audiences reared on superhero comics had come of age, and now demanded cinematic renditions of their heroes.

Regardless of the source of superhero popularity, Fernando Espí Forcén focuses on the psychological appeal of their characters, saying that "psychoanalytically, the superhero can be approached as a grandiose defense against depression" and that "audiences will cathartically relieve their anxieties about theses perceived threats in society through such superhero films."

A curious Netflix series starring a blind protagonist shares similarities with two popular Netflix shows that revolve around Marvel superheroes. Premiering in 2019 and continuing on to the present day (2021), "In the Dark" seems to have capitalized on the popularity of both *Jessica Jones* (2015–2019) and *Daredevil* (2016–2018), for it combines the chief characteristics of each into one person. Jones is a hard-drinking, loose-loving female detective who began life as a comics character before morphing into a Marvel marvel.[6] The star of the show (Perry Mattfeld as Murphy) merges the superpowered Jessica Jones with Matt Murdock, the beloved blind attorney who lost his vision as a child but simultaneously gained superpowers after being exposed to radioactive waste. As an adult, Murdock becomes an attorney but leads a double life as a vigilante known as Daredevil. In spite of her vision loss (and inebriation), Murphy functions as a detective, like Jones, as she tracks down the culprit who killed her friend. Her tenacity, as well as her blindness, recollect Matt Murdock as Daredevil.

In the next essay, a comics scholar and former Hollywood writer who earned a Ph.D. in comics studies presents a different approach to the Daredevil character, and to comics characters in general. Rather than adding psychoanalytic speculation, as per Fernando Espí Forcén, Jaq Greenspon links these blind superhero characters to other superheroes, and to Spider-Man in particular. He emphasizes their comics creators, especially the legendary Stan Lee, who has inspired several recently published academic biographies that supplement the long, long list of fawning fanzines and comics-centric columns, websites, and blogs. We see a point of commonality: these "wounded warriors" acquired disabilities via unintended accidents, sometimes while performing altruistic acts that were followed by untoward and unexpected consequences. Yet they transmute their disabilities into abilities, and into super-abilities at that. What might have become "post-traumatic stress disorder" in someone else turns into "post-traumatic strength disorder" in these characters. And that is consistent with the goal of their creator, for Stan Lee states that "I was trying to think of a hero who would start out with a disability—a hero whose weakness would actually be more colorful, more unusual than his power itself."

Extending way beyond the better-known Daredevil, who enjoyed his own Marvel streaming TV show, Professor Greenspon tackles the curious cases of the three different Drs. Midnight, each of whom accomplishes near miraculous medical feats in spite of vision loss. In some cases, technology comes into play, and in other cases, a low-tech owl acts as a vision aid. Sometimes, another human assists. In several situations, blinded superheroes refurbish gear or costumes that belonged to earlier generations and enhance their superpowers via a variant of supernatural transmission.

One comics character who is not included in this essay about superheroes in comics is "Mr. Magoo," who is comedic rather than heroic and who is currently considered to be politically incorrect, in spite of the popularity he enjoyed in America for decades. Mr. Magoo was created in 1949 by Millard Kaufman and John Hubley for UPA Studios. The aging, groping, and bespectacled gentleman encounters one "comedic" situation after another due to his extreme near-sightedness and his constant refusal to accept his situation. His animated television show in the 1960s was highly rated and well received. However, in 1997, when Disney made a live action film version, the studio was highly criticized for being out of touch with contemporary sentiments. Just the same, Mr. Magoo resurfaced in a French animated series in 2018, undeterred by American antipathy toward denigrating disability.

Having broached the topic of the supernatural a few paragraphs earlier, let us look at the essay provided by pastoral counselor and Episcopal priest, Curtis W. Hart, titled "Pastoral Counseling and Impending Blindness: Vision Loss and a Quest for Meaning." For many years, the Reverend Hart headed Cornell-Weill's department of pastoral counseling. He currently edits the *Journal of Religion & Health*. Straddling the cusp between science-based medicine practiced at major medical centers, and spiritual belief characteristic of the clergy, the Reverend Hart approaches blindness through a unique vantage point. He discusses Milton's initially catastrophic reaction to his vision loss and to his perceived inability to continue with his "one talent." Until then, Milton was a successful poet who served the leadership of the England's Puritan revolution and its Lord Protector Oliver Cromwell.

The Reverend Hart also tells us about the time-honored role of pastoral counseling in addressing major medical challenges, including vision loss. In reading about pastoral counseling of the blind, some readers may be reminded of the curious Woody Allen movie—*Crimes and Misdemeanors* (1989)—which features a nearly blind yet never embittered rabbi who is a patient of a duplicitous, adulterous, and murderous ophthalmologist (Martin Landau) who cannot cure the rabbi's eye affliction but is capable of hiring a hit on his mistress (Anjelica Huston).

Students of history might also be interested in early Christian attitudes toward blindness, including miracle healing of blindness, and the metaphors relating to "spiritual blindness," used to describe non-believers. Authors such as Brenda S. Walter Gardenour, a medical historian, and Carlos Espí Forcén, an art historian, delve into these issues in detail, telling us how medieval Christian sources often ascribed spiritual blindness to heresy and, more frequently, to Judaism. Churches often included the statues of *Synagoga* and *Ecclesia*, with *Synagoga* wearing a blindfold to signify disbelief and spiritual blindness, while her male counterpart *Ecclesia* is fully sighted. In miracle tales, the blindness of disbelief was often intertwined with sinfulness.

In a essay titled "Blinded on the Battlefield," George Higham explores a somewhat forgotten, but nevertheless memorable, 1945 film, *Pride of the Marines*. This black and white film was made during the heyday of film noir, but, with its ultimately uplifting outcome, it stands apart from the usual crime-ridden noirish themes that are set on seedy city streets. A filmmaker and sculptor by training, who has a special appreciation for sculpting skills of any sort, Higham introduces us to this wartime film that revolves around a battle-wounded marine who perseveres in spite of several life-threatening and life-limiting injuries. The protagonist proceeds to win a heroic battle, through a combination of his own military expertise, his ingenious collaboration with other grievously injured team members, his unwavering dedication to the cause and his commitment to America's winning the war. Higham also alludes to the human experiences of actor John Garfield, who played Schmid on screen and lived with Schmid while making the movie about Schmid' heroics. Although Schmid went on to live a long life, surmounting what had been nearly lethal physical and psychological war wounds, Garfield took a downward turn. He died an early death, partly because of his deliberate disregard of his congenital heart defect but also arguably because of the stress imposed by accusations during the McCarthy hearings.

Higham also discusses inventions of Mikhail Margolin in what was then Soviet Russia. Margolin also succeeded against many odds, having endured bitter anti-Semitism and pogroms in Czarist Russia before participating in the Bolshevik Revolution and being relocated to Siberia. He lost his sight when a bullet hit his head, yet he overcame many obstacles, including a poor choice for his earlier vocational rehabilitation. He eventually designed a gun that, among other things, was used by Princess Leia in *Star Wars*.

In the next essay on "Blindness in the Jewish Tradition: From Written Text to Oral Law to Contemporary Medical Practice," radiation oncologist Jerome M. Karp collaborates with Howard L. Forman, a physician and psychiatrist, to produce an assiduously detailed and thoroughly documented review of Judaic attitudes toward blindness. They emphasize Talmudic and Midrashic texts, presenting their many and varied arguments that precede any conclusion. The authors also quote from the Hebrew Bible and rabbinic commentaries as they explain seemingly superficial inconsistencies that mandate compassion and care of the blind while simultaneously banning the blind from serving as temple priests.

In addition to their close textual readings from the Judaic Oral Tradition that was encoded nearly two millennia ago, they broach more contemporary medico-religious controversies, such as organ transplantation, and cornea transplantation in particular. Some Biblical stories that they cite are as familiar to art historians as to historians of religion, for they were popular subjects for many major artists over the centuries. Samson and Delilah is an often-replayed theme that features seduction and vengeance as well as blindness. The story of the blind patriarch Isaac, who was deceived by his son Jacob, is as important to family therapists and anthropologists as it is to Biblical scholars and artists. For the mild-mannered Jacob covered his arms with sheepskins so as to impersonate his more hirsute brother Esau, who was rightfully entitled to Isaac's inheritance, had his mild-mannered yet duplicitous brother not received their dying father's blessing first.

We find a different take on religion, spirituality and culture in the essay by Andrew J. McLean, titled "Native Stories About Vision and Impairment: Western Medicine Meets Aboriginal Mythos." McLean chairs a major university psychiatry department where he focuses on mental health disparities in Indian Country. Writing from his home, which rests on the ancestral lands of the Dakota Oyate and Dakota/Lakota Peoples, he acknowledges those who have resided there for generations and recognizes that their spirit permeates this land. He touches on the complexities of Aboriginal cultures around the world (which number 5,000) and does not restrict himself to nearby Upper Midwest states that are home to him and to many Native peoples. He clarifies that some rites and rituals, myths and memes, recur among different Aboriginal cultures, while some are tribe or region or even gender specific. He informs us that the very concept of "vision" is multi-faceted for Indigenous Peoples, ranging from vision journeys (both intentional and unintentional) to folktales of magical restoration of sight, and to the sad fact that eye conditions and blindness have disproportionately burdened Aboriginal Peoples for centuries. McLean also connects Native vision rites to the present, and to psychiatry's renewed interest in psychedelic drugs as treatment (as opposed to treating only the consequences of recreational psychedelic drug misuse, as was true of the last several decades).

The next essay on "Blind African American Musicians: Insights from a Social Psychiatrist" is written by H. Steven Moffic, a psychiatrist who is affectionately known as "Dr. Jazz," and who was also designated as a "Hero of Public Psychiatry" by the American Psychiatric Association, and who identifies himself as a "social psychiatrist" who focuses on society's impact on psychiatric symptoms. Moffic merges medicine and music in his review of blindness among African American musicians, providing multiple examples of vision impaired musicians and musical groups, many of whom are household names: Stevie Wonder, Ray Charles, the Blind Boys of Alabama and the Blind Boys of Mississippi, and more. He delves into the medical aspects of the blindness of prematurity, which robbed Stevie Wonder and so many others of their sight, and he also attributes Ray Charles' blindness to his untreated glaucoma, which is usually treatable, if not also preventable, but which is four times more prevalent in African Americans than in Caucasian Americans and which progresses faster and strikes earlier in African Americans. He addresses the psychosocial contributors to this music, and speculates about reasons for the overrepresentation of African Americans—and especially Southern-born African Americans—among blind musicians. Referencing Franz Fanon, the Caribbean-born and French-educated psychiatrist whose writings inadvertently inspired America's Black Panther movement several decades ago, Moffic hypothesizes that music offered an acceptable outlet for anger against race-based indignities, and that audiences of other races saw this music a safe venue to witness that rage.

My own essay on "Idioms and Ideas: Meanings and Metaphors" started out as a serious piece but ended up sounding like a spoof as I attempted to incorporate as many allusions to sight as possible, in just a few paragraphs. The idea originated with my own unease in using words that reference sight when treating patients with impaired sight (and I likely treat more such people than many psychiatrists who practice outside of specialized settings devoted to vision-impaired people). While trying to modulate my wording, to avoid offending others, I soon realized that I was attempting a nearly impossible task, given that our language is peppered with so many similes and metaphors and idioms that reference sight.

Having been subjected to psychoanalytic training early in psychiatry residency, I was well aware of the value accorded every nuance, every syllable, every word (even if such an exegesis did not impact clinical outcomes at all). Psychoanalysts typically plumb meanings from unconscious slips of the tongue without necessarily focusing on ways to relieve distressing symptoms. Thanks to my extensive religious education (which led to Certification in Orthodox Jewish Education via the Jerusalem Examination), I was already familiar with Biblical heuristics, and with many Torah commentators who focused on the minutiae of language, and who dissected syllables that might have been dismissed as "typos" or artifacts of "auto-correct," had they occurred outside of sacred sources. Instead, the commentators zeroed in on inconsistencies that supposedly concealed many levels of meaning. Those sometimes-mystical meanings were deemed to be as significant as the manifest meaning. The crossover between Biblical heuristics and psychoanalytic attention is obvious, and that in turns crosses over with "politically correct" speech that strives to safeguard against potentially but not necessarily intentionally offensive language. As linguist and lawyer Debbie Felder pointed out during a conversation, a trained linguist would broach this subject differently, and with greater depth, and might devote an entire academic career to "sense words" that pop up in everyday language.

From there, we move to Caleb Puckett's essay, "Through the Eye(s) of Tiresias: From Thebes and Beyond." Caleb Puckett is a published poet as well as a published academic who apparently absorbed nearly limitless knowledge from the books that surround him in his work as a university librarian. Tiresias of Thebes is one of the oldest extant myths about vision loss, and his character is pivotal to the convoluted original Oedipus plot. Although he is blind, he sees the truth that others cannot. Caleb Puckett traces the origins and evolution of the archetype of the blind seer who surfaced in Greek myth and repeatedly resurfaced in literature and also appears in contemporary films such as the Coen brothers' comedy-drama send-up of the *Odyssey*, *O Brother, Where Art Thou* and Salley Vickers's recent retelling of the Oedipus myth, *Where Three Roads Meet*. We learn that there is not one Tiresias, but many incarnations of the blind seer, adapted by different authors and reinterpreted over time, yet conforming to the essential archetype: Tiresias's remarkable powers of perception result from a supernatural gift, a divine compensation for the loss of his physical sight. Curiously, Caleb Puckett identifies Tiresias in *Oedipus Rex* as the first detective story—even though Edgar Allan Poe is more often accorded this honor—but Caleb Puckett is particularly qualified to make such a pronouncement, given his prior research into Poe, as published in an earlier McFarland essay collection about *Arkham Asylum* (2019).

We learn even more about the ancient world—and about international literature from various eras—in Professor Eric Sandberg's essay titled "'Close your eyes and see': Blindness and Literature." He reminds us that literature itself is essentially blind because it is based on the written word and depends on readers to draw mental pictures in their minds. As per Professor Sandberg, blindness is may be a higher form of vision that allows readers to "see" the unseeable.

Having taught literature in universities around the world, in Europe as well as in Asia, Professor Sandberg taps into his multi-cultural experiences as much as his own scholarly pursuits. His analysis of Nobel Laureate José Saramago's *Blindness* ([1995] 2005) details the collapse of an unnamed civilization in the face of an unexplained outbreak of the "white sickness," or blindness, but it differs from the approach articulated by science fiction experts appearing elsewhere in this collection. He explores the figure of Tiresias in T.S. Eliot's 1922 poem *The Waste Land*, and covers Jorge Luis Borges, the celebrated Argentinian writer who spent three decades with limited vision yet introduced a magical, post-modernist literary fiction style that was unique enough to merit its own rubric, "Borgesian." His discussion of H.G. Wells' short story about "The Country of the Blind" points out an important paradox: even though this story introduces the oft-cited adage, "in the land of the blind, the one-eyed man is king," this assertion proves to be patently untrue for the unsympathetic and presumptuous protagonist in Wells' short story. His section anticipates Professor Walter's post-modernist contention that vision loss is not a de facto disability but is instead an alternative way of experiencing the world.

Not restricting himself to secular literature, Professor Sandberg considers the concept of blindness as divine punishment, quoting the Old Testament curse for disobedience: "The Lord shall smite thee with madness, and blindness, and astonishment of heart. And thou shalt grope at noonday, as the blind gropeth in the darkness..." (Deut. 28: 28–29). While relaying the story of Samson, first betrayed by Delilah, and then blinded by the Philistines, Sandberg compares and contrasts the Hebraic model with the Greek version, where blindness is also a punishment, sometimes brought about through divine intervention, but where mortals also inflict blindness, as when Homer's Odysseus takes revenge on the Cyclops by blinding him with a heated stake.

Straddling the nexus of literature, history, religion, and myth, Professor Eric J. Sterling taps into his extensive academic accomplishments as well as his personal family history to write about "Blindness as Holocaust Metaphor: Elie Wiesel's *A Beggar in Jerusalem* and *The Forgotten*." A professor of English at Auburn University who has published many academic articles on the Holocaust, including an entire university press book on *Life in the Ghettos During the Holocaust*, Professor Sterling is also the son and grandson of Holocaust survivors. Here, he focuses on Elie Wiesel's novels, *A Beggar in Jerusalem* (1969—winner of the prestigious French Prix Médicis), and *The Forgotten* (1992), which each feature an old blind madman who is seemingly human and insane but perhaps is actually a mystical seer who serves as the caretaker and preserver of knowledge of past anti–Semitic tragedies. Influenced by Hasidic tales of mysticism, Wiesel shows that even—or particularly—blind people may serve as witnesses of the past. Professor Sterling then touches on a tangential but unforgettable medical topic related to the Holocaust: Mengele's fanatical twin experiments on the inheritability of iris color. Those studies often ended with the blinding of his unwitting subjects but never ended in useful medical knowledge, in spite of Mengele's formal training in medicine and anthropology. This important essay is as unnerving as it is informative.

Historian of medicine and pharmacy college professor Barbara S. Gardenour Walter taps into her wide areas of expertise, citing physicians as well as philosophers, myths and medicine, as she scans historical changes in the Western view of blindness. Her essay, "In Darkness and Light: The Meanings of Blindness in the West," relates ancient Egyptian myths about Horus, who was blinded by his brother, as well as Sumerian myths about Enki, the god of water, who creates perfect human beings from clay until the goddess Nimnah challenges him to create deformed or incomplete human beings so that Enki can give them a purpose in human society. When Nimnah creates a blind man, Enki gives him inner sight and makes him a royal musician. She also compares ancient Hebrew attitudes toward blindness as sin and punishment to Mesopotamian myths that influenced other Israelite ideas after they arrived in Canaan.

Her historical essay traverses many more centuries, reminding us of early philosophers who did not believe that the blind could cognate adequately, while the French philosopher of the Enlightenment Denis Diderot (1713–1784) averred that the blind were equal to the sighted in their ability to learn about the physical world. As the co-founder and chief editor of the Encyclopedia, Diderot's more "enlightened" position swayed future generations, leading to progress in the early modern and modern periods, when the demystification of blindness and increasing secularization facilitated the founding of schools for the blind (akin to the ones chronicled in Reja-e's memoir of his blind boyhood). As blind culture developed its own identity, sighted culture continued its ocularcentrism, privileging vision over other senses, until postmodernist thinkers argued that the sighted and the act of seeing should not be privileged at all, nor should blindness be defined or controlled by the sighted. When seen through the postmodernist lens that Professor Gardenour Walter espouses, blindness becomes neither a disability nor a medical condition, but an existential experience—and a unique way of knowing—that is different from but as valuable as that of the sighted.

In writing about "Out of Sight: Body and Building from Medical Architecture to Post-Modern Haptic Space," Professor Brenda S. Gardenour Walter returns to a subject that she explored in an earlier McFarland publication about *Arkham Asylum* (2019), where she offered cross-cultural and historical perspectives on the representation of "brick & mortar" mental hospitals in virtual space. Here, her essay about "haptic space" (which uses technology to simulate the senses of touch and motion) expands her earlier focus on institutional architecture, be it in physical or virtual space. She reminds us that "architectural structures are projections and reflections of the human body, the shape and meaning of which shift according to historical and cultural context." In the patriarchal worlds of Ancient Greece and Rome, male architects created spaces that echoed their own embodiment, a pattern that would be replicated across millennia. The father of architecture, Vitruvius, argued that the design of buildings should be founded on the proportions and symmetry of the perfect human form, which he deemed to be the male body, and which he saw as orderly and rational and as "the paradigm of creation."

After tracing the recent shift in the importance of vision for the design of our everyday world, she shows how hospitals and homes are transforming as traditional sightlines in architectural design yield to individualized spaces that simultaneously—and perhaps paradoxically—embrace both nature and technology. These post-modern tactile homes shield the occupant from the "authoritative eye" (known as the "spectator's gaze" in film studies parlance). They do not depend on the line of sight because they offer multi-sensory information that transcends an individual's ability to see. She dismisses the Cartesian concept of vision loss as a "mechanical failure and a disability" as obsolete, in somewhat the same way that the Cartesian dualism that distinguishes the mind from the body has been dismissed out of hand by contemporary neuropsychiatry even though it was championed by psychoanalysis. Professor Gardenour Walter herself veers toward the post-modernist views discussed in her more historical essay, where she denounces "oculocentrism" that privileges vision. Instead, she recommends dispensing with the current body hierarchy, and embracing the differences of human life as a sign of humanity. This approach recollects a parallel emphasis on "neurodiversity" advocated by organizations that speak on behalf of persons with autism.

We can contrast this approach with insights shared with me by Tanya Busailah, a teacher who had been married for 27 years to Reja-e, the recently deceased blind professor whose essay appears in this collection. She relates conversations with her late husband, where he instructed her on ways to heighten her own perception, not in a superhero style like the Drs. Midnight mentioned by Jaq Greenspon, but simply by paying attention to details that the average person overlooks, and which lead many people to erroneously conclude that sightless people have "extrasensory perception."

To quote Tanya Busailah, "he never subscribed to the idea that your other senses became stronger when you were blind." "He said everyone has these 'extra sense' abilities if they would just practice and pay attention! Whenever I [Tanya] lost my keys, Reja-e said, 'Quit using your eyes to find things, use your memory.' He gave me two strawberries and said, 'Put them both in your mouth. One of them is sweeter. Pay attention.'" She reminds us that Reja-e did not view his inability to see as a disability, any more than other people consider their inability to fly as a disability (Daedalus notwithstanding).

I imagine that arguments for and against the post-modernist approach to blindness would be prime fodder for a college philosophy classes, and that those conclusions would be very different from the conclusions that flow from a standard medical model. I also imagine that few of us have the equanimity to accept Reja-e's approach to his situation, even though his acceptance of an unchangeable condition makes the most sense of all.

My purpose here is not to advocate for a specific conclusion, or to promote my own viewpoint, but rather to present different views of the same subject and to let the reader draw his or her own conclusions. I suspect that persons who have encountered their own physical or mental or sensory challenges may react very differently than "armchair advocates" who approach these questions from a theoretical—rather than experiential— perspective. It is also likely that persons who have experienced temporary limitations on their vision or hearing or mobility espouse equally different perspectives than those who never experienced such sensory perceptions, and do not perceive their absence as a loss, as eloquently explained in Professor Basailah's essay about his blind boyhood. In fact, many medical and psychological studies of this subject have been conducted over time, with fairly consistent results that show that persons who are born with limitations adapt more easily than those who lose function at later times in life, and that persons who lose physical functions due to intentional human acts struggle even more than those who lose bodily functions to "natural causes." George Higham's essay highlights how two soldiers adapted to injuries sustained in wars and eventually achieved much more than an average person could ever achieve under ordinary circumstances.

What has changed over time are the rankings of the most feared medical conditions (and I add "blindness" as a medical condition, in spite of post-modernist arguments to the contrary). Currently, blindness is Americans' fourth most feared illness (after AIDS, cancer, and Alzheimer's disease). Yet in the not-so-distant past, before AIDS entered our lexicon and before Alzheimer's became a common concerns for our aging American population, the dread of blindness ranked much higher.

Before ending this unexpectedly lengthy introduction, let me refer back to the opening paragraphs of this introduction, where I mention Freudian concepts about the Oedipus complex, and hint at Freud's subsequent psychosexual explanations of behavior and the "family romance" paradigm implied by the Oedipus Complex. I feel obliged to address a different myth, an "old wives' tale," that attributes blindness to masturbation. Although we cannot attribute this myth to Freud, we also cannot relegate this seemingly atavistic idea entirely to the past because it still occasionally resurfaces in the present. Even though this inaccurate association was dispelled long ago by any number of scientific studies about sexuality (some of which were not as completely scientific as one would like), this once common idea persists in some circles. The question is asked often enough to merit open discussions—along with denials—on various respectable health websites (and on some less credible ones). Not surprisingly, some outliers on the internet still insist that it is true, but we must recall that a wide variety of other unusual and scientifically unsupported ideas also command attention on the internet.

Even though this contention falls under the rubric of "mythology" more than medicine and is no more credible than beliefs about the evil eye as the etiology of blindness (as noted in Professor Busailah's boyhood memoir), we should still consider the fact that several STDs (sexually transmitted diseases) can nevertheless impair vision and cause blindness. That is a medical fact and is non-negotiable. Potential culprits include chlamydia, syphilis, gonorrhea and AIDS.

Neonatal conjunctivitis (opthalmia neonaturm) is most commonly associated with *Chlamydia,* whereas the conjunctivitis associated with gonorrhea (*Neisseria*), which is transmitted from an infected mother during the neonate's passage through the birth canal, is the most visually threatening. AIDS, although less prevalent in America today than it was a few decades ago, remains an important contributor to vision loss, given that 20–40 percent of people with AIDS develop CMV (cytomegalovirus) retinitis, which robs its victims of sight. Acquired and congenital syphilis may seem like relics of a Victorian past, but it remains on the medical horizon even today, and has increased in prevalence in recent decades. Syphilis is associated with many medical, cardiac, dermatological, neurological and psychiatric consequences, along with potential vision loss. Oddly enough, these sexually transmitted diseases require contact with an infected partner, rather than self-stimulation, and directly contradict the contention that masturbation causes blindness. However, not everyone admitted to such activity, which may be one of the reasons why this unsophisticated belief about blindness persisted as long as it did. Perhaps an historian of medicine will excavate the origins of this idea and bury it for good.

As I draw this introduction to a conclusion, I feel obliged to mention some essays that I had hoped to publish, but which did not arrive, largely because of complications from COVID and work and life demands imposed by the pandemic on academics. I had hoped to include more material on early Christian history, and on Muslim, Hindu, Buddhist and East Asian attitudes toward vision loss, including information about the blind swordsman/samurai archetype. In some cases, I was able to interject an extra sentence or two on these critical issues in other entries. I regret that these religions are not addressed in greater detail elsewhere, given religion's overarching role in shaping our ideas about visual loss (and just about everything else in life and death). Religion existed long before science, and its influence will likely outlast many ideas that were once touted as science but were eventually disproven and are now treated as superstition.

For instance, Buddhist stories about the 500 blind beggars deserve at least as much attention as, if not more than, Kurosawa's renowned 1985 film, *Ran*, where a boy is left blind and impoverished, yet consoled by Buddhist rituals. That film was made when the director himself was nearly blind. The Third Eye of Shiva, in the Hindu and Jain traditions, is very relevant, as are Hindu and Jain stories about the blind men and the elephant, which are used as metaphors for the disparities between individual interpretations of manifest reality and for humans' overall inability to perceive the whole truth when we focus exclusively on perceptions that we encounter in our own environment. In fact, that allegory can be aptly applied to this essay collection, given that authors from different academic or artistic backgrounds often tackle the same subject (the *Daredevil* character, for example, or Wells' much-cited short story about "The Country of the Blind" or *The Day of the Triffids* or Nobel Laureate José Saramago's *Blindness*), and they—predictably—see these very same topics through different lenses and present different insights.

Notes

1. Sharon Packer, *A Belated Obituary: Raphael J. Osheroff, MD,* first published in 2013 in *Psychiatric Times*, tells the human side of the story that catalyzed the transition from "beliefs" or dogmas to "evidence-based" medicine.

2. Sholem Aleichem, *Motl the Cantor's Son.*
3. My thanks to Heidi Anne Duerr, M.P.H., of *Psychiatric Times* for granting permission to reprint a redacted version of the original article.
4. Laurie Martin's essay on her sister's hearing loss.
5. M. Leona Godwin, written with Okezie Nwoka. "When People See Your Blindness, They Stop Seeing You as Human." www.catapult.co [accessed online June 7, 2021].
6. For more information about Jessica Jones, see Sharon Packer, "Jessica Jones, Women and Alcohol Use Disorders," in *Jessica Jones: Scarred Superhero,* ed. Tim Rayborn and Abigail Keyes (Jefferson, NC: McFarland, 2018), 64–82.

Sound Over Sight

*Depicting Blindness in Horror Films
(From a Sound Specialist's Perspective)*

Jeffrey Bullins

Darkness, the unseen, the unknown. The fear of what we cannot see is at the core of one of humankind's strongest and primal emotions. Horror films are defined by the emotion that they seek to produce in their audience. When discussing this genre, whether a movie is really "scary" is the determining factor on its success. Everson sees horror as relying on audience response more than other genres, noting, "More than any other kind of film, it depends for its ultimate effect on the scaring of the audience by manipulating their emotions."[1] Certainly over the decades plenty of tactics have been used to frighten the audience: gothic castles in the 1930s, radioactive bugs in the 50s, slashers and serial killers in the 80s and 90s. Yet the fear of the unknown and unseen remains at the heart of many of these frights. In the absence of sight what can we rely on to protect ourselves from the dangers in the dark? We hold our breath and listen closely.

Creative use of sound, then, is often relied on to generate feelings of fear. William Whittington claims, "In general, horror films use music and sound effects to establish emotive intensity and impact far more aggressively and conceptually than any other genre."[2] Sound can help the viewer identify with the protagonist, empathizing with them. It can provide an objective perspective, promoting realism and believability. It can misdirect and then thrill with a jump scare. Some critics surmise that sound was a necessity for the creation of the genre. Roy Kinnard notes sound's role in the creation of the genre, stating, "The horror film as a genre was officially born in the early sound era, on November 16, 1931 [the day *Frankenstein* was released]."[3] However, it was in the sequel, *Bride of Frankenstein* (1935), in which The Monster forms a friendship with a blind hermit. The hermit is not a main character, and his role is more to exhibit the misunderstanding of The Monster. For a moment it seems like the hermit and The Monster could live happily together before they are found by townsfolk. One of them states that The Monster isn't human and asks the hermit, "Good God, man, can't you see!?" Though the hermit is not frightened by what he cannot see, the horror film soundtrack often seeks to by promoting the scariness of the unseen. Further, much of the soundtrack for films with blind characters deal with determining whose perspective is taken. Does it subjectively connect the viewer to a blind character, or does it objectively allow the events to unfold? This essay will examine a selection of soundtracks from films that contain blind protagonists and/or antagonists.

In *The Philosophy of Horror*, Noel Carroll makes a distinction between natural feelings of horror such as "I am horrified by the prospect of an ecological disaster" and what is termed "art-horror," the horror tropes of literature, film, and fine art.[4] Rather than a realistic horror, it is the audience's connection to the narrative and characters that elicits feelings of fright. There are some general assumptions about what it takes to frighten a horror movie audience. Bodo Winter notes, "As people are generally afraid of the unknown, horror movies may be tapping into mental associations between knowing and seeing."[5] Winter argues that the metaphor of "evil is dark," which permeates the genre, is a counter to the concept of "understanding is seeing." When we can see something, we can know or understand it. Thus, the dark and unseen are instinctually frightening, and some horror films have attempted to tap into this ancient fear through the inclusion of blind characters. At times, the audience experiences the story as they do, but in other instances the perspective of the audience is more objective, resulting in sympathy or concern more than identification.

A notable blind protagonist is Susy Hendrix, played by Audrey Hepburn in *Wait Until Dark* (1967). Hepburn received an Oscar nomination for her portrayal of a blind woman whose home is invaded by criminals looking for drugs that her husband was unknowingly given. Not born blind, Susy lost her sight in an automobile accident. This follows a trend from the Victorian period, observed by David Boir, in which authors without visual impairments created characters who are "generally blinded rather than born blind."[6] Is this necessary for a connection between the character and an audience member that is not visually impaired? Or does it explain why Susy perhaps is more vulnerable? Increasing tension and suspense, *Wait Until Dark's* soundtrack fluidly moves between objectively showing the events unfold and giving us subjective insight into Susy's emotions. In an overall negative review from 1968, Stephen Farber does recognize the film as "a work whose tension depends on intimacy."[7]

Susy is not actually introduced until twenty minutes into the film. The opening credits show drugs being put into a doll, a woman bringing that doll through the airport, and then handing it off to Susy's husband Sam when she gets suspicious. Three men, Talman, Carlino, and Roat, are looking for the doll and end up at the Hendrixes' apartment. There is some searching and expository dialog before Susy arrives home. Seeing her approach, Roat tells everyone "Don't breathe!" While the opening credit sequence contained underscore by Henry Mancini, which continued into the film, when Susy comes home the soundtrack becomes noticeably quiet. Even though the music is understood to be non-diegetic, outside of the film world and only for the audience to hear, it must be absent for the criminals' noises to potentially be heard. Thus, the soundtrack becomes more objective in that it realistically presents the sounds of the space. Even though underscore is the usual indicator of emotion and mood, the lack of it here creates tension since any sound the criminals make would alert Susy to their presence. The men go undetected and make it out of the apartment after Susy leaves. Subsequently they begin an elaborate con game in order to get Susy to reveal the location of the doll.

Mancini had been the composer for Audrey Hepburn's previous film *Two for the Road* (1967) and she advocated to her husband and producer, Mel Ferrer, that Mancini be brought on for *Wait Until Dark*. Mancini's score gives insight into Susy's experience as well as creating an uncomfortable experience for the audience. He incorporated out of tune pianos, about which John Caps notes, "that sound goes a long way toward recreating the unsettling world of Suzie [sic], under attack from forces she certainly cannot see nor barely comprehend."[8] The soundtrack is not always dissonant, though, such as during tender moments between Susy and her husband or when Susy and her child neighbor Gloria make up after an argument. Yet what remains is that the vast majority of the soundtrack is constructed to support her point of view. At 50:08 a loud squeak is produced by Roat's shoe as he comes down the short flight of stairs in the apartment. Even though this happens in a close-up, the sound is particularly prominent in the mix. The sound effect is important as a plot point, Susy will recognize the sound again later, but also in showing us Susy's awareness and allowing us to hear as she does.

Similarly, at 1:07:41, Carlino knocks on the door and the sound is loud and reverberant. Susy and Gloria are hiding quietly, and the contrast of the loud knock is particularly effective in producing a startle. While *Wait Until Dark* is not a traditional horror film (no monsters, ghosts or mad scientists), startles such as this are a tried-and-true generic convention. Likewise, as Susy grows more suspicious of the criminals, dissonant underscore becomes more prominent. At 1:22:19 low piano hits accompany

Susy's realization that her phone line has been cut. This reflects her emotional state and is all the more impactful given how subtle the score is in the first half of the film. In preparing to defend herself from the criminals, Susy breaks all the lights in the apartment. The lead up to a final confrontation between Susy and Roat is accompanied by slow, tense music that ends when Susy knocks out the final light in the apartment, plunging everything into darkness. At this point only diegetic sounds (sounds the characters could hear in their space) are heard, giving us the same experience as Susy by listening closely for any important sound. Unfortunately, the sound effects over a black screen are short lived as Susy lights matches. While this may seem a strange thing for a blind person to do, it does have narrative reasoning in that she wants Roat to find her cane and tap the floor, so she knows where he is. Susy manages to stab Roat, and the action is paired with a big music sting. This moment and the big scare less than a minute later when Roat leaps toward Susy are more in line with the typical horror soundtrack trope of "jump scares." As such, while a music sting for the stabbing does highlight the difficulty of Susy's actions, the soundtrack during the climax of this film moves somewhat away from Susy's subjective perspective into a thrilling aural experience for the audience. Yet it is this movement between diegetic sounds, Susy's viewpoint, and the fluidity of the audience's perspective that keeps the soundtrack interesting.

Even though the subjectivity in regard to Susy's perspective can be seen as creating a connection between her and the audience, Johnson Cheu interprets this as "co-optations of the Blind gaze meant to reinforce the dominant power that sight embodies" and that subsequently this co-optation "is the vanishing point of her subjectivity."[9] Following this, the soundtrack can be understood as positioning the audience at an advantage over the blind character and thus increasing the portrayal of helplessness and dependency. While this is somewhat contested by Susy's ability to save herself, the dependency of the blind female protagonist is highlighted in *See No Evil* (1971), which was released just a few years later. *See No Evil* follows the story of Sarah, played by Mia Farrow, who has been blinded during a horse-riding accident and is staying with her aunt and uncle in the English countryside. While she is out, her family is murdered, but being blind, she does not realize this when she comes home. While some moments allow insight into Sarah's perspective, much of the film involves seeing things like broken glass on the floor and wondering if she will step on it. In a 2018 review of the Blu-ray release, Christina Newland cites the tense Elmer Bernstein score and visuals, which include "slow zooms to chilling reveals, well-laid traps to which the sightless woman is prone to fall victim at any moment—the sensationalist scares are enjoyable, if a little cheap."[10] This echoes Roger Greenspun's September 3, 1971,

New York Times review in which he states that the film "has its share of thrills. Cheap thrills, to be sure, but thrills none the less." As such, *See No Evil* falls a bit more clearly into the horror genre with the goal to frighten by showing a helpless woman in dangerous situations.

Sarah was visiting stables when her family was killed. When she returns home, the soundtrack is similar in style to when Susy first comes home in *Wait Until Dark*. That is, objectively presented diegetic sounds. As Sarah unknowingly steps around broken glass and a silver bracelet lying on the floor, there are no musical stings to highlight the danger. Rather, the soundtrack remains objective while we are given visual information of which she is. This follows Cheu's view of the dominance of sight relegating the blind to a position of helplessness. So, even if we are hearing the space as Sarah would, we are getting "cheap thrills" from waiting to see if she is harmed or discovers the corpses of her family. Neither happens at this point and Sarah goes to bed. While she is sleeping we hear more typical dissonant "horror" music, which actually situates the music apart from her in that it is following the terrible murders of which she is unaware. Similarly, a sudden music sting accompanies the sight of Sarah's dead cousin (the two are sharing a bedroom), causing a jump scare while Sarah is oblivious.

Contrasting sharply to this mood is the montage the next morning of Sarah riding with her friend Steve who has just gifted her a horse. When Steve arrives at her house, Sarah is on the cusp of discovering the dead body of her uncle in the bathtub she is filling, but Steve distracts, and the reveal is further postponed. As the couple rides horses by a stream, only underscore is present, no environmental sounds. This illustrates the disconnect between what Sarah is experiencing and reality. While we do get insight into the happiness she is feeling riding with Steve, a cut back to the dead bodies in the house reminds us of the grim truth she will inevitably discover. Charles Derry notes that from the very beginning of the film Sarah is the obvious victim and "we just know that before the movie is over, Farrow is going to undergo a horrific ordeal that we shall vicariously share."[11] However, as the soundtrack indicates, the audience perspective does not hold fast to that of Sarah and many of the thrills in the film come from the generic technique of having information that the victim does not. In the climactic action of the film, Sarah does not show quite the amount of fortitude as Susy and in the end is saved from the murderer by Steve. In regard to producing fright in the audience, this follows Cheu's observation that depicting blind women "as both helpless and dependent shows ableist fears about disability."[12]

The first film adaptation of Thomas Harris' novel *Red Dragon* was released as *Manhunter* in 1986. While the film does not contain a blind main character, the serial killer antagonist Francis Dollarhyde forms a relationship with a blind woman, Reba McClane, who works at a film processing lab. *Red Dragon* was adapted again in 2002 and in both films Reba functions as a victim who, like Sarah, is unknowingly in a dangerous situation. The soundtracks of both films move between subjectivity and objectivity but not really in regard to Reba's perspective. Even though she has a larger part in the newer film, like *See No Evil* the goal is to create tension by giving the audience information she does not have. Steven Rybin notes the importance of sound in *Manhunter* and the "to-and-fro movement" of subjectivity which "is designed to keep the audience, at different junctures in the film, both involved and distanced from the events."[13] Protagonist Will Graham remarks that for the killer Dollarhyde, "It's all about seeing." This is true for the audience as well, with the soundtrack deftly moving between perspectives so that the disturbing events are thrilling but at a safe cinematic distance.

In the wake of Reba McClane, other imperiled blind women show up in 90s crime/thriller/horror films. Helena in *Jennifer 8* (1992) and Emma in *Blink* (1994) fall more into the helpless damsel category than "final girl,"[14] although Emma does end up defeating the killer in the end (thanks in part to her minimal vision). In *Jennifer 8*, Helena is a blind music student who becomes involved in a murder mystery when detective John Berlin suspects her roommate was a victim. Mostly the film follows Berlin's investigation and romantic involvement with Helena. The suspected serial killer preys on blind victims and Helena is put in dangerous situations similar to Sarah's. Also borrowing from *See No Evil*, in which the climactic attack on Sarah occurs while she is bathing, Helena becomes doubly vulnerable after disrobing and getting in a bath. The killer is in the room with her and when he moves there is a music sting. Obviously, Helena is not aware of his presence and thus the soundtrack functions here as a startle for the audience. Similarly, when Helena becomes overwhelmed with the cacophonous noise of a Christmas party, the soundtrack does not increase with intensity as she becomes more anxious. Rather, it seems more about watching her than experiencing it with her. Later in the film, following the death of his partner, Berlin is interrogated by special agent St. Anne, who asks if he "picks on this little blind girl" because he can control her, further situating Helena as stereotypically vulnerable.

Blink also has a police detective, John Hallstrom, getting into a relationship with a blind witness, Emma Brody, who also happens to be a musician. However, at the beginning of the film Emma is undergoing a treatment to restore her sight. Unlike *Jennifer 8*, *Blink* focuses on Emma from the beginning and the soundtrack does exhibit her perspective.

When doctors come to take her bandages off after the procedure, one moves a stool closer to her. An innocuous action, the sound of the wheels is particularly loud in the mix, an indication of her sensitive hearing. Similarly, when she is being interviewed soon after, the reporter puts a pen in her mouth, which is also exaggeratedly loud. As her vision develops, the subjectivity continues through POV shots that are blurry and distorted. In contrast, the portions of the film involved with Hallstrom and the murder investigation are presented much more objectively. Thus, the soundtrack moves between two modes as the story shifts between Emma and the police. Since Emma does rely somewhat on her burgeoning sight, she is less often in unknown dangerous situations like Helena or Sarah. Instead, what she sees is called into question, thus increasing mystery and tension.

A more recent film that follows this same formula is *In Darkness* (2018), in which cowriter/producer Natalie Dormer portrays Sofia, a blind pianist who may have witnessed a murder. The opening scene is a misdirection in that a woman shown being murdered is actually just in a movie and Sofia is playing in the orchestra that is scoring it. As she walks home after the recording session, multi-layered environmental sounds are loud in the mix. In the subway, her footsteps, the scraping of her cane, and the screech of the train all sound more prominent than normal. In a coffee shop, the hiss of the espresso machine and the news on TV are so loud they distract Sofia from the clerk's dialog. The first part of the film thus establishes the heightened sonic world that Sofia lives in, even though she later tells a detective that she heard nothing the night her neighbor died. He even presses her by asking if her other senses are strengthened due to her lack of sight. Mostly the subjectivity serves to show us how Sofia is overwhelmed by intense sounds, but it also sets her up as a capable protagonist when the story moves into an absurdly elaborate plot involving Russian spies, missing USB drives, and Serbian war criminals.

Also released in 2018 was *Bird Box*, a huge success for distributor Netflix. In January 2019, the Associated Press reported that 45 million accounts watched the film in its first week of release. Sandra Bullock plays Malorie, who is seen in the opening of the film fervently telling two children that they must keep blindfolds on, or they will die. The blindness of Malorie and other characters in the film is temporary and self-imposed, a safeguard against monsters (which of course are never shown) who cause those who look at them to commit suicide. Much of the film takes place in flashbacks which show the initial chaos of the monsters' effect and then Malorie's interactions with a group of survivors. While literal lack of sight is a major point of conflict for Malorie and the children, the "blindness" of misunderstanding is the main friction between the survivors. This situation is reminiscent of the horror classic *Night of the Living Dead* (1968) in which survivors hole up together in a farmhouse to avoid zombies.

While Malorie is the center of the story and the only character seen throughout the entire film, the soundtrack does not necessarily support a subjective perspective from her point of view. Rather, it follows a trend in contemporary horror films of creating a soundscape that more directly guides the audience from moment to moment. For instance, when Malorie and the children are headed down a river in search of other survivors, the sounds of their conversation under a blanket in the boat are appropriately close and claustrophobic. But the perspective does not stay with them; rather a high angle wide shot of the boat shows us their dangerous traversal and unnatural sound effects suggest the presence of the monsters. So, the scene becomes less about being trapped with the characters under the blanket and more about seeing their treacherous situation. Like the other films discussed, tension is created from the audience having knowledge that the protagonist does not. As such, the soundtrack of *Bird Box* guides us through plot points and delivers thrills to the audience as spectators, less so participants. Likewise, Karin Lowachee sees the survivors as merely plot devices and states, "Malorie is played as disconnected and no-nonsense, so the viewer is already removed from any sort of beating heart in the film."[15]

So, the film ends up following the ocularcentric device of seeing what our imperiled protagonists cannot. The climactic action of the film, in which Malorie and the kids get separated in the woods, contains interesting use of subjective sound design as all of them begin to hear voices. It is unclear if the monsters are producing the voices, if they are just in the characters' heads, or if this is an indicator of what others have heard from the monsters. None of that really matters as the goal is confusion and their disability from lack of sight. Eventually they regroup and make it to another group of survivors, which happens to be at a school for the blind. This does not really change the film's focus on blindness as a disability but does give us a happy ending for characters that have endured terrible events.

In the horror genre, the majority of blind characters are victims, and their portrayed vulnerability can result in tension and fear particularly when the audience is aware of dangers that the character is not. But what about antagonists? In discussing films that feature sensory loss, Lara Kern states, "While other modern classics of claustrophobia *The Descent* (2005) and *Don't Breathe* (2016) also feature sightless villains, both monster and human, it's more commonly the victim that's impaired."[16] Both of these films have blind antagonists and derive much of their terror from the victims being trapped in a dark place: a cave in *The Descent* and a blind man's house in *Don't Breathe*.

In *The Descent* a group of friends take a spelunking trip in the

Appalachian Mountains. The story is mostly focused on Sarah, who lost her husband and daughter in a car wreck a year before. Dreams and subjective sequences position the viewpoint as mostly hers. The "crawlers," monstrous anthropoids living in the cave, do not show up until almost an hour into the film. Initially it is Sarah who glimpses one, but her friends assure her that it is only the dark "playing tricks on her." As antagonists, the Crawlers are mostly mindless monsters, even though there is some suggestion via the presence of cave paintings that they are perhaps devolved humans (this is never explored or explained, however). Director Neil Marshall, in a 2006 interview, stated that the Crawlers use smell and echolocation to hunt in the dark. However, James Marriott notes a discrepancy, stating, "The fight scenes should be full of the sound of their clicking as they try to work out where the cavers are. But the crawlers are more or less silent during the fights: they simply seem to automatically know the location of their prey."[17] As such, these monsters are more about exploiting the protagonists' fears of being unable to see. That instinctual fear of a predator lurking unseen in the dark is more important in *The Descent* than explaining some sort of origin for the cave monsters.

In *Don't Breathe*, the antagonist is given a backstory, but only after the reveal that The Blind Man (his name is never stated in the film) is not a victim as he is initially depicted. The opening of the film introduces a trio of small-time criminals, Rocky, Money, and Alex, the latter of which uses his father's home security connections to break into homes. They get a tip about a large amount of cash supposedly in The Blind Man's home, a result of a settlement after his daughter was killed in a car wreck. The three break into the house and though Money releases some type of gas meant to keep the Man asleep, he emerges and asks in a breaking voice, "who's there?" But this vulnerability does not last long as he quickly wrests away Money's gun, a reversal that "is all the more startling because of its suddenness, which confounds genre convention." However, later plot twists still occur, such as when the thieves discover The Blind Man has been keeping the woman responsible for his daughter's death locked in his basement.

For the most part, *Don't Breathe* has a soundtrack typical of contemporary horror films: ominous underscore, low frequency tones and drones, deep impacts that accompany scene changes and plot points. As such, the perspective of the film is more that of the spectator audience than any particular character. Since The Blind Man is the antagonist, the focus of the soundtrack tends to be the sounds that the thieves are making and the worry that he will hear them rather than presenting things from his point of view. When Rocky first enters the house through the bathroom window, Foley sound effects are prominent. Every movement she makes is heard, the creak of her leather jacket, the crunch of her foot on a piece of glass. After Rocky walks through the house and shuts off the alarm, her breathing is heard, referencing the title of the film and the fact that she still makes noise even when she is not moving. Alex's breathing is similarly loud in the mix against underscore, tones, and hits, which is necessary to indicate he is still audible. The tension, then, is similar to when the criminals are in Susy's house in *Wait Until Dark*. We are waiting for any sound to betray their presence. Tibbetts compares the two films, saying that the reveal of The Blind Man as a formidable villain would be like Susy "revealed to be Norman Bates's knife-wielding 'mother.'"[18]

When we are not leaning in to hear tiny noises, other aspects of the soundtrack situate the perspective for the audience only. When the thieves first enter the house, after the characters move out of frame a shot lingers on a workbench and a hammer on the wall. A very low frequency tone indicates the future importance of the tool, obviously unbeknownst to the characters. Likewise, when the man shuts off the lights in the basement, a monochromatic "night vision" style is used so that we can still see the positions of everyone, thus increasing tension when the thieves get close to the man. At other times close-up shots of the man's ear are used and the soundtrack becomes suddenly quiet. This results in sharp volume contrasts that create a roller coaster effect, appropriate for the thrills and jump scares the film is trying to produce. In regards to the dangerous space of the house, composer Roque Banos noted in an interview for the Blu-ray release that he wanted the music to sound "as if it was coming from the environment," further evidencing the subjective soundscape being created for the audience to inhabit.

In producing fear and tension, the soundtrack is an important part of any horror film, and almost universally it is critical to films that feature blindness or deprivation of sight. While a soundtrack that is subjective to a blind character could help the audience identify with them, it seems the end result is to highlight the knowledge of the visually unimpaired audience. When Susy is listening closely, we watch the criminals trying not to breathe. When Sarah is filling up her bathtub, we are focused on if she will discover the body in it. As Rocky creeps around The Blind Man's basement, we tensely watch the two almost bump into each other. The horror soundtrack often moves fluidly between objective and subjective as well as between certain characters' points of view, with the goal of thrilling the viewer even if that means promoting stereotypes about the vulnerability of the blind.

NOTES

1. William K. Everson, *Classics of the Horror Film* (New Jersey: Citadel Press, 1974), 2.
2. William Whittington, *Sound Design and Science Fiction* (Austin: University of Texas Press, 2007), 130.

3. Roy Kinnard, *Horror in Silent Films* (Jefferson, NC: McFarland & Company, 1995), 1.
4. Noel Carroll, *The Philosophy of Horror or Paradox of the Heart* (New York: Routledge, 1990), 12.
5. Bodo Winter, "Horror Movies and the Cognitive Ecology of Primary Metaphors." *Metaphor and Symbol* 29 (July 2014): 162.
6. David Bolt, "Aesthetic Blindness: Symbolism, Realism, and Reality." *Mosaic: An Interdisciplinary Critical Journal*, Vol. 46, No.3 (September 2014): 96.
7. John Caps, *Henry Mancini: Reinventing Film Music* (Champaign, IL: University of Illinois Press, 2012), 106.
8. Stephen Farber, "Wait Until Dark." *Film Quarterly*, Vol. 21, No.3 (Spring 1968): 63.
9. Johnson Cheu, "Seeing Blindness on Screen: The Cinematic Gaze of Blind Female Protagonists." *The Journal of Popular Culture*, Vol. 42, No. 3 (June 2009): 484–485.
10. Christina Newland, "See No Evil." *Sight and Sound*. January 1, 2018: 104.
11. Charles Derry, *The Suspense Thriller: Films in the Shadow of Alfred Hitchcock* (Jefferson, NC: McFarland, 2010), 35.
12. Cheu, 493.
13. Steven Rybin, *Michael Mann: Crime Auteur* (Lanham, MD: Scarecrow Press, 2013), 94.
14. Carol Clover coined this term in *Men, Women, and Chainsaws* to describe the female protagonist in horror films that defeats or survives the villain.
15. Karin Lowachee, "*Bird Box* Never Quite Takes Off." *Fantasy and Science Fiction* (May/June 2019): 196.
16. Laura Kern, "Senseless Violence." *Film Comment* (May/June 2018): 22.
17. James Marriott, *The Descent*. Liverpool: Auteur; 2013, 44.
18. John C. Tibbetts, "Don't Breathe review." *Film & History*. 46.2 (Winter 2016): 104.

A Blind Boyhood
Reflections by a Poetry Professor
Reja-e Busailah

The following selections are from my memoir, *In the Land of My Birth: A Palestinian Boyhood,* first published by the Institute for Palestine Studies in 2017. These selections are an attempt to present a narrative in the style and language of a growing blind child. They narrate experiences which I believe most of the blind share; the book, however, narrates and describes much more than the experiences of blindness.[1]

1.

My father is big, much bigger than me. He has a deep voice, deeper than Mother's. It is broad, big, and deep, as if it could split into two voices. Mother's voice is not as big and deep. It is soft and sweet. I like Mother's voice, but I want my voice to be like Father's, big and deep. I cannot make my voice as deep as his. I envy the sounds he makes when he eats or drinks. When he draws the rice into his mouth off the spoon, there is a big, long swish. He slurps the lentil soup and slurps the tea. I do not know how to do that. He slurps the coffee too.

They do not let me drink coffee. Children do not drink coffee. I wonder why. Coffee perks as it boils and smells good. It smells even better when Mother roasts it and grinds it before she makes it. Tea does not smell as good as coffee, but it makes the kitchen warm when it boils on the stove, and I am allowed to drink it. My mother brings the coffee to my father; she does not bring tea. Father brings neither coffee nor tea to Mother.

When she walks, my mother's footsteps are many and fast and loud. When my father walks, his footsteps are not as many. They are slower and not as noisy. When my father speaks while standing, his voice comes from high, from far above. My mother's voice comes from lower down, much closer to me. At night Father's breathing is deep and broad, unlike Mother's, which is soft and thin, and unlike my sister's, which is so soft that it is hard to hear sometimes. When Father pees in the chamber pot, it makes a sound very different from the sound Mother makes. In vain I try to make the sound my father makes when he breathes and when he pees in the chamber pot.

The bathroom is outside, and it is cold out. Inside it is warm under the blanket. We sleep on two mattresses on the floor—one on the left, where my parents sleep, and one to the right, where my sister Najeebah and I sleep. The mattresses are stuffed with cotton batting, but they are very thin. Sometimes I am awake while they sleep. The little clock on the table ticks and ticks and I think of Najeebah and of my father and of my mother. My mother has so much hair on her head, thick and long; it smells nice. My father has no hair on the top of his head and thin hair in the back, and his head has no smell. In the morning Mother folds the mattresses and lays them on top of one another against the wall. When night comes, she unrolls them.

Sometimes at night the clock is quiet. The tick-tock, tick-tock sound it makes is not there. They are all asleep—Mother, Father, and my sister Najeebah—but when the clock is not ticking their breathing sounds different and the room is scarcely the room. Is the clock still on the table? Usually, it stands on the table, ticking away all the time. Maybe Father forgot to wind it. He will wind it tomorrow and it will tick-tock again.

Now it is morning and the clock is on the table ticking away, and I am at the opposite end of the room. To my right is where my mother lays down the mattresses when we go to sleep. To my left is the door that opens to the hall and on to the kitchen on the right; I am standing facing the clock as it ticks away. I can walk straight toward it. I can walk straight all the way, guided by its tick-tocks.

When I enter the room the clock ticks on my left. It is hard to hear it when I am in the hall. If Father forgets to wind it, it does not tick, and then things are different in the room where we sleep. I do not like it when the clock stops ticking. I know everything in the room better when the clock is ticking. I know where I am when the clock is ticking. I am less sure of myself when it does not tick.

The voice of my mother and the voice of my father and the sound of the clock ticking—they all make it easier for me to find my direction and my way. "Here I am, son," says Mother. "Come, come," she says, sometimes clapping her hands. "Walk toward me. Here I am. Follow my voice." I walk toward her, following her voice, and I walk straight, veering neither left nor right. When there is no voice or ticking, I do not walk straight.

It is light, because my face feels the heat of the sun. Or it is light, because I feel the heat coming from the lamp that my mother has lit for the evening. When she turns on the Primus, the kerosene stove, I feel the heat, though sometimes they say there is no light. Or they say it is light, when I felt no sun or the lamp's heat. Light of the moon. Light of the stars. Hard to believe, puzzling. What is light, then? My Aunt Ra'oufeh calls me "light of my eyes." Light of her eyes! And I heard the man say, "His eyes are dim, dark." What is light? What is dark? How can my eyes be dark when I am the light of Aunt Ra'oufeh's eyes? For now it is enough that night is dark and day is light, even though the annoying, even painful, fact is that in reality I knew neither, I experienced neither. I existed neither in the dark nor in the light.

Shadow and color, too, were mysteries. Shadow was sometimes in front of me, I was told, sometimes behind me, sometimes smaller than me, sometimes bigger. My shadow! My playmates tried in vain to catch their shadows and never gave up trying. If you jump, your shadow jumps. If you run toward your shadow, your shadow runs away from you. If you run away from your shadow, it runs after you. If you stop, it stops. They say that my shadow jumps with me, runs away from me, pursues me. But what is shadow if you can't hear it, smell it, or touch it?

The same with colors. I agreed, though not unquestioningly, that the sky is blue, that the grass is green, that the fire is sometimes red and sometimes white, that white is good and black is bad. Everybody says so, so why shouldn't I? Yes, and that so-and-so has a white heart and so-and-so has a black heart. I liked the first. 'Itaf, Najeebah's little playmate, has a white heart. But I felt uneasy about the black heart. My ideas about colors remained separate from the experience of my senses. Colors and their application are something mental, an approximation, something that can only be memorized.

I had better luck with echo, though there was a lot of puzzlement there too. Echoes could be heard. I heard their voices replicate themselves. I heard them as if each had been divided into two. I heard me divided into me and into my voice across the valley or down the water well. Echo responded sometimes immediately; sometimes it took more time. Sometimes the echo was so close, right on the heels of my voice, even attached to it. Sometimes it sounded so distant I thought it would not come back. I enjoyed playing with echo as much as the others enjoyed playing with shadow.

Gradually, I came to realize the value and usefulness of sound's echo. In some cases it helped me judge distance. In other cases I could judge the size of a room or how it was configured—how high its ceiling is, say, or how empty or full it might be. Everything depended on the kind of echo:

the sound of a voice or of a footstep, the snap of the finger, or the click of the tongue. If the sound makes an echo, the room is not full or has a high ceiling.

Maybe it came slowly, but its realization was sudden. I walked and I heard me coming toward the wall, or it coming toward me, and I stopped before walking into it. I walked, we came close to each other, and I passed by. Or, it would be the tree standing tall, or a telephone pole, and I would pass by without bumping into them. It took some time before I realized that the sound of my footsteps warned me about the wall, the tree, the post, the telephone pole. This was confirmed in my mind when I walked barefoot or with rubber-soled shoes on. The sound was muffled then, or quite different, so that neither the tree nor I heard the other, and I got a bruised nose or cut lip. A blockage made one sound; open space, another. Learning the difference was good, of course, but it was not good enough unless I was constantly on the alert. Often I would be inattentive, and often I would get into trouble.

I learned quite early how to utilize the snap of the fingers or the click of the tongue against tall objects, on the move or standing still. The sound produced by my arms and the water in the pool, I came to realize later, would even tell me how far I was from the approaching wall. On the other hand, my footsteps, the snap of the fingers, or the click of the tongue were of no help against low objects like a stool or a coffee table. Echo was of no help then. Nor did it help when there was an unexpected drop or depression. A sudden step down always resulted in surprise, shock, even the sinking of the heart. A deeper depression often resulted in real injury. My mother used to say that I bumped into things a lot when I was younger. This was because I was blind, she said. Yes, I did not know then how to make use of sound in order to avoid hurting myself.

One afternoon when I was a little older, we were walking back from Yousuf's store, myself and two or three other children. I do not remember who it was, but someone said that I was blind, without eyes, and that I could not walk home by myself. I asserted that I did have eyes and that I could walk on my own. My hand touched my eyes. My eyes were there, both of them. My companions took off. I was shocked, but I knew the road very well. I had already walked it many times, so I continued on my own. The path was curvy, rugged, and rocky. I got home; therefore, I had eyes. I was not really blind. I was proud of myself, but I was confused and sad that my companions would leave me like that. Again and again, my hand touched my eyes.

It was a cold and windy afternoon in Jerusalem. Mother, my sister Najeebah, and I were waiting to cross Nablus Road. There was a constant flow of cars. When the flow stopped, my sister rushed across the road, her footsteps fast and loud. I wanted to follow, my impatience rising. Mother held my hand tight, until there was another gap in the flow of the traffic. In front of me there was nothing—the car to my right was moving farther and farther away. I heard the car to my left (a big car, from the sound it made), but I thought it was still far enough away and that there was enough time for us to cross. I tugged at my mother's hand, but she half-yelled, "No, no son!" Before the loud car to the left reached us, a smaller car had moved ahead almost soundlessly. My mother's eyes proved smarter than my ears. Najeebah's eyes proved better than my ears—Najeebah, who was younger than I.

Later, three blind boys (I was one of them) were walking toward Bab al-Zawiya in al-Khalil (Hebron). We wanted to cross the street when a bus or truck passed by. We stopped. Immediately after, I wanted to rush across but my friend Musa, who was a couple of years older, stopped me. "Wait until the noise is completely gone," he said. "There may be another car just behind." And by God, there was! So I learned the rule, or principle, but for a long time I preached it better than I practiced it.

Volume, speed, distance, motion, and time—insensibly I came to realize their interaction and the importance of this interaction to crossing a street or reaching a destination. Eventually, the speed at which an approaching object moved and the increasing volume of its sound came to determine for me its distance, and thus my decision to act: whether to move, and at what speed, or to wait. Slowly, very slowly, I learned to evaluate and judge all these factors together. All would be nullified, however, if noise from the outside—traffic, say, or a high wind—interfered. I did not move if I could not hear, the way the sighted would not move, say, when in a dense fog.

We were in Ramleh, my father and I, waiting for the train that would take us to Jerusalem. We were standing near the house of Uncle Shakir and Aunt Fawziyyeh. Soon I heard the train hooting. I heard it rumbling louder and louder, as if it were broader and wider than its tracks. I was right in its path! It was bearing down upon us! I flinched and leaped back, but my father did not budge. As it drew still closer and closer, it seemed to veer a little bit away from us, and as it slowed down portions of it were moving alongside us. Then it was motionless and I wanted to touch it. I wanted to touch the wheels of this big monster, which now seemed tamable. But my father, or time, was in no mood to oblige me.

We got off at the station in Jerusalem, and I would not walk away from the train until I touched those wheels. My father yielded, and we bent down all the way to the ground. Suddenly, as I explored what I took for a wheel, there exploded upon us a voice strange and foreign. I soon learned that it was the voice of an English officer demanding to know what we were doing down there. We stood up. My father explained in words strange and with voice shaking, making gestures with his hand, now toward him, now toward me, his face equally turning with his voice, now toward him, now toward me. The Englishman suddenly turned soft and gentle. I marveled at how my father was able to make him gentle.

Was it the same train or was it another one? Surely it was a different day, and surely the train was running in the opposite direction, from Jerusalem toward Ramleh. It was a train we often took. It will puff rhythmically, slow at first, then faster and faster. The rhythm will be hypnotic. The train will stop first at Batteer, then Deir al-Shaikh, Artoof, Wad al-Sarar, al-Na'aneh, and Ramleh (I may have forgotten one or two). Sometimes, when the train stops at Batteer on the way back to Jerusalem, Father buys Batteer eggplants, the best in the country.

That day I was on the train with Mother, Father, Najeebah, and my maternal cousin Ahmad. I had a toy with me, a windup car with four wheels. Ahmad and I were standing in the train corridor at the window. It felt cool, and I held my toy outside the window. The train was chugging along—"one-two-three-four, one-two-three-four, one-two-three-four"— when suddenly the toy slipped from my hand. I heard it hit the hard ground, but to my surprise the toy was instantly way behind me. Yet when I drop a rock in front of me while standing still, it falls right at my feet. That day on the train, I was moving, and the difference this made was something like a great discovery.

My awareness of the difference between being blind and being sighted continued to grow. Very early I came to depend a great deal on hearing and touching, but gradually I came to realize that these two senses were inadequate as substitutes for vision. Often, if not always, they seemed not to tell the whole story. Sometimes they even told a different story from what vision told.

My father is talking to me as we sit at the table. I hear my mother's footsteps coming toward us. She says something to my sister, but only when she gets very close do I realize that she is bringing coffee to my father. Sometimes I smell it before I hear its name, and my hearing and my touching become useless. Or again, Najeebah and I are standing outside the house when she exclaims, "'Itaf is coming! 'Itaf is coming!" It takes my ears one or two minutes before they hear 'Itaf's voice and footsteps. Hearing and touch are much slower than seeing.

I feel 'Itaf's hand. I feel her hair. I feel her shoulders. I am taller than she, but I gradually realize that this is not all of 'Itaf. I realize this from the way my sister talks about her. She looks at 'Itaf and she knows all. I have to touch 'Itaf limb by limb, yet I do not know all! My sister takes everything in—the hair, the eyes, the hands, the feet, and more. She takes them in all at once. It takes me much longer, and even then I don't take her all in. There is more to her than her limbs, which I do not get. My sister's glance, like my father's and mother's, is faster, more accurate, more comprehensive.

Similarly, the cat meows and she has a small head and small ears and she has hair all over her. She has a tail and four legs, and when she is contented, she purrs. My family and my friends agreed with all of this, but they seemed to add something I did not get. It was the totality of the cat.

Or, they see a building and talk about it as if they know everything about it—all from a distance. I walk toward the building, around it, and it takes me a long, long time, touching parts of it and missing others. And by the time I am finished, or think I am finished, I am unable to put together in one whole the properties I have acquired through touch and then memorized, the way the sighted seem to do through vision with one glance. As for the sky, the stars, and the moon, I shall forever only hear about them. They are unapproachable, unfathomable.

Thus slowly, I came to realize that recognizing people and objects through hearing and touch gave me a different impression from the one that vision gives to the sighted. I was sure that there was such a difference, but I was never able to identify it. Over time I came to realize another way in which relying on touch is limited. I could touch my mother's hair and my father's bald head, and that made me think that I knew what my sister knew through seeing. But I could not do the same with strangers. It was not proper, I was made to understand. It was awkward, embarrassing. This disadvantage has never completely disappeared.

And with his eyes, my father reads! He reads in the book and the newspaper, yet the book is nothing but sheet upon sheet upon sheet. And the sheets of the book smell quite different from the sheets of the newspaper. The smell of the newspaper sheet is much stronger. The newspaper is made up of two or three sheets, which are very, very large. My father reads in them, he says, but how he reads and what he reads are mysteries. My sister cannot read yet, but she looks at the pictures in the book and the newspaper: she sees a cat, a dog, and even a horse in motion. I touch the book, I touch the newspaper, but I feel no pictures. I am confused, left out as they talk to one another using "this" and "that" without naming it. What is "this"? What is "that"? The same with "there." "Look *there*. It is *there*. *There* it is." But where?[2]

2.

I had lost my eyesight before I completed my first year. According to my father, this was caused by ophthalmia. My mother, however, gives a very different story. My eyes were beautiful, she told me, blue and all. But one day, when visiting in Ramleh, she ran into Imam Ibrahim Busailah. The woman was curious about the baby, Mother said. She looked at my eyes and exclaimed, "*Ya Allah!* They are worth the whole world!" Immediately afterward something went wrong with my eyes. Terrified, my mother ran to my grandmother and explained what had happened. My grandmother said Imm Ibrahim had the evil eye and scolded my mother for not snatching something from her: "a trace—a piece of cloth, a lock of hair, even a single hair—anything belonging to her in order to burn it and so cancel out the jinx." My mother protested that she did not know that Imm Ibrahim had the evil eye.

My parents took me to a hospital where the disease was all but cured, but then a nurse spoiled things. She must have used an eyedropper that was not clean, my parents concluded. They then took me to the hospital's rival, run by a certain eye doctor named Ticho, a Jew, at the time the most renowned in the Middle East. According to my father, Dr. Ticho did his best to save my eyes, but to no avail. It was too late, he said. Mother took me and prayed at the al-Aqsa Mosque, at the Holy Sepulchre, and at the Ibrahimi Mosque in Hebron. Her prayers were not answered. It must have been a bad blow to my parents that this should happen to their firstborn. It was depressing to their friends and neighbors. A friend was so affected by my parents' sorrow that he suggested—to the horror of my father—getting rid of the blind baby altogether by smothering him with a pillow. "How could I do such a thing to what God has given me!" my father said.[3]

3.

According to tradition, anyone who asks God for anything on the twenty-seventh night of the month of Ramadan would have his prayer answered. That was because this was the night the first chapter of the Qur'an was revealed. It was the Night of Power (*Lailatulqadr*), the most important night of the year, better than a thousand months. Heaven's gates would be open all night for the angels to descend to earth and then to ascend back. The angels in the air descending from heaven and ascending back were a marvel. The night would be peaceful and warm and festive with the sound and motion of the good angels—so festive, indeed, that you would feel you are a part of it.

That evening of the twenty-seventh was different from other evenings. It was a joyous one, quick with adults and children bent on using the night to the full. It was almost as alive as a sunny day, but better, because it was night—and the night of the twenty-seventh of Ramadan.

So, when everyone was busy and preoccupied, I slipped out of the house. I went down on my knees and stretched out my hands, my palms upward, and waited for what seemed a long time. I waited until I heard something open in the sky, a click. The angels were coming down; the Gates of Heaven were open. God will surely hear: "Please, my God, I don't want to be blind. Please give me my eyes back. I want to be like Is'haq and Khalil, and like my sister Najeebah."

I waited. I got up and went back inside, where all was quiet. Will it happen? Will it happen? Nothing … As much as I did believe it at the start, I did not believe it now. Why didn't He respond? Was I cursed? Why was I cursed? I knew then that there was no hope, that I was always going to be blind. I knew then that I would have to depend on whatever ingenuity I had—independence with much compromise and adjustments, even with foolhardiness and cunning.[4]

4.

The summer after graduation, more than once I heard my father tell my mother this story: Twice he had gone with Mr. Dajani to the Department of Education in Jerusalem, where both argued that I should be admitted into the prestigious Arab College in Jerusalem. Twice I was denied admission. "How will he take care of himself?" asked Mr. Ahmad Samih Khalidi, the director of the college. "How will he get to class, to the dining room? What if he needs to go to the bathroom?"

"Finally," I heard Father telling Mother, his voice rising, "I went to Mr. Hannoush, the Christian Syriac! Yes, the *Christian Syriac*! Can you imagine?" It was Mr. Hannoush who okayed my admission into Ramleh's High School on condition that I be kicked out after three months if I did not do well. Of my class at 'Alaiyyah School, only Fat'hi and I went on to high school, he in Hebron, I in Ramleh.

So, I am going to be admitted into secondary school, high school, blind, and I am going to be a high school student with the sighted! Before the House for Orphans, they were all I knew, and afterwards I played with them during vacations. But now I am going to study with them. I am going to learn more than I ever learned, and I am going to do well, to learn much. Does not the first verse revealed to our Prophet command that we read and learn? Did not our Prophet say, "Seek knowledge even if you have to travel as far as China for it"? "Seek knowledge from the cradle to the grave," they say. Don't I love learning? I will learn, and I will not be kicked out. Look at Mr. Dajani! Look at Taha Hussein! Haven't they done well? And isn't blind Abu al-'Ala' al-Ma'arri our greatest poet?

So one day in September, I found myself at my new school in a classroom full of the voices of boys. I could tell that the boys were looking at the newcomer, the blind student. They looked and whispered with excitement, a promising excitement. For a while I could sense that I was the object of the students' eyes, while I noted with my other senses some of their peculiarities, especially their voices and speech. I could feel that I was in a new world, wide, rich, ready to be explored.

It was strange and wonderful, like a dream. I was experiencing something similar to what I had experienced when I was little, when I was introduced to the sea for the first time—the scent in the air I had never known, fresh, aggressive, exciting; the mass of sound approaching from afar, becoming more and more distinct, coherent; the feel of the sand under my bare feet, first hard, then loose, then hard, then moist again, unsteady, slippery; the tumult of water and the waves breaking on the sand, then getting noisier and more challenging. And then the feel of the water, first shy and unsure, then rising up my limbs playfully, until I am lifted up in my Uncle Hussein's arms, just above the fray, announcing a vastness, endless and tempting. The class was a new world, a sea, and I was ready to plunge into it. My blindness was temporarily forgotten. It was no insurmountable obstacle. Mr. Khalidi's fears were unfounded. I was determined to make it. I was already making it!

5.

The human tide at first surged forward, but soon it was to slow down and merely to keep trudging on, pushed by the need to survive, to get out of the sun, because thirst and hunger were beginning to make themselves felt and because of the terror from behind, kept alive by the sounds of explosions, gunshots, air bombings, and planes swooping over us. There was also the slow pressure of this sea of men, women, and children, moving inexorably, rendered cruel and ruthless in its helplessness, edging forward in complete disarray, like an elemental force without intelligence. I started out walking with Haider. Soon we began to switch the suitcases we carried from one hand to the other. Soon I began now to lose him, now to find him, now to walk with one guide or companion, now with another, and now to walk alone, both following the noise and leading it, now stumbling over a stone, now getting a shock from a sudden drop, and so forth.

I had walked alone and with blind boys, especially in Hebron. But our walks always took place on roads and in streets, normally quite narrow, which made it easy to walk straight. It was different here, on this day. It would have been impossible for me to walk alone without the huge company I had. I would not have been able to recognize or identify a road. I do not know if there even was a road. The one I followed was as if covered with deep snow or high water. I followed the voices, the way I had done when Mother would call to me so many years ago. It was not long before I realized that the suitcase had to go if I was to go any farther. It carried no gold.[5]

Notes

1. Editor's note: The personal anecdotes about "folk medicine," the evil eye, and other superstitious non-scientific beliefs about the causes and cures of blindness stand in stark opposition to the sophisticated Islamic medical system that dates to medieval times, and that incorporated Galen's views, which were forbidden to the contemporaneous Christian medical world because those Greek medical systems stemmed from "paganism." These advanced Islamic medical systems also influenced the Spanish-born but North African-educated Jewish physician, philosopher and rabbinical commentator, Maimonides (Rambam), who served as personal physician to the sultan Saladin (Salah-a-Din).

2. Reja-e Busailah, *In the Land of My Birth: A Palestinian Boyhood*, first published in Institute for Palestine Studies, 2017, 3–13.

3. *In the Land of My Birth: A Palestinian Boyhood*, first published in Institute for Palestine Studies, 2017, 94.

4. *In the Land of My Birth: A Palestinian Boyhood*, first published in Institute for Palestine Studies, 2017, 38–39.

5. *In the Land of My Birth: A Palestinian Boyhood*, first published in Institute for Palestine Studies, 2017, 237–238.

Blindness in Science Fiction
From Mary Shelley's Frankenstein *to* Star Trek's *La Forge—and Much More*

Jason W. Ellis

Science Fiction (SF) emerges out of discourses rooted in the Enlightenment, Scientific Revolution, and Industrial Revolution. It was in that transitional period that blindness shifted from ideas of curse and gift to those of medical and scientific study. While some SF became a place of testing old ideas against new ones through story-driven thought experiments, other examples retread myths regarding blindness with a technoscientific veneer. The following chronological survey explores the role of blind characters in SF literature, film, and television.

Mary Shelley's *Frankenstein, or the Modern Prometheus* (1818) is arguably the first work of SF,[1] and a blind character features in a pivotal scene. In Volume II, the old blind man De Lacey is key to the Creature's plan to form a bond of friendship between himself and others. Knowing De Lacey could not judge his appearance, the Creature approaches De Lacey when he is alone to make his introduction as a traveler in search of his friends, but "a fatal prejudice clouds their eyes, and where they ought to see a feeling and kind friend, they behold only a detestable monster."[2] De Lacey replies, "I am blind, and cannot judge of your countenance, but there is something in your words which persuades me that you are sincere."[3] Unfortunately, the Creature's plan falls apart when De Lacey's alarmed family returns.

Mary Shelley's *The Last Man* (1826) is about a late-21st-century plague that kills off everyone except the story's chronicler Lionel Verney, who had a developed immunity to the disease.[4] When Verney and a few remaining survivors travel to Switzerland, they discover music coming from a church in Ferney where "a blind old man sat at the bellows; his whole soul was ear; and as he sat in the attitude of attentive listening, a bright glow of pleasure was diffused over his countenance; for, though his lack-lustre eye could not reflect the beam, yet his parted lips, and every line of his face and venerable brow spoke delight."[5] The blind man's daughter, who "since childhood, had been the guide of his darkened steps," plays the organ.[6] His blindness had "permitted her to continue a delusion ... sole survivors in the land, he remained unacquainted with the change, nor was aware that when he listened to his child's music, the mute mountains, senseless lake, and unconscious trees, were, himself excepted, her sole auditors."[7] His blindness hides the horrors of the plague from him until his daughter dies and he subsequently succumbs.

H.G. Wells' "The Country of the Blind" (1904, revised and expanded 1939) takes a long evolutionary view of a community in the Andes cut off from the rest of the world by circumstances of geography where "a strange disease had come upon them and had made all the children born to them there—and, indeed, several older children also—blind,"[8] and over generations, "the seeing had become purblind so gradually that they scarcely noted their loss. They guided the sightless youngsters hither and thither until they knew the whole valley marvelously, and when at last sight died out among them the race lived on."[9] Blindness comes to anchor their society, work, and cosmology to the point that the concept of sight is heretical. Nuñez, a mountaineer, accidentally discovers this community. Realizing these people are all blind, Nuñez acts on the proverb, "in the country of the blind the one-eyed man is king," but he soon discovers that they are fully capable persons.[10] Eventually, the community accepts him, but he is considered an "idiot" with "delusions" because he professes the existence of sight.[11] A doctor examines Nuñez and determines: "His brain is affected" by "those queer things that are called eyes."[12] Even though he is offered surgery in exchange for full admission to the community, Nuñez escapes up the mountainside. How the contagion that first blinds the children goes on to become an inheritable trait is never explained. The TV series *See* (2019) expands some of Wells' ideas into an epic set in the far future in which almost all humans are blind and those with sight are considered heretics.[13]

John W. Campbell, Jr.'s, "Blindness" (1935), originally published under his penname Don A. Stuart, is about Dr. Malcolm Mackay, who was "blinded ... by the three-year-long exposure to the intolerable light of the Sun" during his successful attempt to develop a nuclear fusion reactor that mimics the nuclear processes of our local star.[14] While radiation can damage the eyes and neurological vision systems in various ways, Mackay's advanced age and prolonged exposure to intense ultraviolet light led to his developing what appear to be cataracts: "His eyes turned from deep blue-grey to a pale blue with red, blood shot balls, his skin turned first deep, deep brown from the filtering ultra-violet, then it became mottled and unhealthy."[15] Cataracts are known to be the primary cause of blindness,[16] and Mackay's ultraviolet light exposure would have been far greater than that experienced by anyone on Earth considering the inverse-square law, no protective ozone layer, and technological limitations of his spacecraft.

Robert A. Heinlein's "The Green Hills of Earth" (1947) is about the life of "Rhysling, the Blind Singer of the Spaceways" and how his famous song "The Green Hills of Earth" came to be.[17] Rhysling was a jetman, an engineer who maintained the nuclear-powered spacecraft engines. On a trip to the Jovian moons, one jet critically malfunctioned, so "he slapped the emergency discover and fished at the hot stuff with the tongs. The lights went out, he went right ahead. A jetman has to know his power room the way your tongue knows the inside of your mouth. He sneaked a quick look over the top of the lead baffle when the lights went out. The blue radioactive glow did not help him anyway; he jerked his head back and went on fishing by touch."[18] The blue radioactivity indicates ionizing radiation from a criticality accident or uncontrolled fission reaction, which in addition to causing death can also cause cataracts, depending on exposure.[19] Being newly blind, Rhysling turns to composing and performing songs. Years later, Rysling is on an Earthbound ship and takes over the power room controls after the chief jetman is killed by radiation: "Rysling sensed what had happened. Automatic reflexes of old habit came out…. The place was as light to him as any place could be; he knew every spot, every control, the way he knew the keys of his accordion."[20] Despite saving the ship, he knows that the radiation will soon kill him, so he asks the watch to record his final song.

John Wyndham's *The Day of the Triffids* (1951), which Aldiss calls a "cosy catastrophe," or a story in which "the hero should have a pretty good time … while everyone else is dying off,"[21] is a post-apocalyptic novel that combines two threats to decimate humanity: green flashes of light in the night sky blinds most people, and the triffids, an ambulatory and carnivorous plant life, attack the survivors. Protagonist Bill Masen escaped being blinded by the green lights, because his eyes were bandaged after surviving a poisonous triffid strike to his face.[22] The blind and sighted alike present dangers to the survivors—some of the former trap sighted people to serve as their eyes[23] and the latter create pillaging gangs of the blind each with a sighted person as a guide.[24] Wyndham depicts the newly blind as generally helpless while the already blind are imperturbable. For example, Masen hears "a sharp new sound—a steady tapping not far away, and coming closer…. A man, more neatly dressed than any other I had seen that morning, was walking rapidly towards me, hitting the wall beside him with a white stick. As he caught the sound of my steps he stopped, listening alertly."[25] Masen narrates, "I felt relieved to see him. He was, so to speak, normally blind. His dark glasses were much less disturbing than the staring but useless eyes of the others."[26] The blind man's reproach to Masen, "Stand still, then…. I've already been bumped into by God knows how many fools today."[27]

Bob Shaw's *Night Walk* (1967) begins on the planet called Emm Luther where Sam Tallon, a spy from Earth, has stolen the route through null-space to a newly discovered Earth-like planet. During an attempted escape, a local intelligence agent destroys Tallon's eyes by point-blank shots fired from a non-lethal hornet gun: "Tallon, completely immobilized by the drugs, could not even blink as the darts ripped viciously into his eyes, robbing him forever of light and beauty and stars."[28] Imprisoned, he joins forces with Winfield, another blind prisoner, and Ed Hogarth, a sighted engineer, to construct devices to help Tallon and Winfield see the world (and escape)—a sonar torch, which "generated a narrow beam of inaudible high-frequency sound and had a receiver to pick up the echoes,"[29] and the more advanced eyesets, which take a visual signal from another person or sighted animal and direct it to their optic nerve.[30,31] After Tallon successfully escapes, he hijacks the *Lyle Star* in an attempt to return to Earth. Alone, he relies on his memory and standardized control layouts to make use of the ship, similarly to Rhysling in Heinlein's "The Green Hills of Earth."[32] Lost in deep space, Tallon's eyeset delivers unexpected dividends. His blindness and his eyeset technology permitted him to collect previously unknown data and visualize relationships within null-space in a new way. The final piece of the puzzle was his finding a stowaway—a rat—that he could pair with his eyeset and use as his "new eyes" for the more complicated process of mapping null-space to real-space.[33]

In Robert Holdstock's *Eye Among the Blind* (1976), a crisis unfolds on the Earth-like planet known as Ree'hdworld, home to three intelligent species—the animalistic Ruudii, the ecologically-focused Ree'hd, and the ancient Pianhmar. The latter's plan to self-devolution is disrupted by the import of human culture and capitalism. Kevin Maguire, a born-blind man with "pearl-white orbs" for eyes, had first come to Ree'hdworld 700 years earlier as an emissary of Earth tasked with finding and meeting with the Pianhmar.[34] A blind person was required for this position, because the Pianhmar refused to be seen, much less photographed. Unexpectedly, Maguire disappears. During the intervening years he secretly traveled the galaxy, visiting long forgotten outposts of this ancient people with a Pianhmar spirit guide who telepathically acts as his eyes. Maguire explains to fellow traveler Robert Zeitman, "there's one with me, always has been. Unconscious, unintrusive. You'll see better than any human because you can see an object in whatever way you want to.... The Pianhmar have a very expansive visual sense—even in the ghost-form. They won't return your own sight, but you'll find that's no loss."[35]

John Varley's "The Persistence of Vision" (1978) is about a southwestern community established by deaf-blind people born during the 1964 rubella outbreak in the United States.[36] The story weaves the history of the commune with the unnamed 47-year-old sighted protagonist's experiences, including his attempt at learning their four stages of tactile signing communication: hand-talk (International Manual Alphabet), body-talk (communicating via all parts of the body), shorthand (a higher bandwidth version of hand-talk), and Touch—"an incredible blend of all three other modes ... and the essence of it was that it never stayed the same."[37] The narrator leaves, frustrated by his inability to take part in a communal practice of the deaf-blind people referred to as "***," indicated by "three sharp slaps on the chest with the fingers spread."[38] According to Pink, a sighted child of a deaf-blind couple and the narrator's inappropriately aged (she is 13 years old when he first arrives) lover, "***" means "the gift whereby one can expand oneself from the eternal quiet and dark into something else ... vision and hearing preclude or obscure it."[39] The narrator returns a few years later to learn that the deaf-blind adults had transcended this world and disappeared during a *** session. Pink, 19 and with an infant, and the other previously sighted children are now all deaf and blind. She communicates to the narrator, "I will give you a gift," and "reached up and lightly touched my ears with her cold fingers. The sound of the wind was shut out, and when her hands came away it never came back. She touched my eyes, shut out all the light, and I saw no more. We live in the lovely quiet and dark."[40] This story turns the disability-as-barrier narrative on its head: sight and hearing become barriers to belonging.

Kim Stanley Robinson's "The Blind Geometer" (1987) develops a fully realized lifeworld of the protagonist, born-blind mathematician Carlos Oleg Nevsky in an exciting story about spies trying to manipulate him and steal his unpublished work.[41] Nevsky was born with "almost total blindness (I can tell dark from [bright] light)," because his mother was infected with rubella while he was in utero.[42] Working and living in Washington, D.C., he navigates the sidewalks, enjoys a social life, plays sports, and ultimately, takes on the spies. He relates how, as a mathematician, he sees: "all my work, no doubt, is an effort to envision things in the inward theater. 'I see it *feelingly*.' In language, in music, most of all in the laws of geometry, I find the best ways I can to see: by analogy to touch, and to sound, and to abstractions."[43] "The Blind Geometer" and Varley's "The Persistence of Vision" are among the strongest stories examined here that describe fully realized lives and experiences of blind people—the former through a blind character and his narration, and the latter from the perspective of an outsider joining a community of deaf-blind people, and interestingly, perhaps given the age of the writers, both use rubella as the cause for their respective characters' vision loss.

Geordi La Forge (LaVar Burton) in *Star Trek: The Next Generation* (series 1987–1994, and films 1994, 1996, 1998, and 2002) is perhaps one of the most well-known blind characters in SF. The character is noted as having been born blind.[44] In his earlier appearances, he is instantly recognizable by his VISOR, or Visual Instrument and Sensory Organ Replacement, and its golden screen trimmed in silver and punctuated by a circular circuit pattern over each temple. His VISOR interfaces with cybernetic implants in his brain to give him vision that surpasses normal human capabilities to, as La Forge puts it in the first episode of the series, "see much of the EM spectrum ranging from simple heat and infrared through radio waves."[45] Yet, he grapples with pain from his implants and considers (but ultimately rejects) offers to have functional organic eyes from the well-intentioned Dr. Katherine Pulaski (Diana Muldaur) in "Loud as a Whisper,"[46] Commander William Riker (Jonathan Frakes) who had been given god-like powers in "Hide and Q,"[47] and the healing effects of the planet Ba'ku in *Star Trek: Insurrection* (1998).[48] Later, however, La Forge receives ocular implants that look like normal eyes but provide their own enhancements to his vision.[49]

In Joe Haldeman's "None So Blind" (1994), Cletus Jefferson, a Black polymath and genius, develops and performs a radical surgical procedure on his white, blind-from-age-five wife Amy Linderbaum as an answer to a question that had driven his intellectual development since adolescence: "Why aren't all blind people geniuses?"[50] His stated intent was to attempt to return her sight, but she realizes afterwards this was untrue: "The sole intent of the operations was to subvert the normal functions of the visual cortex in such a way as to give me access to the unused parts of my brain."[51] Utilizing these unused parts of the brain elevated Amy's intelligence beyond that of Cletus and everyone else. Not to be left behind, he has the operation performed on himself, but it comes with the cost of his vision as the eyes "blocked surgical access to the optic nerves, which would be his conduits through the brain to the visual cortex. Physical conduits, through which incredibly tiny surgical instruments would be threaded."[52] Soon, the "secondsight" operation becomes a virtual requirement for intellectual workers to keep up with the increased intelligence of colleagues and competitors who already had the surgery.

José Saramago's *Blindness* (1995, trans. 1997)[53] is an apocalyptic novel by the Nobel Prize-winning writer that imagines the effects of a highly contagious disease resulting in blindness, described by the character known as the Doctor, "this blindness is white, precisely the opposite of amaurosis which is total darkness unless there is some form of white amaurosis, a white darkness, as it were."[54] The microcosm of characters locked away in an asylum gestures toward the societal breakdown revealed to have occurred while they were imprisoned. Fear of the contagion leads to neglect and profound tragedies. The doctor and some of the first patients are aided by the doctor's wife who seems to have a natural immunity to the contagion. Like John Wyndham's *The Day of the Triffids*, Saramago's newly blind are depicted as generally helpless. At the novel's end, the surviving blind regain their sight on a changed world.

Blindness and other blindness narratives include Desiderius Erasmus' adage, "In the country of the blind, the one-eyed man is king."[55] As shown in H.G. Wells' "The Country of the Blind" and John Varley's "The Persistence of Vision," the saying does not go very far when sufficiently scrutinized. Nevertheless, the proverb appears in many SF stories—those directly related to blindness and others that use it metaphorically or allegorically. Its use can reinforce stereotypes about blindness. A case in point is Damien Kilby's "Travelers" (1990), which is about a time traveler from the future named Sean who travels to the present time of the protagonist Jessica.[56] In this otherwise innocuous story, Sean alludes to it to explain his power to manipulate people in the present: "Here, I find myself in a world of millions of blind people—all banging around, crashing into each other. In theory, I can take anything I want."[57] SF Reader Christine Faltz Grassman, who was born blind and has since gone on to become an educator and lawyer, wrote to the editor taking issue with Kilby's use of this stereotype: "If the portrayal of blind characters were more diverse, if we were depicted as ordinary human beings more than once in a while, I would not be complaining about this tiny excerpt from this one short story.... However, statements of this nature send subliminal messages which do nothing but strengthen and justify the stereotypes and prejudice I must face on a regular basis."[58] Eighteen years later, she released *The Sight Sickness* (2009), which is framed as an "anti-sequel to [José Saramago's] *Blindness*" that serves as her "personal response to the public's fear of blindness."[59]

Neo (Keanu Reeves) in *The Matrix Trilogy* (1999–2003) experiences layers of blindness and sight. The cultural touchstone of the first film is the metaphor of the red pill (truth) and the blue pill (ignorance) offered by Morpheus (Laurence Fishburne) to Neo. Neo chooses the red pill, which helps the crew of the *Nebuchadnezzar* hovercraft locate and withdraw his body from the Machine's power plant. Safely aboard, Neo asks, "Why do my eyes hurt?" to which Morpheus replies, "You've never used them before."[60] This is because the Matrix is a simulation experienced directly in the brain via a computer interface implant. Neo's battery-like, atrophied body including his eyes would have never been used while he was contained his is individual body pod in the power plant. He loses his metaphorical blindness to the Matrix and his real blindness in the pod, and he gains sight in the real world. The next layer is revealed at the end of the first film after Neo's resurrection. He sees the falling lines of code underlying the apparent materiality within the Matrix, which the others cannot unsee. This gives him greater control within the simulated world. The final layer occurs in the last film aboard the hovercraft *Logos*. Bane (Ian Bliss), a human who had been reprogrammed as a copy of Agent Smith (Hugo Weaving), a rogue program from the Matrix, violently cauterizes Neo's eyes with a burning cable during a fight over control of the ship. Robbed of his eyes, Neo sees the ghost-like true forms of the Machines. In this case, Neo sees a phantasmagoric Agent Smith instead of Bane, and later, he uses his vision to guide Trinity (Carrie-Anne Moss) to the Machine City.[61]

The Book of Eli (2010) is a post-apocalyptic film set after a nuclear war laid waste to the surface of the Earth and damaged its protective atmosphere. Eli (Denzel Washington) is on a mission from God to take the last remaining copy of the Bible to a cultural sanctuary. The film features two blind characters. The first one is Claudia (Jennifer Beals), who Eli asks, "Did you get blinded in the war or by the sun after?"[62] She replies, "I was born this way. I think probably I'm lucky, because I was already used to being like this by the time it happened."[63] This implies other survivors have lost their sight from the nuclear blasts and a damaged ozone layer. In the film's final act, we learn that Eli is also blind. Throughout the film, he displays an extraordinary ability to act seemingly by sight in the world, but he is likely born blind also due to the fact that the Bible he carries throughout the film is revealed to be written in braille. However, Eli has committed its text to memory, so he fulfills his mission when he asks Lombardi (Malcolm McDowell) to transcribe the book as he recites it. Casting Denzel Washington as Eli and LaVar Burton as Geordi La Forge in *Star Trek: The Next Generation* is perhaps prescient, because African Americans have a higher rate of blindness than any other demographic and in raw numbers are second to non–Hispanic White individuals with blindness.[64]

Rogue One: A Star Wars Story (2016) follows the Rebel spies who steal the Empire's secret plans of the first Death Star. An important team member is Chirrut Îmwe (Donnie Yen), a blind warrior who adheres to the religion of the Force. While his eyes are glazed, white orbs, he demonstrates a preternatural ability to sense and act within his environment, such as when he calls out to Jyn Erso (Felicity Jones) across a crowded thoroughfare when he sensed that she was wearing a necklace with a kyber crystal, single-handedly defeat a Stormtrooper patrol, and destroys an in-flight

TIE fighter with a blast from his lightbow.[65] The sighted mercenary Baze Malbus (Jiang Wen) accompanies him on their adventures. Ultimately, Chirrut's self-sacrifice on the planet Scarif metaphorically opens Baze's eyes to his lost faith in the Force.

This essay explores only some of the many examples of blind characters in SF. While further research needs to be done on representations of blindness in SF, even more work needs to be done to ensure blind culture is presented respectfully and biomedical plausibility is advanced.

Notes

1. Brian W. Aldiss, *Billion Year Spree: The True History of Science Fiction* (Garden City, New York: Doubleday & Company, 1973), 3.
2. Mary Shelley, *Frankenstein: Annotated for Scientists, Engineers, and Creators of All Kinds*, ed. David H. Guston, Ed Finn, and Jason Scott Robert (Cambridge: The MIT Press, 2017), 112, https://doi.org/10.7551/mitpress/10815.001.0001.
3. Shelley, 112.
4. Mary Wollstonecraft Shelley, *The Last Man*, ed. Anne McWhir (Orchard Park, NY: Broadview Press, 1996), 271.
5. Shelley, 328.
6. Shelley, 329.
7. Shelley, 329.
8. H. G. Wells, "The Country of the Blind," *The Strand Magazine*, April 1904, 401.
9. Wells, 402.
10. Wells, 405.
11. Wells, 412.
12. Wells, 413.
13. Francis Lawrence, "Godflame," *See* (Apple TV+, n.d.).
14. Don A. Stuart, "Blindness," *Astounding Stories*, March 1935, 99.
15. Stuart, 105.
16. Alberto Modenese and Fabriziomaria Gobba, "Cataract Frequency and Subtypes Involved in Workers Assessed for Their Solar Radiation Exposure: A Systematic Review.," *Acta Ophthalmologica (1755375X)* 96, no. 8 (December 2018): 779.
17. Robert A. Heinlein, "The Green Hills of Earth," *The Saturday Evening Post*, February 8, 1947, 32.
18. Heinlein, 142.
19. Thomas P McLaughlin et al., "A Review of Criticality Accidents 2000 Revision" (United States, May 1, 2000), 12, https://doi.org/10.2172/758324.
20. Heinlein, "The Green Hills of Earth," 146.
21. Aldiss, *Billion Year Spree: The True History of Science Fiction*, 294.
22. John Wyndham, *The Day of the Triffids* (New York: Carroll & Graf Publishers, Inc., 1993), 7.
23. Wyndham, 64.
24. Wyndham, 129.
25. Wyndham, 55.
26. Wyndham, 55.
27. Wyndham, 55.
28. Bob Shaw, *Night Walk*, eBook (London: Gollancz, 2011), 14.
29. Shaw, 21.
30. Shaw, 24.
31. Tallon and Winfield's original plan involved a video camera directly connected to

each eyeset. Due to complications, they made do with their tuning-into-other-vertebrate's vision systems technology. Lionel Davidson's contemporary spy novel *Kolymsky Heights* (1994) develops this science fictional idea further. The narrative's MacGuffin is a Russian weapons lab developing an electro-optical fiber technology to give the blind sight, which is a tangent from their electromagnetic pulse (EMP) equipment protection research. Davidson details the development process involving genetic engineering of Neanderthal, ape, and human hybrids, studying their visual systems, and grafting a successful electronics-fiber optic vision system into the hybrids. The potential of this development is a robust intervention giving the blind sight. See chapters 41–44 and the Epilogue.

32. Shaw, *Night Walk*, 84.
33. Shaw, 94.
34. Robert P. Holdstock, *Eye Among the Blind* (Garden City, New York: Doubleday & Company, Inc., 1977), 120.
35. Holdstock, 215.
36. Meredith Wadman, "The Physician Whose 1964 Vaccine Beat Back Rubella Is Working to Defeat the New Coronavirus," Science | AAAS, March 21, 2020, https://www.sciencemag.org/news/2020/03/physician-whose-1964-vaccine-beat-back-rubella-working-defeat-new-coronavirus.
37. John Varley, "The Persistence of Vision," *The Magazine of Fantasy and Science Fiction*, March 1978, 43.
38. Varley, 44.
39. Varley, 44.
40. Varley, 50.
41. Kim Stanley Robinson, "The Blind Geometer," *Isaac Asimov's Science Fiction Magazine*, August 1987, 145.
42. Robinson, 146.
43. Robinson, 147.
44. Corey Allen, "Encounter at Farpoint," *Star Trek: The Next Generation* (Paramount Pictures, September 28, 1987).
45. Allen.
46. Larry Shaw, "Loud as a Whisper," *Star Trek: The Next Generation* (Paramount Pictures, January 9, 1989).
47. Cliff Bole, "Hide and Q," *Star Trek: The Next Generation* (Paramount Pictures, November 23, 1987).
48. Jonathan Frakes, *Star Trek: Insurrection* (Paramount Pictures, 1998).
49. Winrich Kolbe, "All Good Things…," *Star Trek: The Next Generation* (Paramount Pictures, May 23, 1994); Jonathan Frakes, *Star Trek: First Contact* (Paramount Pictures, 1996); LeVar Burton, "Timeless," *Star Trek: Voyager* (Paramount Pictures, November 18, 1998); Frakes, *Star Trek: Insurrection*; Stuart Baird, *Star Trek: Nemesis* (Paramount Pictures, 2002).
50. Joe Haldeman, "None So Blind," *Isaac Asimov's Science Fiction Magazine*, November 1994, 65.
51. Haldeman, 72.
52. Haldeman, 71.
53. Translated into English in 1997. Originally published in Portuguese as *Ensaio sobre a cegueira* in 1995.
54. José Saramago, *Blindness*, trans. Giovanni Pontiero (New York: Harcourt Brace & Company, 1997), 20.
55. Saramago, 98; Desiderius Erasmus, *The Adages of Erasmus*, ed. William Barker (Buffalo, NY: University of Toronto Press, 2001), 276–77.
56. Damian Kilby, "Travelers," *Isaac Asimov's Science Fiction Magazine*, February 1990, 97.
57. Kilby, 93.
58. Christine Faltz, "Dear Dr. Asimov, et Al.," *Isaac Asimov's Science Fiction Magazine*, February 1991, 15–16.
59. "The Sight Sickness," accessed August 11, 2020, https://www.goodreads.com/work/best_book/6649133-the-sight-sickness.

60. The Wachowskis, *The Matrix* (Warner Bros., 1999).
61. The Wachowskis, *The Matrix Revolutions* (Warner Bros., 2003).
62. The Hughes Brothers, *The Book of Eli* (Warner Bros., 2010).
63. The Hughes Brothers.
64. Rohit Varma et al., "Visual Impairment and Blindness in Adults in the United States: Demographic and Geographic Variations From 2015 to 2050," *JAMA Ophthalmology* 134, no. 7 (July 1, 2016): 802–9, https://doi.org/10.1001/jamaophthalmol.2016.1284.
65. Gareth Edwards, *Rogue One: A Star Wars Story* (Walt Disney Studios, 2016).

Looking at the Unseeing

Blindness in the History of Art

Carlos Espí Forcén

Blindness in Ancient Art

The depiction of blind people has played a major role in the history of art, with some of the most frequently represented subjects including a blind person as one of the main characters of the story. In ancient art, it is not easy to find depictions of blind people, for art was many times understood as a form of propaganda of the ruling power. Thus, sick people were not always considered worthy of representation. Nonetheless, after Alexander the Great defeated the Persian Empire and extended Greek culture from Egypt to India there was a growing interest in a realistic representation of decrepitude and abject reality in Hellenistic art.[1] A good example of this new style is the so-called "Blind Homer," a 2nd-century-BCE bust portrait of the allegedly blind poet, who was presumed to be the writer of the *Odyssey* and the *Iliad*. Homer may have been a fictional character, but in Antiquity he was believed to be real and was widely admired in the Hellenistic age. His bust portrait was an imaginary construction that purported to re-create the ideal image of a learned man, with a wrinkled face, a beard, messy hair, and blindness. The blind Homer bust graced many libraries in Ancient Greece, and the model has survived thanks to some preserved Roman copies of the original Hellenistic model today housed in some prominent museums such as the Prado in Madrid, the Louvre Paris or the British Museum in London.[2]

The arrival of Christianity substantially changed the artistic panorama in the Roman Empire. New images were necessary for a new creed that incorporated the Bible as an immense iconographical resource for this newly arrived religion. Whereas Judaism and Islam forbade the use and creation of images in their cult, Christianity gradually allowed the use of images for its rites and the representation of iconographic cycles as an adaptation to former pagan customs.[3] It did not do it without overcoming important obstacles such as the Byzantine iconoclast controversy,[4] but the triumph of figurative images in Christian culture guaranteed the existence of a rich art historical tradition that allows us to study the role of images and iconography in different periods of the Western World.

The Iconography of the Old Testament

I will now proceed to analyze the depiction of blindness in a period dominated by Christianity since its spread throughout the Roman Empire in the 3rd century CE to the Enlightenment of the 18th century. Firstly, we will focus on the iconography of the Old Testament and secondly on the episodes that involve blindness in the New Testament. One of the first episodes in Christian iconography that contains the story of a blind man is curiously apocryphal. It involves the death of Cain, the son of Adam and Eve. The book of Genesis says that the forefathers first had Cain, who cultivated the land; and afterwards, they had Abel, who chose to keep the flocks. After a while they both made an offering to God: Cain offered the fruit of the land and Abel the firstborn of his flock. God rejected Cain's offering and this caused him envy to the extent that he killed his brother and committed the alleged first homicide in history. The Lord condemned Cain to be an eternal wanderer on Earth, but he marked him so that everyone could recognize him but could not attempt to kill him (Genesis 4: 1–16). The mark of Cain has been an object of debate over the centuries. Sometimes it was thought to be a constant trembling or even black skin, which for some explained the origin of black people. A popular version of the story in the Middle Ages maintained that Cain had horns like a wild animal. A horned Cain was represented in medieval images in a fatal episode: the death of Cain. The primitive law of retaliation (eye for an eye) demanded that if Cain had killed his brother, he had to be murdered by a close relative. There is no information regarding the death of Cain in Genesis, but rabbinic interpretation of the story maintained that he was killed by a member of his offspring called Lamech. Since Lamech was blind, he needed the assistance of his son Tubalcain to be able to go hunting. One day Tubalcain saw two horns in the bushes and thought he had found a stag, so he quickly told his father to shoot an arrow in that direction. Misfortune made a blind Lamech kill his ancestor and thus the law of retaliation was fulfilled. A 12th-century Romanesque capital in the abbey of La Madeleine of Vézelay in France contains a bearded Lamech about to shoot his arrow, his blindness graphically depicted through his closed eyes and the fact that his face is not focused on the target (fig. 1). Sometimes Cain was depicted without horns; this is the case with a sculpted 12th-century frieze on the façade of Modena cathedral. However, the blindness of Lamech has been clearly depicted while he kills Cain with an arrow in his throat.[5]

Blindness plays an important role in another chapter of the book of Genesis: Isaac's blessing of Jacob. Once Isaac got old, he lost sight and was scared of dying without blessing his successor. Isaac wanted to bless his elder son Esau, so he told him to go hunting and prepare him some delicious food before his blessing. Isaac's wife Rebekah heard his husband's intentions and carefully planned to cheat him so that her favorite son Jacob could be blessed instead. Rebekah told Jacob to get two young goats from the flock so that she could cook them, and Jacob could offer them to Isaac pretending that he was his brother Esau returning from the hunt. Jacob expressed his concern, since he was a smooth-skinned man and Esau was hairy, but Rebekah solved the problem by covering Jacob's arms and neck with the skins of the goats. This treacherous trick worked, and the blind Isaac blessed Jacob instead of Esau, who discovered the betrayal after he offered dinner to his father (Genesis 27: 1–38). The scene was included in some interesting 12th-century Italian iconographic cycles. The arcades that separate the naves in the cathedral of Monreale (Sicily) contain two scenes of this story on golden mosaics: blind Isaac ordering Esau to bring him game and Jacob deceiving his father (fig. 2).[6] Another contemporary example is in the 12th-century Saint Mary's church in Ceri (near Rome), a fresco on the walls of the nave depicts Isaac blessing Jacob, while Esau arrives with a dead hare. Despite the Bible's insistence on Isaac's blindness, he has been rendered similarly to the rest of the characters of the scene. As art evolved, this scene turned more faithful to the biblical account, as it can be observed on a late 13th-century fresco painted in the upper church of the basilica of Saint Francis in Assisi (Umbria, Italy) by the so-called Isaac Master—a painter identified with Pietro Cavallini or a young Giotto. Two scenes represent the story: Isaac blessing Jacob and Isaac rejecting Esau. These images are much more naturalistic. A note of realism can be noticed in the fact that Isaac has been depicted completely blind in both scenes: his eyes are half open and his eyeballs are white.[7]

Another blind man in the Old Testament is the judge Samson, whose legendary biography can be read in the Book of Judges (13–16). Samson was the strongest man among the Jews, which enabled him to kill a lion with his bare hands and defeat the Philistines on several occasions. After being tempted by Delilah, he revealed to her that the secret of his strength lay in the fact that his hair had never been cut. Blackmailed by the Philistines to betray him, Delilah made him fall asleep on her lap and had his hair cut so that the Philistines could bind him (Judges 16: 1–21). Samson was further humiliated by having his eyes pulled out by the Philistines, a scene that has been depicted several times in the history of art. A late 12th-century capital in the cloister of the cathedral of Monreale, Sicily, contains the exact moment in which Samson has been bound on the lap of Delilah and one of the Philistines pops out his right eye by sticking his finger into the eye socket (fig. 3).[8] The most popular depiction of this subject was painted by Rembrandt in 1636 (Städel Museum, Frankfurt).[9] The Philistines have subdued Samson and one of them stabs his right eye with a dagger, while Delilah flees away with Samson's hair in her hand. Samson was also frequently depicted as a blind man chained in the temple of Dagon, where God restored his strength, and he was able to destroy the building and kill many Philistines (Judges 16: 25–30).

A popular blind man in Christian iconography is Tobit, whose story is narrated in the biblical Book of Tobit. The legend places Tobit in Nineveh in a period in which Jews were being persecuted by the Assyrian king Sennacherib. The Bible tells us that Tobit was blinded while he was sleeping in his courtyard on a hot night. Two sparrows standing on the top of the wall of his courtyard defecated on his eyes and the excrements covered them with a white film that blinded him. His condition impeded his continued working and his wife had to start weaving to sell cloth. One of her clients paid for her services and also gave her a goat, which made Tobit believe that she had stolen it (Tobit 2: 9–14). The family quarrel was beautifully represented by Rembrandt (fig. 4. Rijksmuseum, Amsterdam). Tobit is sitting on a couch in front of his wife with the goat. His eyes are open, but he is not looking at her because he cannot see. The artist has scrupulously followed the biblical narrative: his eyeballs are covered with a white film that does not allow us to see the iris nor the pupils, visible instead on his wife's eyes.[10] Tobit was also represented as a blind man in several popular iconographic scenes such as the parting of his son Tobias to Media to collect a debt. Tobit's blindness was finally healed by his son Tobias following the instructions of angel Raphael to put fish's gallbladder on his father's eyes, a scene that was represented during the Baroque (Tobit 11: 7–14).[11]

The Iconography of the New Testament

So far, I have analyzed blindness in Old Testament stories, but there are two episodes involving blindness in the New Testament that had a deep impact in the history of art. According to the Gospels, Jesus was an acknowledged healer: he cured lepers, a woman with a flow of blood, a paralytic. He exorcized demons and performed several resurrections.

More interesting for us are his healings of blind men. The Gospel of Mark reports that Jesus cured a blind man from Bethsaida by spreading saliva on his eyes (Mark 8: 22–26), Matthew writes that Jesus healed two blind men by touching their eyes (Matthew 9: 27–31) and John states that Jesus restored sight to a man born blind (John 9: 1–12). These miracles had a significant impact to increase the popularity of Christianity within the Roman Empire. Early Christians carefully pictured Jesus as a healer and redeemer; thus he was gradually accepted by a majority of pagans that were eager to abandon polytheism. Healings and miracles were the most frequently depicted scenes in early Christian art. The healing of a blind man is very frequently included among Christian miracles in Roman sarcophagi, mosaics and frescoes. The Roman sarcophagus of Bethesda was set on the west façade of the cathedral of Tarragona in the Late Middle Ages. It contains several miracles of Jesus that include the healing of blind people, two of whom approach to him so that he can cure them by touching their eyes (fig. 4).

Physical blindness was metaphorically referred to the spiritual blindness of those that did not recognize Jesus as the Messiah, i.e., Jews that remained faithful to the Mosaic law. The first blind Jew that recovered sight through conversion was Paul of Tarsus. The Acts of the Apostles set Paul persecuting Christians in the area of Jerusalem in the context of the lapidation of Saint Stephen. When Paul was on the road to Damascus, a bright light blinded him, he fell from the horse and Jesus asked him: "Saul, Saul, why do you persecute me?" (Acts 9:4). After this miraculous apparition Paul was blind for three days until Jesus sent one of his disciples to his house to restore his sight and baptize him. The conversion of Saint Paul was represented throughout the history of art, but its most popular examples are probably the two versions of the subject painted by the Baroque Italian artist Caravaggio: one belongs to the Odelcaschi collection in Rome and the most famous painting is in the Cerasi chapel in the Roman church of Santa Maria del Popolo. In the second painting Paul has fallen from the horse in a daring and beautiful foreshortening masterfully crafted by the artist: his eyes are closed, but his spiritual and physical blindness will be restituted after baptism.

Allegories

Caravaggio created a new naturalistic style that was to be followed by many painters all over Europe. One of his closest followers was the Spaniard José de Ribera, whose style is easily recognizable for his dark paintings illuminated in specific spots, namely the *chiaroscuro* technique, and the realistic appearance of his characters. Not all the representations of blindness were strictly religious in the 17th century; Ribera abandoned the biblical narrative to paint allegories of the five senses. Two different allegories of touch are attributed to Ribera, both showing a mature blind man that touches a classical bust with his hands. "The Allegory of Touch" (Museo del Prado, Madrid)—also known as the blind sculptor—contains a moving scene, the extreme naturalism of the old, bearded man with closed eyes feeling scrupulously every detail of the sculpture with his bare hands, that has induced the idea that Ribera was painting a real blind model.[12]

The Depiction of Blindness After the Enlightenment

The Enlightenment required new subjects besides the traditional Christian iconography. Royal Academies of Art were created in France, Britain, Spain and other European countries to define the tenets of what could be considered high art. Students were meant to learn to draw and paint according to what was strictly taught in the academy. The most appropriate subjects for painting were historical, mythological or religious; this allowed a wider array of themes in comparison with the traditional Christian subjects. The most notable painter of the French Academy was Jacques-Louis David, who painted both historical episodes and contemporary events since he was the official painter of Napoleon. One of his most well-known paintings involves an apocryphal legend that involves the Byzantine military general Belisarius, who had defeated the Vandals in North Africa and the Ostrogoths in Italy to restore part of the former Roman Empire in the 6th century AD. In the 18th century it was believed that by the end of his life, Belisarius was blinded by Emperor Justinian and fell in disgrace. Jacques Louis David made a painting of the subject in 1781 (Palais des Beaux Arts, Lille), in which an old and blind Belisarius is begging for alms in the street in the company of a child, while a woman is throwing a coin into his helmet. By chance, a former soldier of Belisarius observes the dramatic event and raises his hands for the miserable condition of the former leader.[13]

Subjects from popular culture were common in the late 18th century to decorate the houses of wealthy layers of society. One good example of this genre of paintings is Francisco de Goya's "The Blind Guitarist" (Museo del Prado, Madrid). It contains a blind singer playing the guitar, who wandered around towns and cities to announce tragic news in the company of a child.[14] A blind guitarist was also a subject chosen by probably Goya's fellow Spaniard Pablo Picasso. In his "blue period," Picasso chose to paint in blue, grey and black hues to exorcise his pain for the death of his closest friend Carlos Casagemas in 1901. In "The Old Guitarist" (The Art Institute of Chicago) he depicts a poor old blind man playing guitar barefoot in the streets of Barcelona. At the time Picasso was also poor and was always surrounded by beggars and prostitutes that became the most popular subjects of his paintings. Another good example of Picasso's blue period is "The Blind Man's Meal" (Metropolitan Museum of Art, New York), which shows a desolate and skinny blind man, who can only have a piece of bread and some water as a meal.[15]

Blind men and amputees were common in German painting between World War I and World War II as an indictment of the catastrophic consequences of the war and the miserable condition of war veterans. One of the most significant paintings of this period is "The Match Seller" (Staatsgalerie, Stuttgart) painted by Otto Dix. A realistic style was chosen by German artists of the period over avant-garde to denounce social injustice in a movement known as "The New Objectivity." Otto Dix depicted a blind amputee without arms and legs condemned to sell matches in the street in the presence of anonymous members of the bourgeoisie that feel no pity for him. The dramatic situation transforms the war veteran into a sort of ignored object on the street; this concept is graphically stressed by the fact that a dachshund is peeing on him.[16]

Notes

1. John Onians, *Art and Thought in the Hellenistic Age* (London: Thames and Hudson, 1979).
2. Gisela Richter, *Portraits of the Greeks*, vol. 1 (London: Phaidon, 1965), 51; Sheila Dillon, *Ancient Greek Portrait Sculpture. Contexts, Subjects, and Styles* (Cambridge: Cambridge University Press, 2006).
3. André Grabar, *Les voies de la création en iconographie chrétienne. Antiquité e Moyen Âge*. Paris: Flammarion, 1979; Hans Belting, *Bild und Kult. Eine Geschichte des Bildes vor dem Zeitalter der Kunst*, Munich: Beck, 1990.
4. In the 8th century the Byzantine emperor decreed the destruction of all Christian images, see André Grabar, *L'iconoclasme byzantine*, Paris: Flammarion, 1984.
5. Ruth Mellinkoff, *The Mark of Cain* (Wipf and Stock: Eugene, OR, 1982), 5–18, 59–63; Louis Réau, *Iconografía del arte cristiano. Iconografía de la Biblia. Antiguo Testamento*, vol. 1 (Barcelona: Del Serbal, 1995), 122–125 (originally in French: *Iconographie de l'art chrétien*, Paris: P.U.F., 1955). For the sculpture in Vézelay see Linda Seidel, *Legends in Limestone. Lazarus, Gislebertus, and the Cathedral of Autun* (Chicago: The University of Chicago Press, 1999).
6. Otto Demus, *The Mosaics of Norman Sicily*, New York: Philosophical Library, 1950; Ernst Kitzinger, *The Mosaics of Monreale*, Palermo: S.F. Flaccovio, 1960.
7. Alfred Nicholson, "The Roman School at Assisi." *The Art Bulletin* 12 (1930): 270–300.
8. Reau, *Iconografía del arte cristiano*, 291–292; Beat Brenk, "Zur Programmatik der Kapitelle im Kreuzgang von Monreale. Rethorik der varietas als herrscherliches Anspruchsdenken," en K. Bergdolt and G. Bonsanti, eds., *Opere e giorni. Studi su mille anni di arte europea dedicati a Max Seidel*, Venice, 2001, 43–50.
9. Jakob Rosenberg, *Rembrandt. Vida y obra*, Madrid: Alianza, 1987, 195–197 (originally

in English: *Rembrandt. Life and Work* (New York: Phaidon, 1968); Simon Schama, *Los ojos de Rembrandt* (Barcelona: Plaza y Janés, 2002), 467–471 (originally in English: Rembrandt's Eyes (New York: Knopf, 1999).
 10. Schama, *Rembrandt's Eyes*, 473–476.
 11. For the iconography of Tobit and Tobias see Reau, *Iconografía del arte cristiano*, 368–379.
 12. Alfonso Pérez Sánchez, *Ribera (1591–1652)* (Madrid: Museo del Prado, 1992), 24–30.
 13. Klaus Weschenfelder, "Belisar und sein Begleiter. Die Karriere eines Blinden in der Kunst vom 17. bis zum 19 Jahrhundert." *Marburger Jahrbuch für Kunstwissenschaft* 30 (2003): 245–268.
 14. Valeriano Bozal, *Goya y el gusto moderno* (Madrid: Alianza, 2002), 57–96.
 15. James G. Ravin and Jonathan Perkins. "Representations of Blindness in Picasso's Blue Period." *Arch Ophtalmol* 122 (2004): 636–639.
 16. Michael MacKenzie, *Otto Dix and the First World War. Grotesque Humor, Camaraderie and Remembrance* (New York: Peter Lang, 2017).

Visual Loss in Cinema
A Psychiatrist's Viewpoint

Fernando Espí Forcén

In the history of cinema, stories of persons with disabilities who overcome difficulties have inspired audiences through the decades. One of the first films with blind protagonists is *The Masseurs and a Woman* (1938) by Japanese director Hiroshi Shimizu. In this movie, Toku is a blind man who works as a masseur with other fellows who are blind too. They take pride in their job as masseurs and seem happy. One day, a woman from Tokyo intrudes in their lives and threatens the symbolic order. This woman seems to awaken Toku's sexuality. However, for the most part Toku takes a passive role. He never makes a sexual pass. Perhaps he has the cognitive distortion that blind men cannot be suitable partners. Nonetheless, at some point in the film, this woman is accused of theft. Once she needs someone to save her, Toku tries to help her escape. Here the setting will change Toku's behavior. He obviously loves her and fantasizes about her but will not take any action as his sexuality is too repressed by society. However, when the new goal is to save her rather than seduce her, he will not hesitate to take the step and break society's rules to save her. Perhaps he is also attempting to keep her away from other more suitable sexual partners as one of the clients is smitten with her and tries to seduce her.

The masseurs as portrayed in the film seem to suffer from congenital blindness probably related to some congenital disease or a childhood infection. In the United States, one film that includes a character that becomes blind after a perinatal infection is *The Miracle Worker* (1962). Based on the stage play by William Gibson, which itself was based on Helen Keller's 1959 autobiography, *The Story of My Life,* the film was directed by Arthur Penn. The movie narrates the story of Helen Keller, a blind and deaf young girl, and her teacher Anne Sullivan. Helen lost her sight and hearing after encephalitis during the first days of her life; therefore her development was largely affected by her disability. She never learned how to speak and communicate in a proper manner. Her parents let her wander in the house and do as she pleases, but after she flings the cradle of her baby sister to play with her as a doll, her parents decide to hire Anne Sullivan, a special tutor who has experience working with blind children. Despite the complexity of the case, Anne teaches her to communicate by pairing an object with a word as written with her fingers on Helen's palm. Helen has an intellectual disability secondary to lack of stimulation, but Anne opens a new way of communication that will allow Helen to learn and acquire new cognitive and social skills. Thus, her attachment to people and impulsive tantrums also improve. While in therapy, Anne uses positive reinforcement to enhance the chances of the desired outcome by pairing the learning of the word spelling via writing on her palm with the desired reward (milk, doll, etc.). Positive reinforcement is the main tool in behavior therapy. This therapy is particularly helpful with children with oppositional defiant disorder, conduct disorder as well as children with autism and other intellectual disabilities. When the desired behavior is followed by a reward, it is more likely to be repeated.

In the midst of the civil rights movement, Guy Green directed *A Patch of Blue* (1965).[1] It tells the story of a Selina, a young Caucasian blind lady who falls in love with Gordon, an attractive African American man, played by Sidney Poitier.[2] In the film, Selina lives with her abusive mother, who tells her she is disfigured, and her grandfather, who has an alcohol use disorder. She strings beads to supplement the family's little income. One day at the park she meets Gordon, who helps her with the beads and buys her a pair of sunglasses. For the first time, Selina meets a person who treats her with respect. Selina seems to be a little naive; however, one day she shares with Gordon the tragic story of her blindness at the age of five. She also shares that she was raped by one of her mom's boyfriends. Gordon empathizes with her story and becomes a close supportive friend. Selina's mother is portrayed as pure evil. She is racist and disapproves of Gordon. She constantly abuses Selina physically and psychologically and exploits her. One day she makes a plan to prostitute Selina, but Gordon rescues her and enrolls her in a school for the blind. That night, Selina tells Gordon that she loves him, but Gordon proposes they wait at least one year. Selina then leaves Gordon's apartment to start her new school.

In this motion picture, Selina has been repeatedly abused by her mother but does not seem to display symptoms of post-traumatic stress disorder (PTSD). In that way, she seems to be resilient. The film portrays Gordon as an educated man which contrasts with Selina's naiveté. Due to that, he can foresee possible problems that would interfere with their relationship. That is probably why Gordon suggests waiting one year so that

Selina can be exposed to normal social interactions. Gordon intends well and does not want to take advantage of her. Only time will tell what will happen between them.

Another film based on a stage play was *Butterflies Are Free*. After its success in Broadway, Milton Katselas directed a major motion picture in 1972. The setting is the city of San Francisco during the hippie cultural movement that had defined the decade. Here, Don is a blind young adult who struggles with independence. Don was born blind and therefore he is not frustrated that he is blind as he has not experienced the alternative. What concerns him is to be treated differently for the mere fact of being blind. He has just moved to an apartment on his own and although he seems able to carry on activities of daily living fairly well on his own, his mother keeps calling to check on him, something that he finds frustrating and even enraging at times. Don's new neighbor is Jill, a hippie and naive young lady who just divorced a man after a few weeks of marriage. Jill is portrayed as a sexualized object that Don cannot see. Both Don and Jill enrich each other. Whereas Jill takes him around and help him explore the world and enjoy life, Don helps her grow emotionally towards a healthy romantic relationship. Their love is tested when Mrs. Baker, Don's mother, visits unexpectedly, intruding as a threatening maternal superego attempting to restore the symbolic order. Soon, rivalry between Jill and Don's mother starts. Now Jill will help Don achieve the long-desired independence. From a developmental perspective, this film raises thoughts on Margaret Mahler's separation individuation theory. During the rapprochement phase, children 15 months and older understand that their physical mobility will imply a psychic differentiation from their caretakers. As such, children are able to differentiate from their mothers. From a psychodynamic point of view, an argument could be made here that Don was not able to differentiate fully from his mother as he was born with a congenital disease. Therefore, his vision was impaired, affecting the comprehension of the physical separation from his mother and also making him more dependent on her. Don's mother became overprotective knowing that her child's disability has perpetuated the dependence and did not permit a full differentiation.

Historically, common causes of blindness and disability were the injuries and calamities that came with wars. Anti-war film *Johnny Got His Gun* (1971), directed by Dalton Trumbo, was based on Dalton's own novel with the same name, first published in 1939. It tells the story of Joe Bonham, a young American soldier who becomes blind, deaf, and mute and lost his arms and legs after an explosion while in combat during World War I, becoming a prisoner in his own body. Joe cannot commit suicide because he has no arms and legs. He cannot even asphyxiate himself because he has a tracheostomy done. The doctors initially believe he is not suffering and is decerebrated. He lies in a hospital bed and is kept a secret. However, the viewer can hear his thoughts and dreams. Joe is trying to understand what happened to him. He tries to reorient himself in order to not become delirious. With a little sunlight that warms up his skin he can tell the difference between day and night. He can also tell who is coming into the room through the vibration from the steps of the people that enter. He can also tell when his favorite nurse, the only compassionate one, arrives. He also develops techniques to differentiate daydreaming from sleeping and fantasy from reality. Finally, Joe figures out a way to communicate with his caretakers by moving his head in Morse code. Initially the physicians think he is having spasms, but his nurse is able to understand that he is trying to communicate something. Once they bring a Morse expert, Joe tells them that he wants to be exposed to people so that they can see the consequences of the war, but the U.S. army is hesitant to grant his wishes. After that he asks to be killed but for religious reasons, they do not want to do that either. Joe's nurse tries to euthanize him in mercy by closing his tracheostomy tube, but she is stopped by the army officer. After that Joe realizes that he is going to be left alone in that room until he dies one day. The film soon gained a cult status, especially after future president Jimmy Carter asked his new state cabinet members to watch the film shortly after he was elected governor in Georgia. A new wave of popularity came after metal band Metallica wrote the song "One" in 1988, based on the film. They utilized those film clips in their music video "One."

Another film portraying a blind veteran is *Scent of a Woman*, a remake of the Italian film *Profumo di donna* (1974). It was remade in 1992 by director Martin Brest and adapted from the novel by writer Bo Goldman. This Hollywood version became extraordinarily successful, and Al Pacino's interpretation of Army Lieutenant Colonel Frank Slade earned him an Academy Award.

In *Scent of a Woman*, Frank is a veteran who became blind after a mishap with a grenade, when he was slugging live grenades to show off while he was intoxicated. Frank now is disabled due to his blindness and lives with his niece and her family who take care of him in small town of New England. Frank's life now seems to have no meaning. He is angry and volatile, unfriendly and detached from his family. As a result, he has decided to commit suicide but before that he takes a week of luxury and hedonism in New York City with his newly hired caretaker Charlie, a boy from the nearby popular boarding school for the wealthy. Charlie comes from the working class but has a scholarship and is working on Thanksgiving weekend to pay for his flight back to Oregon for Christmas. The idea was to stay in town, but Frank has everything planned differently: he has bought two flights to New York City and booked a room at the Waldorf-Astoria. He has made reservations at the best restaurants in the city and an appointment with a high-class escort. By the end of the week he gives Charlie his flight back, but he is committed to stay as he has planned his suicide. Charlie can give Frank a new meaning to his life. He tells him that he is deeply worried as he had seen his classmates setting up a prank for the headmaster. He is now called to testify against them, and the maleficent headmaster has threatened him to expel him from school if he does not testify against his classmates. Instead, if he does, he will recommend him at Harvard. Charlie is overwhelmed with the new ethical dilemma, to break the codes and report or to not report and lose the opportunity to have a brilliant future. Charlie convinces Frank to not commit suicide and go back with him to town. The day of the appeal, Frank shows up unexpectedly to support Charlie in place of Charlie's parents. In the end, Charlie decides to not report his classmates. The headmaster recommends the committee to expel Charlie, but Frank gives a memorable speech about the importance of not being a snitch, of respecting the codes and choosing the right path in life, even if it seems too hard. Frank publicly expresses his admiration for Charlie's persona.

A therapeutic relationship takes place between Frank and Charlie. Frank is depressed by his disability because of his trauma at war (which famed film critic Roger Ebert described as "stupidity" rather than trauma). Charlie instead does not have a father figure in his life. In that sense, Frank becomes a therapeutic father and a model. Frank is a war hero and represents the importance of respecting the ethics codes, the importance of honor as a path to virtue. Frank also gives him support by showing admiration for him, something that will be especially important for Charlie. Instead, Charlie gives Frank's life a new meaning. After the speech in the school, a lady from the committee goes to meet them to show her admiration for Frank. He is now ready to explore an intimate romantic relationship. He does not seem depressed or angry anymore. He is ready to keep on living and make the changes needed.[3]

Like in *The Masseurs and a Woman*, in the United States, *At First Sight* (1999) by Irvin Winkler tells the story of a blind man who makes a living as a masseur, based on an essay written by Oliver Sacks about the true story of Shirl Jennings, a man with congenital cataracts who recovered his sight after a surgical intervention but found it overwhelming to learn how to see again.[4] Here, Virgil is a blind man who works as a masseur in a small town. Amy is an architect who takes a vacation from the city and falls in love with him after a massage. After she is back in the city, she learns through a doctor about the possibility of a surgery that could restore Virgil's sight. Both Virgil and his sister are hesitant as in the past they tried multiple doctors and nothing worked, but Amy continues to persuade him until he finally agrees. After the surgery, Virgil recovers some sight and is able to see some things with the help of this intervention. Now, he has to learn how to see again and coordinate, something he finds overwhelming at times. However, as he also has a degenerative disease of the retina, he is never able to see properly and continues to lose his sight. Finally, he ends up blind again and goes back home. Amy reconnects with her narcissistic ex-husband but finally decides to stay faithful to Virgil. In the meantime, Virgil goes to meet his father who left him when he was a child. Virgil's dad tells him that he felt he was a failure and that is why he left. Virgil goes back to town to live with his sister while he is trying to see as many things as possible before he goes blind. Amy later reconciles with him.

An interesting point in the film is Virgil's hesitance to undergo the surgical procedure. He explains that he went to many doctors when he was younger, and nothing worked. He seems hopeless that a new procedure will save his sight. To recover his vision will imply significant changes in his life and he seems happy with what he has at that point. A new change, even if that implies to recover his vision, might be too overwhelming at this stage of his life. In addition, he might be traumatized by his experience of going blind as a child. He went to a lot of doctors and likely he was perceived as the sick or the problem child by his parents. After doctors could not find a cure, his father left him. Though Virgil's father explains that he left because he felt he was a failure, Virgil probably perceived it the other way around. Virgil likely felt that he was the failure who could not have his vision restored and that is why his father left him. Parents can be overwhelmed by having a sick child and a flee response can be common as they do not feel ready to cope with something like that. Often guilt can happen as they feel responsible in a magical way for passing the wrong seed or the wrong genes. Nonetheless their children, like in this case, may feel quite different about that. Another interesting aspect is Amy's persistence in convincing Virgil to undergo surgery. Perhaps her struggle is related to having a disabled man as a partner. Jealous, her narcissistic ex-husband ridicules her efforts to find the right partner when she reveals that Virgil is blind. Amy might be consciously trying to save Virgil with this new surgery but unconsciously trying to make him a more suitable partner for her in society.

The tragic story of Selma in Lars von Trier's *Dancer in the Dark* (2000) tells the story of another woman with a congenital disease-causing blindness. The film might also reflect a criticism of the United States health care system. Set in Washington State in 1964. Selma is a Czech immigrant who works in a factory and lives with her son in a trailer rented at the property of local police officer Bill and his wife Linda. Selma has a degenerative eye disease and is losing her sight. She struggles with her disability while working extra hours at the local factory to save as much money as possible before going blind. Her goal is to pay for surgery that will save her son from losing his vision too as her disease is hereditary. Selma escapes from stress by daydreaming about musicals, her true passion in life. One day, Bill reveals that he is going bankrupt as Linda spends a lot of money and he does not know how to say no to her. Knowing that Selma is blind, he spies on her to see where she hides her money to pay for her son's surgery. After that he takes the money to pay his debt to the bank. When Selma goes back home and sees that her money has been stolen, she immediately goes to Bill's house as she knows he has been the one taking it away. Bill is hesitant to give her the money and once she takes it back, Bill asks her to kill him. Bill had thought of committing suicide but could not do it. However, being killed might be for him a way of solving the situation in a way that he would look better to his wife. Selma helps him with his mission but after that she gets accused of murder. Before being arrested, she deposits all the money at the doctor's clinic to pay for her son's surgery. Once on trial she does not defend herself properly as she does not want to expose Bill and also does not want people to know about the money and the surgery. She wants to protect her son's future. Subsequently she is sentenced to death by hanging. Selma's friend Kathy finds out about Selma's true motivation and finds a lawyer to give her a fair trial. However, Selma refuses to use the money she had saved because her main goal is to save her son's sight. Selma reveals that she feels guilty that she had a son despite knowing her disease was hereditary. She feels she was selfish to have a son despite knowing it and now she wants to undo her deed even if that means dying. She prefers to die rather than living in jail if that way she can save her son's vision. Another interesting character for psychological discussion is Bill. For him, to be unable to provide for his wife's caprices means a significant narcissistic injury. He has been hiding his financial problems for years but now he is trapped. To disclose or not to disclose. He considers suicide but he is not sure if that is the solution because eventually his wife will find out. However, being killed and becoming a victim seems the easiest way of solving the problem. That way he will not have to deal with the potential shame of disclosing to his wife and he will become a victim in her eyes. Selma will help him with his purpose as soon as she can save her son even if that will mean her own sacrifice.

In 2003, two films portraying a blind superhero saw light in the theaters: *Daredevil* by Mark Steven Johnson in the United States and *Zatoichi* by Takeshi Kitano in Japan. In the latter, Kitano plays the blind samurai himself. There is far more to be said about Zatoichi, as noted in the introduction.[5] Psychoanalytically, the superhero can be approached as a grandiose defense against depression. Psychologically, in times of financial or political instability, society enjoys watching films about superheroes that provide a sense of safety and stability. Audiences will cathartically relieve their anxieties about these perceived threats.[6]

Another Japanese film portraying a blind samurai is *Love and Honor* (2006) by Yoji Yamada. The original title was *Bushi no Ichibun* (*A Warrior's Honor*) but in the West the film was released with the title *Love and Honor*. In the motion picture. Shinnojo is a low ranking samurai who works as a food taster at a feudal castle. Misfortune follows after he tastes a sashimi out of season, and he becomes blind from food poisoning. Shinnojo lives with his loyal wife Kayo and his dutiful servant Tokuhei. Due to his disability they have no means of supporting themselves. One day Kayo goes and meets with Toya Shimada, a high ranking samurai and duty officer who offers to help by providing the family with rice. However he takes advantage of her sexually and tells her that if she does not meet with him more times, he will tell her husband. Scared, Kayo agrees to meet him other times, but she is discovered by Tokuhei. At that moment Kayo tells Shinnojo what happened. As she has dishonored her husband, Kayo feels she deserves to be decapitated by her husband, but he instead asks her to leave the house and not come back. When Shinnojo finds out that Shimada had nothing to do with maintaining his stipend since the help was coming from the chief of the clan, he decides to avenge the dishonor of his wife Kayo and sends Tokuhei to set up a duel. Shimada agrees to meet but does not want to fight a blind man from a lower rank; however, after Shinnojo provokes him, he agrees to fight. Shinnojo seems well trained and prepared. Shimada tries to take advantage of his blindness and jumps off from a stable, but Shinnojo is able to cut off his arm. After that Shimada commits harakiri without telling anyone what he has done. In a different scene, Tokuhei brings a new cook home, which turns out to be Kayo. Shinnojo recognizes her cooking immediately and welcomes her back home. The film is set up in rural Japan. As we can see the values in society can vary depending on the social and historical context. Here a good wife must be loyal, dutiful and submissive. Even when Shimada takes advantage of her, Kayo is not seen as a victim but as a person that according to the ethical code can even face an execution. Nonetheless, the film does a good job at explaining the importance of honor for Japanese Samurai. Like in the case of Shimada, harakiri can be a way of saving one's honor by suicide. For this society suicide is better than to live in dishonor. As compared to western societies where suicide is generally seen as the result of a mental illness, in this sector of Japanese society suicide has a totally different meaning and purpose. In fact, it can be an extremely useful tool. A

Japanese samurai would rather die in honor than to live in dishonor. Philosopher G.W.H. Hegel talks about the values in society that we can learn from the past. For instance, he argues that we can learn from medieval societies about the importance of courage and honor.[7]

There are few horror films portraying a blind man. In 1967, Terence Young directed *Wait Until Dark*, starring Audrey Hepburn as a blind woman terrorized by three criminals who search for a heroin stuffed doll in her apartment. The film *Don't Breathe* (2016) directed by Uruguayan Fede Alvarez narrates the story of three burglars who plan a robbery at the house of a blind man who presumably has a fortune. However, this blind man turns out to be an antisocial adversary. He keeps a woman at his basement to have a child with her. This idea reflects on the fear and terror evoked in society by the Cleveland kidnappings between 2002 and 2013. Horror films allow the audience to re-experience their anxieties but with a sense of control. Psychologically this catharsis together with the sensation seeking theory might well explain why people might enjoy horror movies.[8]

As reflected in this manuscript, the portrayal of blindness in film has varied through the decades depending on the historical context of the time and the cultural values in the societies where films were made. A wide range of causes of blindness and situations can be seen such as congenital blindness, traumatic blindness and so on. These films explore the psychological struggles people affected with blindness may face. Nonetheless, most of these stories show how blind protagonists are able to overcome difficulties and carry on a meaningful life. In that sense, films that portray blindness can be useful for persons with blindness, their families and friends and people involved in the care of patients with blindness.

Notes

1. Ernest Callenbach. 1965. "A Patch of Blue." *Film Quarterly*.
2. See introduction for additional data about Sidney Poitier.
3. Danny Wedding, *Movies and Mental Illness: Using Films to Understand Psychopathology* (Gottingen, Germany: Hogrefe, 2014).
4. See introduction for additional data.
5. See introduction for more details.
6. Sharon Packer, *Superheroes and Superegos: Analyzing the Minds Behind the Masks* (CT: Praeger, 2009).
7. Watanabe, Tomio. Kobayashi, Yukata, and Hata, Sekenobu. 1973. "Harakiri and suicide by sharp instruments in Japan." *Forensic Science*—Elsevier.
8. Fernando Espi Forcen, *Monsters, Demons and Psychopaths: Psychiatry and Horror Film* (Boca Raton, FL: CRC Press, 2016).

Unsighted Superheroes
Insights from Comics, Films and TV

JAQ GREENSPON

Stan Lee, the man who gave us the quintessential superhero line "with great power there must also come—great responsibility"[1] with the first appearance of Spider-Man is also credited with creating some of the most memorable and influential characters of the Silver Age[2] of comics. After giving the world the Fantastic Four, The Incredible Hulk and the aforementioned Spider-Man, he set his sights on doing something completely different:

"I was trying to think of a hero who would start out with a disability—a hero whose weakness would actually be more colorful, more unusual than his power itself. Not the easiest thing to come up with, perhaps, but I was in there trying."[3]

For Lee, the real problem was coming up with a disability which would be believable, even considering the fantasy nature of the medium itself. Credibility had been the hallmark of his earlier creative endeavors and so, too, this one must as well. "And then it hit me," he says in the 1975 *Son of Origins of Marvel Comics*. "I remembered some books I had read years ago, mystery stories about a blind detective named Duncan Maclain. If a man without sight could be a successful detective, think what a triumph it would be to make a blind man a comic book superhero." He immediately set about to answer the questions he had raised: "But how were we to make a reader believe that a man without sight could actually perform the hazardous feats of heroism that would be required? This was the problem I was faced with—the problem that had to be solved."[4]

The solution, of course, was Daredevil, the red suited, horn headed, crime fighting alter ego of blind attorney Matt Murdock. Except not really. The problem of making Lee's groundbreaking concept of a superhero without sight easily believable had been answered two decades earlier with the creation of Dr. Mid-Nite by writer Chuck Reizenstein and artist Stan Asch (né Aschmeier).[5]

In 1941, a mere three years after the first appearance of Superman, the superhero industry had taken off. Aside from adding the characters to daily newspaper strips, superheroes were showing up on screen in movie serials and animated shorts, radio programs and, most importantly, a multitude of comic books. Characters were not relegated to eponymous single titles, but instead, the bigger names, like Superman and Batman, The Flash and Green Lantern were joining forces[6] in groups or as part of generically titled anthology series. These types of books provided the luxury of allowing publishers to try out new characters, to bring them in for a short adventures as back up stories in books anchored by a more popular name. Then, once these characters had proven themselves, they would be brought in to become part of a superhero group or given their own title or, often, both. With this kind of popularity, the major publishers of the time, particularly National, which would later become DC, were constantly on the lookout for new and interesting takes on the characters in the genre.

Reizenstein and Asch were part of a growing number of freelance creators coming in to pitch their ideas. In a fictional world populated by aliens, speedsters, and various other enhanced individuals, it seemed like the easiest thing to do was throw out every idea which came to mind, set it in motion with a six-to-twelve-page story and see what happened.

Such was the case, it seems, with Dr. Mid-Nite, whose eight-page origin story cribs from a number of already established heroes. Mid-Nite started out as pre-eminent surgeon Dr. Charles McNider, who made his first appearance as the fifth backup story in *All-American Comics* #25 (cover dated April 1941[7]). McNider is called upon in the middle of the night to save "an important witness" against mob boss "Killer" Maroni. While attempting to save the man, Maroni's henchman, Mike, lobs a grenade into the room, killing everyone inside with the sole exception of the good doctor. McNider does not get away clean, though. While still alive, he has been blinded and his much-vaunted medical career, along with his tremendous humanitarian work, is over.[8]

McNider's fate is not sealed, however. At the top of page three, in panels two and three, which takes place several weeks after the career ending accident, we get the following exchange between a bandaged McNider and his nurse (and later lover) Myra Mason:

McNider: Myra, you've been a good assistant to me in my research—I want you to work with me—
Mason: But doctor—your eyes….
McNider: There are still things left for me to do—I always wanted to be a

writer—I will write now—stories that will help to bring justice to the downtrodden and oppressed.

Yes, Mason immediately offers to be McNider's eyes. "Dictate your stories to me," she tells him. "I will read to you and help in any way I can." But the importance of the passage clearly shows that McNider refuses to let his loss of eyesight prevent him from completing any task he sets his mind to and Mason, really, is just continuing the assistant work she had been doing for him pre-accident. Within 23 panels, slightly over 25 percent of the way through the story, we've already established both the public and private character of the man. And we then see that McNider is successful, publishing his exposés as "a writer fighting for the public good."[9]

The panels immediately following show us, in microcosm, the public opinion of the sightless when "Killer" Maroni is presented with McNider's prose takedowns of his criminal empire. Maroni even refuses to allow Mike to finish the job he started a page earlier, explaining "Aw, let him make a monkey out of himself if he wants to—no one's going to pay attention to a guy who can't even see what he's talking about!"

Even if the origin story stopped there, we would have enough to give us the world's first blind (and probably first disabled in general) comic book hero. But in order to bring the "super" into it, we needed one more page. There, while pondering what else he can do in case his words are not enough to help rid the world of evil, McNider is attacked, Batman like, by an owl crashing through his window. Instinctively ripping the bandages from his face, he realizes he can see ... but only when the lights are out. The metaphor of the owl is soon understood by McNider, who explains it to the readers while talking to the bird: "Both of us are blind by daylight and can see only by night."

Reizenstein then gives us a scientific explanation for McNider's ailment, but we do not need or want it (although it does solve Lee's "believability" issue nicely, as we'll discuss further when we get to Daredevil). It is better to know McNider overcomes his impairment by continuing to play to his strengths, which he does. He spends the remaining four pages of the initial story devising a costume and the "blackout grenades"[10] which would become his stock in trade weapon of choice. Then he captures the bad and makes sure "Killer" Maroni is placed behind bars for a long time.

It is an auspicious beginning for the first blind hero, but he still has more to teach us and a legacy to hand down yet.

Dr. Mid-Nite ran in the back pages of *All-American Comics* as a supporting feature for the following seven years, until issue number 102 (cover dated October 1948) when most of the continuing characters and stories were replaced by westerns.[11] But, as was noted earlier, this did not mean his adventures were confined to eight-page jaunts as filler for Green Lantern. Less than a year after his initial appearance, in January of 1942, the good Doctor also found himself in the pages of *All-Star Comics* number 8, becoming (along with Starman) the newest member of the Justice Society of America.[12]

In his first outing as a member, Dr. Mid–Nite does not break any new boundaries or strike blows for the "handicapped." Instead, he is shown working with his secretary, the ever-present Myra Mason, and leading a normal life.[13] This representation, especially for 1941, is wonderful. There is no cessation of everyday duties, just an adjustment in how McNider interacts with the world. McNider is quite conscious of the fact that even though he can see in the darkness, when the lights are on, he is quite blind.[14] He does not try to hide his disability, even as Dr. Mid–Nite, to those who know his true identity. This is in direct contrast to Daredevil, as we will see.

McNider's run as a member of the original JSA lasted as long as the group itself, ending in 1951 when *All-Star Comics*, like *All-American Comics* before it, was converted to westerns. After more than a ten-year hiatus, Mid–Nite came back as a minor character, showing up in support of A-listers like The Flash and still as a member of the JSA, whenever they would appear in crossovers with the Silver Age and more modern Justice League of America.[15]

The next time Charles McNider becomes relevant to our discussion, though, is in 1985 in issue 19 of *Infinity, Inc*.[16] By this point, the Dr. has aged into a slightly elder statesman of the superhero set. While he may still be Mid–Nite, now he is spending more time as a physician, charged with the rehabilitation of what we have now started calling "meta-humans." And he happens to be on call when a hero group known as Infinity, Inc. bring in some wounded soldiers. However, it is not McNider who actually interests us here. Instead, it is his protégée, a young woman named Beth Chapel. On page six, he refers to Dr. Chapel as "potentially the most brilliant surgeon I've ever seen," so immediately we notice she is treated with respect and, while raw, still with deference to her abilities. We understand from the context that McNider has absolute faith in the abilities of Chapel, so much so we get the idea that were he to retire, she would be the ideal candidate to become a veritable "doctor to the super-powered."

Chapel herself is introduced as an interesting figure. In addition to being a woman, she's African American and is immediately misidentified as a nurse rather than a doctor, and she takes offense. Her offense may or may not be warranted, and we could certainly spend some time discussing the stereotypical roles of African American women in hospitals, but it is her response which does warrant note. On the top of page four, before we have even really been introduced to the character aside from an anonymous floating head on the previous page (we will get her name in the next panel), a disembodied voice responds to the charge of being a nurse with the line "Give yourself an 'E' for 'eyesight.'" This is an odd phrase to use here. Even something as innocuous as "can't you read" while pointing to her doctor's ID would have made more sense, until one keeps reading.

When McNider does show up a page later, declaring they will save the injured superhero who has been brought in, then qualifies his claim with "at least we will if it's humanly possible for a blind physician to do so," Chapel's first response is to not only identify the speaker as McNider, but then to exclaim "I—I didn't see you there."

Even considering the oddity of the first phrasing, this should not, and does not, raise any alarms. And, in fact, Beth Chapel does little else in that issue. She is a competent physician but that is all. It is not until the next issue,[17] when we see her interacting positively with "Hooty," Mid-Nite's sidekick owl, that we begin to get suspicious. Then, when the hospital in which she and McNider work is destroyed by an earthquake, Chapel proves her mettle by assisting the costumed superheroes in saving trapped civilians—even at the possible expense of her own life when she is caught in an oxygen tank explosion.

By the end of the issue, Chapel is on her way to recovery, with one exception: The explosion blinded her. We see her, the same way we saw McNider 40 years earlier, eyes wrapped and wondering about the state of her medical career.[18]

"This isn't the end of your career, Beth. You're still a doctor..." she's told by two of the heroes who were part of the rescue effort.

"Oh, sure!" she responds. "And if a certain JSAer ever retires, I can even take over *his* business. In which case you can call me—Dr. Midnight!"

Now everything makes sense. The writer, Roy Thomas, knew where this was going, knew Beth Chapel would become the new incarnation of the blind hero and was setting us up from her introduction. The fact she changes the spelling to Midnight is a way to set herself apart while still maintaining a respectful link.[19]

Everything comes to a head in issue 21 of *Infinity, Inc.* when the blind Chapel has gone back to her parents to wallow in her new status. This is honest and plays as such. The loss of sight is a major disruption to the status quo, obviously, but all it takes for her to come around is the visit of one of the heroes who helped her at the hospital (Rick Tyler, the son of the original Hourman, an original JSA member, who is now replacing his father). While discussing future options on page 22, Chapel, Hourman and Chapel's brother John, are attacked. Hourman is laid low, and John immediately jumps to his sister's aid, yelling "I can't leave you—I won't!"

And Chapel's response is immediate and unwavering: "No, of course you won't leave me—" she says. "—Because I'm helpless and blind, right?" Then, with no thought of superpowers, she rips the bandages from her eyes. Even sightless, she is displaying the courage and tenacity needed to be a hero, like McNider some 40 years earlier. But, also like McNider, when, in the course of the battle, the lights are turned out, she discovers she can make out shadows and shapes. "My eyes—They feel different, burning! Burning and—yes! This isn't the same kind of vision I used to have, but—I can see!"

By the end of the issue, Chapel has acquired a costume and assumed the Doctor Midnight moniker (she also picked up some of the blackout grenades courtesy of Rick Tyler). By the next issue, Chapel and Tyler have fully integrated their mid-80s personalities on heroes from the 40s and the next generation is ready to do battle.[20]

There is, however, one more Mid-Nite to come.

The final incarnation of Doctor Mid-Nite (note he is back to the original spelling of Mid-Nite, but now spells out "Doctor") came in 1999, courtesy of writer Matt Wagner and artist John K. Snyder in a three-issue mini-series detailing the hero's latest origin. The similarities between this version, Pieter Cross, and the earlier pair are striking. Once again, he is a righteous physician who is blinded in a freak explosion and who, in a pique of instinct, rips the bandages from his eyes only to discover his preternatural ability to see in the dark—or, how Cross himself sees it "the lower spectrums are mine."[21]

Here, Wagner pays homage to the original Mid-Nite[22] while at the same time, giving Cross his own distinct personality and drive. Even before the accident, Cross is already a driving force for social change, calling himself the "Midnight Doctor" he makes the rounds in the seedier parts of town, taking care of those who cannot take care of themselves, or who need his special attention.

However, unlike his predecessors, while Cross seems the most likely to become a superhero, he is the one who has the hardest time adjusting to his blindness. His associate, Camilla, narrates: "Following the accident, Pieter Cross vanished from the outside world. He discontinued all interactions with his former patients and social causes. It was like the darkness that claimed his eyes had opened up and swallowed him whole." Disconcertingly, he rejects the notion of who he was, going so far as to reprimand Camilla when she calls him "Doc" by telling her not to call him that, since he is no longer a doctor.

Not until he understands what has happened to him does he embrace the advantages he might gain from the world thinking he cannot see. "Don't you see," Cross says, and again Wagner, like the creators before him, plays with visualization puns in the dialogue. "This new ... condition grants me the freedom to finally operate under a true cover of darkness." With this line, Cross decides to become a costumed crime-fighter.

And yet, this version of Doctor Mid-Nite has become even more known for his medical knowledge and personality than for his crime fighting. When he joins the modern version of the JSA, not only do the writers continue the puns ("Seeing is believing," "Looked into it," "We do tend to see things in a different light.") giving Cross more of a sense of humor than Wagner may have originally intended, but also focus on his medical knowledge, allowing him to beat opponents who far outmatch him physically (as well as constantly tossing off medical bon mots about the dangers of smoking or poor diet).

Even so, in *JSA Classified* #19, on the top of page 16, we still understand that Cross' visual impairment is a real and lasting issue. He explains through the narration that "without my mask, I'm blind under the surgical lamps. But I've operated enough to do this without eyes. By necessity, I've learned to rely on other senses."[23]

With the exception of the three issues which introduced Cross, Doctor Mid-Nite has never carried his own title. And even though Charles McNider was the first blind hero by more than twenty years, the most recognizable sightless super is the Man Without Fear—Daredevil himself.

As noted at the beginning of this essay, Stan Lee was hoping to create a hero "who would start out with a disability." This word "hero" is actually an important distinction since several months earlier, Lee had given the world The X-Men, lead by "the crippled Professor Xavier."[24] Xavier, though wheelchair bound, and with powers in his own right, is *not* considered a superhero. Instead, he is the leader of a group of mutant heroes, and while each of them might be disabled in their own way (including Cyclops, who has force beams emanating from his eyes) they were not, in the eyes of Lee, "disabled." That difference is really the crux of the matter. What he is saying, in effect, is that while having wings or a tail might make you different, the real-world concept of not being able to see is a far more debilitating issue—which comes back to the idea of believability.

Being a green rage monster or having skin which looks like orange rocks or being able to stretch to near infinite lengths[25] cannot possibly exist in our world so by extension, they do not come with the same credibility gap. Being blind, on the other hand, is something we all have experience with in one way or another. Since we as readers could envision the reality, then the fictive would need to be especially careful.

With Matt Murdock, Lee succeeds (although the character does not really hit its creative stride until Frank Miller takes the reins in the '80s). Young Murdock loses his eyesight for the noblest of reasons—he is saving an old man from being hit by a truck. Instead, Murdock takes the brunt of the impact, getting hit in the face with a canister containing radioactive material.[26] Like Doctor Mid-Nite, the innate "heroness" is already present and his injuries come as a direct result of placing others before himself.

Unlike Mid-Nite, though, who gets a quasi-scientific explanation for his unique abilities, Murdock's enhanced senses[27] come directly (Lee and Everett, Daredevil 1964) from the radioactive materials (and later, from training by another blind character called "Stick."). Additionally, by having the accident occur while Murdock is still a teenager, Lee has given him some time to get used to not only the disability itself, but also the ways to use it, relying on the classic preconceived notions of what it means to be blind in order to support the future abilities. For example, at the top of page 10 of *Daredevil* #1, the blind Murdock is working out in the gym when he notices "It's as though nature made all my senses far more powerful, to compensate for my blindness!" Then, after hypothesizing that the radioactive compound *might* be the cause, he continues at the bottom of the page to tell us just how perceptive his remaining four primary senses are—He can hear heartbeats, never forgets an odor and so can recognize a person, can determine how many bullets are in a gun by the weight of the barrel and, in what must be the most unusual and possibly useless adaptation of all, can taste exactly how many grains of salt are on a pretzel.[28] With all that, no matter how the enhancements were achieved, we are still in the realm of possibility. Where he gets beyond those senses though, is where we enter the mystic. As Murdock points out "my most important new ability is in the form of a built-in radar" which enables him to walk without bumping into anything.[29]

Powers in place, all it takes is the proper catalyst for Murdock to spring into superheroic action. With Lee behind the typewriter, that catalyst takes the form of a dead parent,[30] in this case Jack Murdock, who is killed for *not* throwing a fight. Murdock now begins a dual life, fighting crime as Daredevil but also fighting crime as an attorney. And it is here, on page 19 where we see the other side of what Murdock will have to deal with, more so than any of the Mid-Nite characters, when Karen Page, the young blond secretary at his newly opened law firm, declares, "What a pity such a wonderful, handsome man is so handicapped."[31]

As was stated though, it is really not until some 20 years later, during a story arc titled "Born Again" by Frank Miller, where the character really gets fully tested, because here, the fight is not about the hero, but about the man. The antagonist, Kingpin, discovers Daredevil's true identity and goes about destroying Murdock rather than fighting the Devil himself. Interestingly, he never questions the sightfulness of Daredevil, assuming instead that it is the blindness which is the act. And that act, if nothing else, sports a grudging respect—enough so that the Kingpin assumes if Murdock falls low enough, he might be able to hire the former defender of justice: "Any man so dedicated as to pretend to blindness in daily life has surely developed a range of methods and techniques that would be an asset to my enterprises."[32]

All of which is fascinating in and of itself, but Miller takes it one step further. One of the threads of the story arc involves Ben Urich, a reporter trying to get to the bottom of the frame Kingpin has put around Murdock. At one point, Kingpin has an associate threaten Urich with violence should he continue his investigation, but the way it is accomplished is via another being killed as Urich listens on the telephone. This simple little device works wonders, not only putting Urich into the same position as a blind man but also placing the reader there, witnessing his reaction. We are now in a place of exquisite empathy for what Murdock has been going through and it works beautifully.[33]

For the most part, these characters exist and thrive on the printed page. Recently, though, Daredevil has made the leap to the small screen in his own series[34] as well as part of a team called The Defenders. But like in the comics which spawned them, Mid–Nite has been reduced to a bit player. He has shown up in the WB "Arrowverse"[35] and on several animated series and films, but still has yet to break through to stardom.

Ultimately, it seems Lee solved his problem more successfully than any of the blind characters who came before. He gave us a character still going strong more than 50 years after his debut. A character who let the reader believe that a man without sight could actually perform the hazardous feats of heroism that were, and continue to be, required.

Notes

1. Lee & Ditko, *Amazing Fantasy #15*, 12.
2. The Silver Age is most often considered to date from 1956, with the first appearance of Barry Allen as The Flash in Showcase #4. The ending date is in question, but most will consider it ending anywhere from 1970–1975.
3. Lee, *Son of Origins*, 112.
4. Lee, *Son of Origins*, 112.
5. Markstein, *Toonopedia*, Dr. Mid-Nite.
6. At this point, "groups" meant a framing device for the individual characters to have their own adventures as part of a larger storyline, i.e., they would all meet, discuss a plan, then each would go their own way, execute their part, then return to debrief the rest of the group.
7. The common practice then, as it is now, is to cover date the comic several months ahead of actual publication in order to give it a longer shelf life on the newsstands.
8. Reizenstein and Asch, *All-American Comics*, 1–8.
9. Reizenstein and Asch, *All-American Comics*, 1–8.
10. These grenades cause a cloud of total darkness to envelope the area, allowing for Mid-Nite to retake an advantage.

11. Markstein, *Toonopedia*, Dr. Mid-Nite.
12. This was possible due to the leaving of Hourman and The Flash as regular members. Interestingly, the same issue which saw Doctor Mid-Nite become a permanent member of the JSA, also saw a backup feature introducing the world to the creation of William Moulton Marston: Wonder Woman.
13. Fox and Asch, *All-Star Comics #8*, 1–8.
14. A visual example of this can be found in Peter Schaffer's one-act play *Black Comedy*, where the lighting is designed in reverse, i.e., whenever the lights of the fictional world are on and the characters can see, the stage is completely dark, and the audience cannot. When there is an "in-world" blackout, the stage is illuminated for the spectator while the characters stumble around in "darkness."
15. Markstein, *Toonopedia*, Dr. Mid-Nite.
16. Thomas, *Last Crises*.
17. Thomas, *Stormy Weather*.
18. Thomas, *Stormy Weather*.
19. And in later issues, once it has been established that Chapel has known McNider's secret all along, he does, in fact, train her.
20. Thomas and Thomas, *Shadows at Midnight!*
21. Wagner and Snyder, *Doctor Mid-Nite-D.O.A.*
22. Both directly, having Cross openly acknowledge McNider in his choice of name and costume, and indirectly as Cross also trains a "seeing eye owl" whom he names "Charlie" in honor of McNider. As well, it is discovered in later appearances that McNider himself was the doctor who delivered Cross as a baby.
23. Beatty and Morales, *Skin Trade-Part One*.
24. Lee, *Son of Origins*, 16.
25. Respectively: The Incredible Hulk, The Thing, Mr. Fantastic—all also co-created by Lee.
26. The radioactive material which escapes from the canister ends up leaking into the sewers where it mutates four turtles and their sensei master, the rat Splinter, turning them into superheroes in their own right—the Teenage Mutant Ninja Turtles.
27. Murdock's physical prowess is also never in question. His father is a washed-up prize-fighter so we see the teenage Matt, before the accident, training his body as a fighter would.
28. Lee and Everett, *Daredevil*, 10.
29. Lee, *Son of Origins*, 113.
30. Also used to great effect in Spider-Man, a character Daredevil was initially modeled after.
31. Lee, *Son of Origins*, 122.
32. Miller and Mazzucchelli, *Daredevil-Born Again*, 24.
33. Miller and Mazzucchelli, *Daredevil-Born Again*, 88–89.
34. The series ran for three seasons on Netflix, and as of this writing, a new series titled *Daredevil: Born Again* is expected to debut on Disney+ in 2024. The less said about the 2003 feature film, however, the better.
35. However, in his third, and final appearance, this version of McNider has been transported to the future where, for some reason, he uses advanced technology to restore his eyesight.

Pastoral Counseling and Impending Blindness

Vision Loss and a Quest for Meaning

Curtis W. Hart

An individual suffering from vision loss may or may not belong to or have a relationship with a faith community. Regardless, they may seek out a priest, minister, rabbi, or imam to help them adjust to their condition whether it stems from macular degeneration, glaucoma, traumatic injury, or other source. No matter the cause of vision loss or the patient's relationship to any particular spiritual community they may avail themselves of the skills and insights of trained pastoral counseling professionals, congregational clergy, or volunteers who extend outreach and emotional support to those in the broader community who are in need. All those afflicted may engage in the sorts of questions common to those with vision loss or impairment regarding their self worth, their future, and the meaning of illness, including questions that relate to the God of their understanding. Such issues involve dependency such as "Will I, or am I, an undue burden to my loved ones and my neighbors?" or, in some cases, "Is my vision loss meant for some purpose?" In any case, such questions take on a significance that can only be understood as existential in character.

It is probably not well known among healthcare providers that those in the pastoral counseling community are represented by the following professional organizations: the American Association of Pastoral Counselors, the Association for Clinical Pastoral Education, the Association of Professional Chaplains, the National Association of Jewish Chaplains, and the National Association of Catholic Chaplains. All have undertaken supervised training for the counseling of individuals, families, and groups. Some have also undertaken advanced degrees to prepare them to serve in institutional, congregational, and clinic settings. This training includes emphases on loss and spiritual growth. Moreover, this training prepares those certified in the field to work collegially with others in the helping professions and with mental health professionals in particular. They can be a resource for counseling and consultation, and likewise these individuals may refer to other professionals and groups in the healthcare community. The purpose of these organizations is summed up in the *Mission Statement* of the American Association of Pastoral Counselors with these words:

"The Mission of the American Association of Pastoral Counselors is to bring healing, hope, and wholeness to individuals, families, and communities by expanding and equipping spiritually grounded and psychologically informed care, counseling, and psychotherapy."[1]

These words offer an insight into the perspectives of these professional groups prepared to focus on service in a contemporary multicultural world.

Severe illness changes everything, For example, a rabbi who served at Memorial Sloane Kettering Cancer Center asked patients, once he had gotten to know them, "how has cancer changed your life?" This same question, or one similar to it, could be posed to a person suffering from vision loss. Persons with vision loss might pose such a question themselves as a natural and very human part of coming to grips with significant loss. But vision loss has its own special meaning and character in the way it provides a challenge to an individual's religious or spiritual grounding and their perceived place in their world and web of human interactions. And, most particularly, it poses the abiding question of the place of suffering within the context of the human condition.

John Milton, Our Contemporary

It would be impossible to enumerate all the examples of loss and healing in sacred texts from all traditions as they relate to vision loss or its symbolic expressions and references to such things as light and darkness to be found there. A cataloging of this order might prove interesting but not as useful as turning instead to a very famous case example that will assist a probing into vision loss and its relationship to the challenges of a search for meaning.

In 1652 after having become blind due to what is thought to have been undiagnosed glaucoma, the English poet John Milton (1608–1674) penned the memorable sonnet "When I consider how my light is spent."

> When I consider how my light is spent
> Ere half my days in this dark world and wide,
> And that one talent which is death to hide
> Lodged with me useless, though my soul more bent
> To serve therewith my Maker, and present
> My true account, lest He returning chide;
> "Doth God exact day-labor, light denied?"
> I fondly ask. But Patience, to prevent
> That murmur, soon replies, "God doth not need
> Either man's work or his own gifts; who best
> Bear His mild yoke, they serve Him best. His state
> Is kingly. Thousands at His bidding speed
> And post o'er land and ocean without rest:
> They also serve who only stand and wait."

This text has been extensively analyzed, commented upon, and rightly celebrated as among the finest poetic works in English. Among other things, it is a heartfelt lament at the loss in Milton's case of his capacity to see and thus to write. His "one Talent," as he calls it, has become "useless" and he questions how and whether he will be able to move forward and "serve therewith my Maker."

To that point in life Milton was a successful poet who had served the leadership and purpose of the Puritan revolution in England and its Lord Protector Oliver Cromwell. But now because of his blindness he will not be able to continue. Milton's inner state and reflective nature bring forth what he records in the figure Patience's response to him, "God doth not need/Either man's work or his own gifts." This response allows the poet to understand that, in Milton's famous phrase, "They all so serve who only stand and wait." Wait for what? In this state of blindness and acutely felt deprivation what of value can the poet anticipate doing with his life? He cannot know or literally see it. One response is that there may be much for Milton yet to do; for now he must accept his state and wait. Whether Milton intuited at this point that his greatest works, including the epic poem *Paradise Lost*, were yet to be written we do not know. What he appears to be searching for is reassurance that can only come in time from the hand of God and not from within his own inner resources alone. The arc of the poem moves, then, from loss of "Talent" and purpose to a dimly perceived hope for a new life of service. Here Milton must find value for more than just his writer's gifts. He continues to serve but must wait for the resolution or outcome of the burden his vision loss has laid upon him and to do so without guilt or a sense of failure.

This reading of the poem is certainly not the only one. It brings into focus how Milton's inner struggle as portrayed in ""When I consider how my light is spent" represents an archetypal path for what goes on for a person who loses their vision. The arc of the poem moves from a statement about devastating loss to a place of greater self-acceptance. This expression is what those who have lost vision, or are losing it, need to hear from their counselors—physicians, nurses, clergy, and others. There is hope and a future beyond despair. For the present, it is understandable and appropriate to hear the words "only stand and wait" as a comforting message that confirms the reality of suffering and loss but, by implication at least, anticipates a potentially usable future.

This use of Milton's poem as a therapeutic roadmap may appear odd or unusual. It provides, however, direction for the pastoral or "shepherding" instinct in the care of souls. Milton's case is remarkable in that in a fourteen line sonnet he lays out much of what the caregiver must understand when dealing with someone who is suffering from the loss of vision: recognition of the condition, an articulation by the patient regarding loss and suffering, and a response that meets the patient at their point of need.

It should be added that a careful reading and careful analysis of "When I consider how my light is spent" might serve as a useful teaching tool for medical residents, medical students, and seminarians who are destined in their professional lives to deal on countless occasions with situations that mirror Milton's poetic representation.

The Caring Community

There is a community dimension to the pastoral care of souls. It is a moral obligation, in fact, to care for the "least of these" as that is understood in all religious and humanistic traditions. Pastoral care cannot be limited to one on one relationships, crucial as they are, for it must have a broader social context to serve the common good. This obligation has been taken seriously by religious bodies and communities in their historic roles and charitable roles in building hospitals and funding agencies to care for the poor and immigrant populations. Quaker efforts to care for the mentally ill in both the United States and England beginning in the 18th century are classic examples of putting faith into practice. That same moral sentiment must now be focused upon issues in the area of prevention through more locally based programs that have access to and the trust of underserved populations. Churches, mosques, and synagogues offer health fairs and screening on a periodic basis to those who otherwise cannot afford it and at times when individuals and families are able to attend. Typically, these events include blood pressure screening, nutritional advice and counseling, screening for diabetes, kidney disease, HIV counseling and other issues. One important addition to any and all of these programs is screening for vision disorders like glaucoma as well as referral for treatment. Children must receive special attention as they approach school age or move into adolescence. The needs of our increasingly aging population are paramount as well. The connection between diabetes and blindness must always be assessed and timely referrals made.

One of the newer and most important aspects of health care has to do with increased awareness of the need for community health workers. These individuals are trained and mandated to make contact with local organizations and leaders and thus are able to enter into the homes of those in need. The American Public Health Association has endorsed this developing concept. Religious institutions may aid in fulfilling this need and its inclusion of eye exams and vision care through partnering with other institutions that can provide educational, organizational, and other support. One notable program that has gone on for over a decade is the Lay Health Educators Program at Johns Hopkins Bayview Medical Center in Baltimore. There local churches, mosques, synagogues and other agencies have forged a working partnership with medical professionals dedicated to a common task, the building of healthy communities. This program utilizes church members to help educate local communities and individuals about health care needs, most particularly prevention. Thus the pastoral task expands through the use of trained and supervised laypersons carefully screened and prepared for their task. To date there is significant data outlining the value of the Lay Health Educators Program at Johns Hopkins Bayview.[2]

This model of pastoral care as a community obligation including a component devoted to eye health can and should be replicated in similar forms in other venues. It should be presented and developed in a manner appropriate to each community's perceived and stated needs. Never a substitute for government's role or the expertise of standing institutions and professional groups, community based pastoral care should play an important role in the education and care of the citizenry and the upholding of the common good.

Notes

1. http://www.aapc.org.
2. Panagis Galliatsatos, Health Promotion in the Community: Impact of Faith Based Lay Health Educators in Urban Neighborhoods. *Journal of Religion and Health*, Springer online, 2016.

Blinded on the Battlefield
True Superhero Stories of Mikhail Margolin and Al Schmid

GEORGE HIGHAM

"Where are my many promised gifts and spoils of war?
Where are my bold [sic] and silver cups?"—Aeschylus

"War is hell." Few would disagree with these words attributed to General William T. Sherman, a succinct phrase that remains as relevant today as when spoken by the Union General best known for his "scorched earth" tactics that helped to end the American Civil War.

Acts of valor or cowardice are basic reactions to the inevitable carnage and loss that all wars bring. The losses are many—life, limb and livelihood have all been sacrificed for freedom, which is never free. Those who do not forfeit their lives on the battlefield often lose life as they knew it. Some traumas are physical. Some are mental ... but most are both.

It is impossible to quantify which disabling trauma may be better or worse than others, but surely an occurrence of severe injury resulting in the sudden loss of sight would be a spirit-breaking event to a young, healthy soldier merely twenty years of age. Yes, it would be a very rough situation to overcome, to rebuild one's life, re-integrate into society and raise a family while adapting to the monumental challenges that were once simple acts taken for granted, such as walking around and eating.

Yes, that would indeed be quite an inspiring story of triumph ... and following are *two* of them:

Russia one century ago: Not all the casualties of war are sent home in body bags. Some limp, some roll and some move with furtive movements guided by the tapping of a cane as they struggle to navigate their once-familiar hometowns, places now made foreign in their darkened world. This is how Mikhail Vladmirovich Margolin returned to Kiev, the land of his birth, in 1922. A wounded war veteran at barely twenty years old, Margolin's life was just beginning.

Hailing from Kiev, Mikhail Margolin chose to fight at a very young age. Aligning himself with the Bolsheviks (Red Army) during the Russian Civil War was a reaction to the pogroms that scarred the formative years of this Jewish youth.[1] Disparate factions vied for control in those turbulent years, and anti–Semitic propaganda was often employed by the White Army, stripping the Jewish population of their belongings while murdering them by the thousands. The chaos following World War I and the Russian Revolution forced both sides of the split nation to scrape together soldiers from the peasantry and weapons from conflicts that dated back into the late 1800s.

The lack of an organized well-stocked armory forced the Bolshevik soldiers of the day to utilize a variety of firearms. The lack of specific weapons training was truly a trial by fire as their survival was dependent upon this diverse selection of guns. Mechanically inclined from a young age, the still young Margolin thrived in this environment. Habitually disassembling and reassembling the assorted weapons that came his way, he developed a "feel" for the complex mechanisms as well as invaluable knowledge about their intricate functions that would serve him professionally in the coming decades.

War, being what it is, forever changed the young man's life. The waning days of the conflict found Margolin commanding a Lewis machine gun platoon in the mountains of Abkhasia. It was there that an anti–Bolshevik partisan bullet struck him in the head rendering him permanently blind.

When able to travel with the whole of a now uncertain life ahead of him, Margolin returned to the city of his birth. Convalescing in Kiev, his restlessness and depression got the better of him. The People's Commissariat of Social Security offered Margolin admission to the sanatorium in Kharkov as both a patient and a trainee. His vocational rehabilitation would include one year of training as a massage therapist. Not really knowing what that was, he eventually accepted that he needed help getting back to some sense of a satisfying life, so he left Kiev behind in 1925. This was a way to use his hands and to build up his strength—both for his physical recovery and a mental one.

Margolin disliked being a masseur. He completed the training, but it did little to help his mental status, perhaps even making his despondency worse. His depression swelled and it was not until the suggestion of a roommate that he try his hand at sculpting that he finally found some relief. Utilizing clay, Margolin fashioned small creatures in realistic form. It did not take long, however, for his hands to be guided by his natural inclinations. He was soon attempting to fashion mechanical pieces and the inner workings of firearms. The pliability of modeling clay does not lend itself well to the small moving parts that he was trying to create, but Margolin would not be deterred. It was a major step forward when he abandoned the material but not his hopes. He set up a vise in his room and began to utilize rigid materials for his designs—aluminum, wood, and stiff cardboard. As his designs took form so did his plans for the future. Intrigued by the mechanical workings of firearms, he opted to embrace his obsession and make it his life's work.

Inspired by the achievements of visually impaired yet renowned engineers, doctors, and scientists, Margolin set a rather lofty goal for himself. Not only was he blind, but he lacked the fundamental education in mathematics and formal studies in materials and mechanics—all required as the foundation for any arms designer. Neither discouraged nor a fool, Margolin made acquiring this knowledge a top priority. In 1926 he settled in Moscow to re-integrate into society while starting a family. Mature and focused, he realized that accepting his condition was the only way to overcome it.

He learned braille and continued to advance towards his goal. Aided by friends and his wife, who read to him aloud from textbooks and historical treatises on firearms, he advanced towards his goal. He collected guns, both old and new, and true to his nature he continued to take them apart and re-assemble them. He identified ways to improve them, cataloging his ideas to utilize in his own designs.

Far from being self-absorbed, Margolin also became very involved in community work. He became affiliated with the Central Committee of Komsomol. The Communist youth organization was founded during the Russian Civil War with the goal of providing education and sports programs to the youthful generation while grooming them for the full-fledged Communist party as they entered adulthood. Margolin initiated a military office with the Komsomol, and soon took a lead position there. In 1928, he led the Komsomol battalion on a parade march through Red Square, coordinating his movements by the sound of the drummers. Other times he trained the youth brigade in the use and care of firearms and body armor.

Through his association with the Komsomol, Margolin made the acquaintance of Brigade Commander Alexander A. Smirnsky. Smirnsky had been an artillery officer and gained some fame as an Olympic marksman in the previous decade. He remained a proponent of recreational shooting while becoming a successful gun designer himself, specializing in sporting arms. In 1927, Smirnsky established the NIIS OAKh (Nauch-no-Ispvtatelnaya Issledovatclskaya), the Scientific Research Station and Proving Grounds of the Central Council of OSCAVIAKHIM in

Kuskovo, South of Moscow.[2] While recreational shooting was the main purpose of the NIIS, the organization retained close ties to the military.

Despite his impaired vision, Margolin was assigned to the firearms training section at the NIIS. Smirnsky saw the potential in Margolin and suggested that he to focus his design aspirations on sporting arms. He thought it would be good for both Margolin and the sport, which lacked dedicated designers and would benefit from innovation.

Ultimately Smirnsky was correct—but Margolin's success was still a hard two decades ahead of him.

Unable to draft his own designs, Margolin was forced to describe his concepts in words and gestures to a draftsman. Utilizing this often-frustrating technique in conjunction with his own constructed mockups, all while continuing to study in depth about the many aspects of the field, Margolin completed his first gun in 1934. It was a success for him to have completed it, but the .22 caliber semi-automatic sporting rifle was deemed a mediocrity.

Undeterred, Margolin continued his efforts and in 1938 was offered a position at the prestigious Tula arsenal with the KBP design bureau. He was now amongst the best Russian arms designers, specializing in .22 caliber guns. The smaller caliber was not a weapon of war, as it lacked the raw power of larger-caliber guns that fired heavier lead projectiles with exponentially more force. But the .22 was an excellent training gun, and the perfect choice for target-shooting by sporting marksmen.

In 1940, Margolin submitted a pattern for a modified .22 target pistol that was accepted for production on June 21, 1941. The next day, on Jun 22, 1941, Germany launched Operation: Barbarossa.

The Nazi invasion of the Soviet Union signaled the start of the "Great Patriotic War," as announced by Josef Stalin—but by any name, the result was a series of barbaric battles punctuated by genocide, atrocities, and famine for the coming years. Such a world had little use for a low caliber "target pistol" and Margolin's design was soon forgotten about.

Lacking the benefit of vision, one might assume that Margolin would have little to contribute to the war effort ... but his achievements stand as remarkable when judged against any person, sighted or not. Serving as an Air Raid Warden in Moscow, Margolin threw a German incendiary device off the rooftop on which he was stationed, directing its detonation into the empty streets below. Margolin's lack of sight was actually a benefit when he led over 120 inhabitants to safety through the darkened subterranean tunnels beneath a bombed-out boarding house as it was engulfed in flames. Margolin's wife and son were amongst those rescued that night, along with the other women, children and elderly that have him to thank for the existence of their future generations.

In late 1941, as Moscow deteriorated, Margolin and his family were sent to Siberia where he dedicated his efforts to artillery design. As Russia slowly forced back the German invasion, he returned to Moscow, and Tula, in 1943. Utilizing his vast acquired knowledge of mechanics and weapons, he became an expert in captured German arms and was tasked with repairing "trophy" weapons for the Soviet Union. He continued this work after the war and was able to pursue his passion once again—the design of a low-caliber target pistol. He withdrew his design that had been accepted at the start of the war, determined to now create a pistol incorporating his observations (both mental and tactile) from the past five years.

The MCM .22 semi-automatic pistol featured some very bold innovations that were met with considerable resistance and was originally written off as the folly of a blind gun designer ... but anyone that held and fired an MCM immediately appreciated the efforts that perhaps *only* a blind gun designer was capable of. The extraordinary sense of balance was the first impression. The elevated sightline facilitated a more stable firing position by keeping the pistol at shoulder-height, ergonomically aligned with the human body, allowing for increased accuracy when fast-firing in rapid shooting competitions. The pistol barrel's counterweight raised the forward sight higher than usual in addition to serving as an upward-pointing muzzle-break that directed the exploding gases up. This reduced the recoil associated with most firearms, a force responsible for jerking the shooter's arm up and back upon firing. Margolin also raised the rear sight to keep everything lined up, and daringly mounted it to a small bridge-like structure that remained fixed to the pistol grip. The slide reciprocates backwards through it as the spent casing is ejected and the next cartridge is chambered.

Produced in 1948, Margolin's pistol was accepted for use in the USSR Shooting Championships in 1949. The team practiced with it for five years, training for the 1954 Olympics held in Caracas, Venezuela. Margolin's pistol was put up against such well-known world standards as the German Walther and the American Colt. The Russian marksman Nikolai Kalinichenko led the Soviet team to victory, setting new world-records in the rapid-firing competition, thanks to the efforts of a man that persevered over decades of hardship and prejudice due to his perceived disability by those more blind than he was.

Margolin continued to improve upon his designs, creating ambidextrous handgrips that appear to swallow the shooter's whole fist, and worked on several other firearms including an upside-down pistol that became nicknamed the "hacksaw" for reasons obvious to anyone looking at it. Official recognition came later in life. The silver medal "For Achievements to the National Economy of USSR" was awarded to Margolin in

1960, and in 1965 he received the highest scientific award, "Merited Inventor of the Russian Soviet Federative Socialist Republic of the USSR." He worked as a weapons consultant for the State Historical Museum and at the Police Research Institute. He also authored several short works concerning the repair of sporting guns and his military experiences.

Mikhail Vladimirovich Margolin passed away in 1975, two years before his original MCM pistol design would secure its place in popular culture. The awkwardly titled "Drearian Defense Conglomerate Defender sporting blaster pistol" wielded by Carrie Fisher as Princess Leia in *Star Wars* (1977) was a minimally modified Margolin MCM. Briefly used in the film's opening battle, the pistol was also featured in some very popular publicity stills featuring Mark Hamill as Luke Skywalker. In accordance with the film's budget constrictions (it is hard to think of *Star Wars* in that way), the sci-fi weapons were all based upon whatever real guns were available in Britain in the mid-seventies, receiving varying degrees of enhanced decoration to fit in better with the other-worldly space adventure.

This association created a bit of a cult-following for the MCM, as evidenced by the 2004 release of a high-quality prop replica by the Master Replicas company, with a limited run signed by Carrie Fisher. The MR release sold out very quickly, now fetching thousands of dollars on auction sites if any are even found.

Legendary firearms designer Mikhail Kalashnikov (best known for the AK-47 assault rifle) commended Margolin, praising his "strength of will, passion and dedication" to succeed in a field that proves difficult for even sighted individuals, further saying: "Margolin almost never talked about how many failures he had to endure on the thorny path of design, how much offensive distrust he had to endure from bureaucrats who rejected the very possibility of a blind inventor to create and create."

As fascinating as Margolin's tale is, his is not the only story of a blinded veteran to leave its mark on popular culture. In 1945, Warner Bros. released *Pride of the Marines* featuring John Garfield as Pvt. Al Schmid, a soldier blinded during a battle in 1942 on the island of Guadalcanal during the tide-turning Battle of Tenaru.

Japan's attack on Pearl Harbor changed to the United States forever. Twenty-one years old, employed at the Dodge Steel Company in Philadelphia and in his first serious relationship, Al Schmid's initial reaction upon hearing the news radio broadcast (after disbelief) was probably shared by many Americans—"Where the hell is Pearl Harbor?" As Mark Twain once observed, "God created war so that Americans would learn geography."

Al's next reaction was also shared across the nation—an immediate willingness to sign up with the Armed Forces as the United States joined what would become known as World War II. His ever present humorous and playful nature made Al good company. His courtship with Ruth Hartley would need to be put on hold, each believing that within one year he would return, and all would be normal again. The movies, dancing, picnics, and trips to the amusement park were typical dating activities that each enjoyed. Al had a particular fondness for the several shooting ranges located at their favorite haunt, the Willow Grove amusement park. An avid hunter, Al could never resist firing the .22 caliber rifles at the duck targets and was quite skilled at it. Al did not commit to Ruth until his brief visit home between boot camp and his clandestine deployment to "destination unknown" with the U.S. Marines. He used his bonus from the Dodge Steel Company to leave her an engagement ring along with his promise to return.

Eventually he did return but he was a changed man. A Japanese grenade robbed him of his sight and his good humor. In less than one year, the cheerful young man became a wounded, morose war veteran whose every move sent shocking waves of pain throughout his body. It would take years of countless surgeries to remove the metal shrapnel fragments that tore through his skin and remained embedded beneath his flesh. One of his eyes was completely gone, while the other was severely damaged.

Lost in a profound darkness—both literal and figurative—Al felt incapable of returning to his old life. He abandoned Ruth but she did not abandon him. Depression and denial about his vision loss clouded his judgment, but Ruth was as tenacious as he was and refused to give up. With her help, Al regained the will to live.

It had been nearly one year since he had last "seen" Ruth and much like Margolin's return to Kiev, Al's return to his hometown of Philadelphia was merely the first step of his long journey to regain his identity. Both men refused to accept that their traumatic blindness was permanent. Both men were fiercely independent and each angrily refused help, but eventually realized that they would be beaten by despair if they continued their bitter isolation.

Each suffered an emotional detachment upon their return home. Unlike Margolin, however, Al Schmid had been declared a national hero. During his five-month stay at the San Diego Naval Hospital prior to his transfer to Naval Hospital Philadelphia, the U.S. Marines publicly released the details of private Al Schmid's heroic actions from the Battle of Tenaru on August 21, 1942. Al did not want the celebrity status forced upon him, nor the accolades of being a "hero." "When I came back, I was the most disgusted man you ever saw. I did not want to bother to do anything. I could see people looking away from my ugly scars. They would not want to associate with me. I even told my girl it was all over."

This quote from Al Schmid's obituary webpage from Arlington National Cemetery (www.arlingtoncemetery.net/schmid.htm) is of importance because he references being able to "see" people recoil from his scars upon his return to the United States. Eventually, Schmid did regain very limited vision (shapes and colors) in his one remaining eye in 1943 but was totally blind during the referenced period. Also of note is Al's self-perception of his looks. There is little doubt as to the extent of facial damage that he suffered during the battle. His face was compared to shredded "hamburger" by his shocked eventual rescuers, but the reconstructive work done during his treatment in San Diego was nothing short of remarkable. Contemporary press photos from his return to Philadelphia survive as first-hand evidence, contrasting the intense despair and internal torment that left their own scars within the soldier.

Al had simply referred to his experience at Guadalcanal as "I was in a bit of action," but America needed heroes in those dark days and the All-American boy that chose to fight for his country at the risk of everything he held dear certainly fit the bill. That, and it was one hell of a story. The U.S. Marines press release was picked up by newspapers nationwide. For *Life* magazine (March 22, 1943) Roger Butterfield presented a very detailed account of Al's "life," culminating with his being awarded the Navy Cross, one of the highest military honors, while still undergoing treatments at the Naval Hospital Philadelphia and once again courting (or being courted by!) Ruth Hartley. Ruth stayed by his side to describe the parades in his honor that he could not see and was a very frequent visitor to the hospital. Butterfield followed-up his exposé with a book that further delved into Al's experiences, including his extensive rehabilitation as a disabled veteran.[3] Butterfield's book *Al Schmid, Marine* was fast tracked for a film adaptation by Warner Bros., who released it as *Pride of the Marines* (1945). A financial success, it was directed by the prolific Delmer Daves while several screenwriters developed the project (A.I. Bezzerides, Alvah Bessie and Martin Borowsky). Albert Maltz finalized the script, which received an Academy Award nomination for Best Adapted Screenplay.

Also instrumental in getting the film made was its star, John Garfield, who played Al Schmid on the silver screen. Garfield had been denied enlistment due to a severe heart condition and had since directed his efforts to support the U.S. Military in every way possible. He had met Al during his original rehab and developed a friendship and respect for the man he would eventually immortalize in the movies. Garfield reprised his role as Schmid on the radio for both *Lux Radio Theater* (December 31, 1945) and *Academy Award Theater* (June 15, 1946). The *Lux Radio Theater* show featured a telephone appearance by Al Schmid, conversing with Garfield.

The film remains startlingly true to the actual events and has always been praised for its authenticity, only taking liberties with a few occurrences concerning Al's return home to Philadelphia while still being treated for his injuries. The logistical details of the Battle of Tenaru on Guadalcanal remain accurate, short of the sickening carnage that soaked everything in blood and viscera by the battle's end. Al's difficult recovery makes up the entire second half of the film, presented as a long process filled with uncertain procedures along the way.

With half a year of training in the U.S. Marines behind him, Pvt. Al Schmidt was assigned to a three-man machine gun crew with Cpl. Lee Diamond (Dane Clark) and PFC Johnny Rivers (Anthony Caruso). Al knew Johnny from Philadelphia and was assigned to load the belt fed Browning M1917A1, a water-cooled machine gun, as Johnny fired it while Lee "spotted" targets. The Marines had arrived on the island of Guadalcanal to secure and protect Henderson Airfield as part of the first substantial push across the Pacific Ocean following Japan's attack on Pearl Harbor. The U.S. Marines arrived in mid–August 1942 and faced little resistance upon landing ... but within one day, a Japanese naval fleet launched a surprise attack and destroyed the U.S. ships moored off Guadalcanal that still had the supplies needed by the men already ashore. In effect, the marines were stranded but pushed on with their objective, knowing that another attack directed towards them would occur soon.

Al, Johnny and Lee set up a foxhole along the Tenaru River at what would be the frontline of the battle. The small, camouflaged pit would house the three men in cramped quarters with the large Browning M1917A1 and many boxes of ammo belts, each holding 250 rounds of caliber .30 ammunition.[4] In the dark of night, the Japanese infantry attacked, constantly mocking and taunting the Marines with the little English they knew—"Marines—tonight you *die!*" The sound of their shrill taunting would haunt Al for years.

Johnny Rivers was shot early on, and Lee Diamond soon after. Johnny died instantly but Lee was able to keep spotting for Al, who now loaded and fired the Browning without help. An enemy grenade damaged the gun while severely injuring Al, blinding him on the spot. As tenacious as Garfield is in his performance of Al Schmid onscreen, in reality Al was even more relentless. He continued to fire the damaged machine gun while totally blinded by following the orders given by Lee and by shooting in the directions of the taunting voices. By dawn, the river and beachhead were filled with the slain Japanese soldiers as America claimed its first real victory against Japan in this war.

Pride of the Marines places the battle scene in the middle of the film, then follows Al Schmid through his recovery and treatment—first at the San Diego Naval Hospital then in his hometown at the Naval Hospital Philadelphia. In San Diego he remains in denial, angrily throwing away an instructional braille card given to him by a surgeon after a failed eye operation. He does not want to bother learning any techniques to aid his daily sightless existence, convinced it is only temporary. He refuses to eat with the other veterans due to his lack of coordination and inability to see his food … and nastily belittles an orderly that has agreed to help feed him in a janitor's closet when the man tries to orient Al to the position of the food on his plate by likening it to the hands on a clock.

Tough as nails, Al would not let anyone feel sorry for him but himself. His biggest battle was overcoming self-pity and his biggest fear was re-integrating into society. He feared both acceptance and rejection, not able to distinguish the genuine concern of his friends or the admiration of the masses from condescending charity or pity, which angered him. He knew that his employment opportunities had vanished along with his vision—who would hire a blind man?

And who would marry one? He accepted the help of Red Cross Nurse Virginia Pfeiffer (Rosemary DeCamp) to write to his fiancé Ruth Hartley (Eleanor Parker) in an effort to cut off their relationship, sparing himself of her "pity." Not wanting to even return to Philadelphia, Al planned on moving to Chicago to start a "new life." Both onscreen and in reality, it was the efforts of Nurse Pfeiffer that eventually brought the couple back together.

Al's anger and fear were shared by his fellow disabled veterans during their rehabilitation. The hospital stay gave them all the opportunity to anticipate the worst from an uncertain future. Regardless of this bond, they were each isolated in their own private hells. How could the GI Bill help them if their old jobs were no longer needed? If they could not work to support their families? If their wives had affairs or left them? Some felt that the government owed them for the sacrifices made, while others argued that serving their country in the military should not entitle all to a free lunch for the rest of their lives. When Lee Diamond tries to convince Al and the others of their potential, sighted or not, he mistakenly says, "Don't tell me we can't pull together. Don't you see it?"

"I don't *see* none of those things!" Al angrily retorts as he exits.

Accompanied by Lee Diamond on the train ride back east to Philadelphia, Al's bitterness and self-pity continue to infuriate his comrade. Lee confesses that the admiration that he felt for Al in the foxhole on Guadalcanal when he refused to give up, even when blinded, is now in question. Lee's respect for Al's tenacity and valor has been replaced by suspicions of wild abandon in the heat of the moment. He accuses Al of being an adrenaline-junky, enlisting as a thrill seeker. The viewers must now share this suspicion, when recollecting Al's enthusiasm when signing up for the military early in the film. An avid hunter, Al proclaimed, "I bet it would be more fun shooting Japs than bears."[5]

While the film may leave this question of motivation unanswered, Al Schmid, Jr., did not. From his deathbed in the winter of 1982, Al Sr. spoke frankly to his son, who struggled to understand why his father did what he did some forty years earlier on the other side of the world.[6] Al Schmid chose to be at the forefront of the Battle of Tenaru of his own free will. He had a valid excuse to *not* be there, and actually disobeyed medical orders to fulfill what he felt was his moral obligation. A gangrenous infection in both legs caused by infected blisters resulted in reassignment to the rear by a medical officer. Under the pretense of retrieving some personal belongings from his foxhole at the Tenaru River, Al returned to the front and resumed his position amongst his three-man machine gun crew. As told by Al Jr., "He knew the battle was going to happen ... he said it was his job. It was what he was sworn to do. And Johnny Rivers was there. He and Johnny were very, very close.... He just had to do it."

Al's assessment was correct. In the dark of night, he began noticing coconuts floating in the water. Then more of them, bobbing along. Then lots more, and he realized it was an act of deception by the Japanese to provide confusing cover for their own soldiers that were treading water while advancing, their own heads above water, indistinguishable from the mass of coconuts....

Early in the battle, Al's best friend was "ripped from top to bottom" by enemy gunfire. Johnny Rivers' remains were spread throughout the tight space, splattering all over Al and Lee. Infuriated, Al took over Rivers' position as gunner while Lee spotted and fed the ammo belts. When Lee was shot and could no longer load, Al did that too as Lee continued to spot. When the water-cooled housing on the machine gun became damaged, Al maintained control by only firing short bursts to avoid overheating and jamming the mechanism. When an explosion blinded Al and sent countless metal fragments into his face and upper extremities, he still managed to fire the machine gun for a bit while following Lee's directions. And when the machine gun finally failed and all seemed lost, Al drew his .45 sidearm. Lee thought that this signaled the end for his blinded and mangled friend, but Al assured him "Hell, don't worry about that. I'm going to shoot the first Jap that comes in here ... just tell me which way he's coming from and I'll get him."

The Battle of Tenaru was the first major victory for the U.S. Marines and a vital strategic accomplishment to gain a foothold in the South Pacific islands in the pushback against the Japanese forces. Al Schmid was credited with over 200 kills, equating to approximately 25 percent of the Japanese forces the night.

Pride of the Marines climaxes with Al's unwilling return home and a bit of contrived subterfuge involving deceiving the blind man into returning to his old house instead of the naval hospital on his agenda, begrudgingly accepting Ruth's help and regaining a small bit of vision in his one eye.

In reality, Al had come to grips with his fate prior to his return and was glad to be greeted by his father, stepmother and Ruth at the Philly train station—even inquiring about his dog "Jeff" upon arrival, disappointed that he was not there. Al and Ruth were wed, had a son, and Al continued his war efforts by agreeing to numerous public appearances. He despised being called a "hero" but continued to be what America needed, inspiring others while raising war bonds.

He grew to appreciate the efforts of the medical staff that had helped him get through the trauma and tried to share some encouraging words with other wounded veterans that still had the worst ahead of them. "My body was full of shrapnel and I was blind—the toughest part, the blindness. I lay there in the hospital and I didn't give a damn about anything. I didn't even want to live." In an interview with the *Los Angeles Examiner* from 1944, he continues—"I'd like to tell the other fellows who come back all bunged up, maybe with an arm or a leg missing, that it doesn't mean the end. I learned that the hard way."[7]

He was promoted to sergeant, named "Father of the Year" in 1946 and had his whole life ahead of him.

Fate decreed that both Mikhail Margolin and Al Schmid would be blinded on the battlefield at a young age. The rest was up to them. Eventually realizing—and *accepting*—the help offered to them, each fought their way back from the darkest depths of despair. While history distinguishes them as "the blind gun designer" and "the blind marine," they proved to be so much more. The many years lived following their adventures recounted here proved to be the best years of their lives.

If this book proves anything it is not to make assumptions about the abilities of those without sight. Blind people may have lost their vision … but not their *vision* for the betterment of themselves and society.

Notes

1. John Doyle Klier and Shlomo Lambroza, *Pogroms: Anti-Jewish Violence in Modern Russian History* (UK: Cambridge University Press, 1992), 301–307.
2. George Morgan Chinn, *The Machine Gun: History, Evolution, and Development of Manual, Automatic and Airborne Repeating Weapons, Volume 2: Part 7* (Washington, DC: U.S. Government Printing Office, 1951), 11.
3. Roger Butterfield, *Al Schmid, Marine* (New York: W.E. Norton & Company, Inc., 1944).
4. Ian V. Hogg, *The American Arsenal: The World War II Official Standard Ordnance Catalogue* (South Yorkshire: Frontline Books, 2014), 227.

5. Immediately following Japan's attack on Pearl Harbor, it was common for such racist and derogatory language to be used in the press, entertainment, and certainly casual conversation by angered U.S. citizens.

6. Al Schmid, Jr.'s deathbed interview with his father occurred in late 1982 and was published ten years later as the cover story "War Hero" in *The Philadelphia Inquirer*, August 16, 1992.

7. U.S. Navy Bureau of Medicine and Surgery Historian André B. Sobocinski provided these quotes in *The Story of Sgt. Schmid and Navy Medicine's Rehabilitation of the Blind in World War II* available at https://navymedicine.navylive.dodlive.mil/archives/12748 Sobocinski's account details the ground-breaking rehabilitation work done at Naval Hospital Philadelphia, which was designated as the center for all bilateral blind patients from the Navy and Marine Corps.

Blindness in the Jewish Tradition
From Written Text to Oral Law to Contemporary Medical Practice

JEROME M. KARP *and* HOWARD L. FORMAN

The Jewish tradition has long contemplated the role of vision in the human condition and what it means for a person to lose his or her vision. Starting from Judaism's most sacred texts, the books of the Old Testament, one notes an unusually large number of central characters who were blind: the patriarchs Isaac and Jacob in their old age, the Temple priest Eli, the powerful Samson, the prophet Ahijah, and others. When enumerating disabilities in narrative or legal contexts, the Old Testament frequently lists blindness first; Steinberg sees this as a reflection of the high incidence of vision loss in biblical times as well as the severe functional impact of blindness in that era.[1] Later rabbinic texts, starting with the Talmud, the foremost compilation of Jewish law completed in the 5th century CE, frequently discuss the impact of blindness in Jewish law. Numerous Talmudic sages were blind, including Naḥum of Gimzo (*Taanit* 21a), Bava ben Buta (*Bava Batra* 4a), Dosa ben Harkinas (*Yevamot* 16a), and the frequently cited scholars R. Joseph and R. Sheshet (*Bava Kamma* 87a); as were many Talmudic scholars who lived centuries later. Indeed, the abundance of references and overt discussions of blindness in Jewish sources prevent offering a singular view of blindness in Jewish thought.[2]

Perhaps representative of the wide range of views toward blindness in Jewish sources is the plethora of exegetic insights found in the Midrashic literature, which compiles rabbinic interpretations of biblical text, regarding Isaac's blindness. Why, ask the authors of the Midrash, was Isaac blind? The sheer volume of discussion of this question and numerous answers suggested might reflect the profound difficulty in accepting that one of the patriarchs, the earliest followers of God, could have been stricken with blindness. And ultimately the answers to the question diverge wildly in their approach to the nature of Isaac's blindness. Some suggest that it was the result of a negative force in Isaac's environment: the smoke emanating from the pagan sacrifices offered by his son Esau's wives (*Aggadat Bereshit* 41:4; *Midrash Tanḥuma* 1:6:8; see commentary of Rashi to Gen. 27:1), or simply Isaac beholding the face of his wicked son Esau (*Megillah* 28a; *Tanḥuma* 1:6:8). Others propose more radically that blindness was a form of punishment for Isaac, perhaps for eating food brought to him by Esau, which constituted a sort of bribe, metaphorically (and consequently, literally) blinding him to Esau's wicked behavior (*Midrash Tanḥuma* 1:6:8 based on Deut. 16:19). Conversely, Isaac's blindness may have been protective, shielding him from the horror of viewing Esau's wickedness, or even ensuring that he stayed indoors so that he would not be embarrassed in public when onlookers might associate him with his son's impropriety (*Bereshit Rabbah* 65:10). Or Isaac may have been blind due to his extreme piety, perhaps a remnant of the spiritual zenith of his life when he was offered as a sacrifice by his father Abraham that exposed him to the blinding tears of the angels (*Bereshit Rabbah* 65:10), or because God mercifully allowed him to experience punishment during his life to spare him from any residual punishment in the afterlife (*Bereshit Rabbah* 65:9). Still other authors of the Midrash view Isaac's blindness in purely utilitarian terms: Isaac had to be blind so that he would mistakenly bestow the blessing upon his righteous son Jacob rather than Esau (*Midrash Tanḥuma* 1:6:8). Finally, others view in Isaac's blindness simply the travails of old age, not a punishment or a reflection of Isaac's life circumstances but a malady that could befall any person (*Midrash Tanḥuma* 1:10:10). Such an assortment of theories to explain how one of Judaism's greatest heroes might suffer from blindness betrays the sense that the corpus of Jewish thought is divided on what blindness might signify. Whether blindness should be understood as a curse, a punishment, an unfortunate fact of life, or even as a hidden blessing is left unanswered.

Ultimately, however, there can be no question that early Jewish sources view blindness, at least in some instances, as a curse. In the definitive biblical inventory of curses, that pronounced by Moses upon the Israelites if they do not follow God's word, blindness features prominently and frighteningly. "God will strike you with madness, blindness, and confusion. You will grope in midday as a blind man gropes in the dark, and you will not be successful; you will be constantly exploited and robbed with no one to save you" (Deut. 28:28–29). The toll of blindness on an individual was not lost on the sages of the Talmud, who wrote, "Four are likened to the dead: the destitute, the leper, the blind, and the childless" (*Nedarim* 64b). The scourge of blindness, its impact upon those who are stricken with it, led the Talmud to refer often to a blind individual as *sagi nahor*, "one with too much light," a euphemism intended to avoid directly mentioning the curse that was blindness; the term *sagi nahor* eventually morphed into a linguistic term for euphemism, serving as a reference to the paradigmatic euphemism which describes a disability in terms of its opposite. The awareness of the isolation of the blind was accompanied by a realization that a blind individual might be acutely conscious of the need for protection by others. Such insight emerges in a Talmudic discussion of lighting a candle, even on the Sabbath, to provide light for a woman in labor, where it is specifically noted (*Shabbat* 128b) that this dispensation extends even to a blind woman giving birth. Although the woman cannot benefit from the light directly, her anxiety is alleviated by knowing that others around her can better assist her with the light.

Though passages in biblical and rabbinic literature allow us to speculate regarding the outlook of Jewish tradition on the impact of blindness, Jewish law itself provides perhaps the best glimpse into the Jewish worldview on how one ought to relate to loss of vision. Two examples of practical questions in Jewish law aptly illustrate this worldview.

First, what ideals may be sacrificed to prevent someone from becoming blind? A rich rabbinic literature is devoted to the question of whether one may violate the Sabbath to prevent an individual from losing his or her sight. Normally, Sabbath violation is condoned only to save a life, based on the premise discussed in the Talmud (*Yoma* 85b) that observance of Jewish law should be compatible with life, rather than causing its end, and moreover that violation of the Sabbath to save a life will result in a net gain of additional Sabbath observance by the individual whose life is saved. What is the law, then, when one wishes to violate the Sabbath to prevent another from becoming blind? At the very least, Jewish law certainly permits violating a rabbinic, non-biblical stricture regarding the Sabbath in this case, as loss of sight represents the loss of function of an organ; threatened loss of an organ or limb is sufficient justification for violating rabbinic law (*Shulḥan Arukh*, *Oraḥ Ḥayyim* 328:17). However, discussion of one Talmudic passage among later commentators raises the notion that the threat of blindness might even allow violation of the biblical Sabbath laws. The discussion revolves around the Talmudic statement (*Avodah Zarah* 28b) that one may apply medication on the Sabbath to a swollen eye. To justify this dispensation, the Talmud offers that "eyesight is connected to the *uvneta* of the heart"; although the meaning of the word *uvneta* is debated, many, including the influential 11th-century commentator Rashi, understand that it refers to the cardiac muscles. This statement does not likely correspond with any modern conception of anatomy or physiology, though several explanations have been proposed to interpret the suggested systemic bridge between the visual and cardiovascular systems in light of modern medicine.[3] The lack of precise explanation of this Talmudic statement notwithstanding, later codifiers including Rabbi Joseph Karo (1488–1575) ruled that one may desecrate the Sabbath in order to treat a patient with an ophthalmologic condition (*Shulḥan Arukh, Oraḥ Ḥayyim* 328:9).

What is left for the modern reader is to ascertain why the Talmudic sages were willing to allow desecration of the Sabbath for a swollen eye. One is tempted to assume that the concern was due to the risk of blindness, suggesting that Jewish law recognizes the risk of blindness as being of such enormity as to permit breach of the Sabbath. But another explanation is, admittedly, more likely: the Talmudic principle is based on a concern that there is a physiologic bridge between the physical eye or its musculature and the heart. Thus, if the eye is in danger of losing its function, but there is no visible macroscopic damage to be seen—or if modern medicine sees no true risk of mortality in a given ophthalmologic condition—one could not violate the Sabbath to prevent blindness. Despite this, the nineteenth-century scholar Rabbi Shlomo Kluger suggested that blindness itself, not necessarily damage to the eye, could provide dispensation for Sabbath violation (*Ḥokhmat Shlomo, Oraḥ Ḥayyim* 328:46). Remarkably, his position is based primarily on the concern that becoming blind would preclude the individual from future Torah observance, especially according to the position (discussed below) that the blind are not obligated in Jewish law. This position was also advanced more recently by twentieth-century scholar Rabbi Eliezer Waldenberg, consulting authority on Jewish law for the religious hospital Shaarei Zedek in Jerusalem, who added that the blind are at increased risk for future accidents which could endanger their lives, and thus Sabbath violation at present might be said to be saving a life in the future (*Tzitz Eliezer* 22:23). However, most contemporary Jewish scholars have adopted the more conservative position, allowing only violation of rabbinic strictures if a patient's vision is at risk but there is no concern for systemic illness, such as for a patient with retinal detachment.[4] To be sure, these scholars recognize the toll of blindness—but the inviolability of the Sabbath overrides even this.

A second, related question is what dispensations Jewish law might provide to enable a blind individual to regain sight. Specifically, contemporary Jewish scholars have debated the question of whether it is permitted for a blind individual to receive a cornea transplanted from a cadaver. This question constitutes a special case of the more general analysis regarding cadaveric organ donation in Judaism. Organ donation is among the most complex topics in Jewish law, chiefly because many Jewish scholars view brain death as having no legal significance in Judaism, thus restricting the possibility of organ donation to cadaveric transplants. Even in this restricted case, some scholars prohibit receiving organs from deceased donors, as there is a prohibition to benefit from the deceased.[5] However, the majority of scholars, including two prominent twentieth-century scholars, Rabbis Moshe Feinstein and Shlomo Zalman Auerbach, permit cadaveric organ donation since the value of saving a human life overrides the consideration of prohibited benefit from the deceased.[6] This naturally leads to the question of whether restoring a patient's vision would also override the same consideration. Several twentieth-century authorities on Jewish law permitted this. For some, corneal transplant could be permitted for technical reasons—perhaps the size of the cornea is too small to qualify as appreciable benefit, or perhaps this benefit should be classified as "atypical" such that it could be permitted in a case of illness, or perhaps transplanting the tissue into a live person reperfuses it such that one could consider use of the tissue benefiting from the living and not from the dead.[7] Echoing Rabbi Waldenberg's ruling above, Rabbi Yeḥiel Yaakov Weinberg, a twentieth-century European scholar, proposed that restoring the transplant recipient's vision was indeed saving his or her life, as this might prevent the recipient from a fatal accident (*Seridei Eish* 2:120).

Having examined the range of Jewish views on how the threat of blindness might affect Jewish law, we turn to how Jewish law treats an individual who is blind. Only one biblical passage comments explicitly on any limitations imposed on blind individuals in the service of God. Specifically, the blind are precluded from participating in the sacrificial duties in the Temple (Lev. 21:18). The exclusion of blind priests from Temple service is included among a list of other physical disabilities that pertain to the priests, as priestly service in the Temple is restricted to those who show no disfigurement. Aside from this, no clear limitations on participation of the blind in Jewish practice appear in the Torah.

Given the lack of explicit biblical guidance in this regard, the Talmudic sages questioned whether the blind were in fact bound by Jewish law. The Mishnah (the rabbinic text compiled in the 3rd century CE on which the Talmud comments) frequently lists individuals who are deaf and mute or mentally disabled, as well as minors, as prototypical examples of those who are not bound by Jewish law; they are not required to abide by biblical restrictions, and they are also unable to perform various Jewish rituals, such as ritual slaughter (*Shulḥan Arukh, Yoreh De'ah* 1:5) or baking matzo for Passover (*Shulḥan Arukh, Oraḥ Ḥayyim* 460:1). This exclusion is presumably due to these individuals' inability to fully comprehend the laws of the Torah, such that they are not expected to abide by them. It should be noted that during the times of the Talmudic sages, educating an individual who was both deaf and mute was extremely difficult, and this individual would be approached similarly to one with an intellectual disability. The blind, however, are not mentioned among those excluded from Jewish observance, and so later Talmudic sages questioned whether they should be categorized similarly. Ostensibly, the fundamental question is whether blind individuals can be expected to participate in Jewish ritual life given their disability. The Talmud (*Bava Kamma* 87a) records that R. Judah suggested that the blind were indeed exempt from Jewish law, though other sages disagreed. The analysis of R. Judah's opinion is followed by a captivating perspective on R. Judah's opinion by R. Joseph, a Talmudic sage who was himself blind. "Initially, I used to say, 'If someone would rule in accordance with R. Judah, who states that a blind person is exempt from commandments—I would make a feast for the rabbis!' Why? Because I am not commanded, and yet I still perform the commandments. But I have since heard the statement of R. Hanina: R. Hanina said, 'Greater is he who is commanded and does, than he who is not commanded and does.' Now, I say, 'If someone would tell me that the law is not in accordance with R. Judah, I would make a feast for the rabbis.' Why? Since I am commanded, I receive greater reward." R. Joseph's statement is not only the contextualization of R. Judah's opinion in the broader framework of Jewish legal theory, but perhaps also represents a fascinating window into the psyche of the blind individual on the question of inclusion in Jewish ritual. Of course, the individual would like to be exempt from Jewish law, as any performance of Jewish ritual would consequently be going beyond expectations. And yet, R. Joseph would ultimately rather be considered among those commanded, subject to the same high standards applied to others, despite the additional difficulty encountered in meeting those standards.

Ultimately, virtually all Talmudic commentators and later Jewish scholars ruled that the blind are fundamentally obligated to observe Jewish law, disregarding the view of R. Judah.[8] However, numerous obligations and rituals in Jewish law are still not incumbent upon the blind. These include rituals which a blind individual is unable to perform due to physical limitations, such as public reading of the Torah (*Shulḥan Arukh, Oraḥ Ḥayyim* 53:14, 139:3),[9] ritual slaughter of animals (*Shulḥan Arukh, Yoreh De'ah* 1:9),[10] and reciting a blessing upon viewing a light at the conclusion of the Sabbath (*Shulḥan Arukh, Oraḥ Ḥayyim* 298:13). Moreover, several commandments do not apply to blind individuals for technical reasons, usually based on exegetic analysis of biblical passages discussed in the Talmud. For example, a blind person may not testify in court, since the Torah mentions that the witness must note what he "saw" (Lev. 5:1). Similarly, a blind individual is not obligated to participate in the pilgrimage to the Temple during the Festivals, as the biblical directive surrounding this obligation notes that pilgrims "shall be seen by the Lord your God" (Deut. 16:16). The Talmud (*Ḥagigah* 2a) infers from the Hebrew word *yera'eh*, "shall be seen," which could have been alternatively vocalized to mean, "shall see," that only those who are able to see are obligated to make the pilgrimage to the Temple. Aside from those few exceptions, the blind are included in all Jewish rituals. In contemporary Jewish communities, blind Jews participate fully in synagogues and may lead prayers, made possible by the advent of Braille prayer books. Owing to this, a pre-eminent twentieth-century American scholar of Jewish law, Rabbi Moshe Feinstein, was asked whether service dogs may be brought into the sanctuary or would serve to defile its sanctity. His response (*Iggerot Moshe, Oraḥ Ḥayyim* 1:45) contains a lengthy exposition noting that contemporary synagogues have been built on the assumption that they can be used for mundane activities such as eating and drinking, and thus certainly for entrance of service animals. Notably, he ends by remarking that there is no greater need than ensuring that the blind individual can participate in the community and partake in communal rituals—especially as the alternative means condemning the blind community member to isolation and depression during the holiest days of the Jewish calendar. Although others disagreed vociferously with Rabbi Feinstein's legal analysis, they encouraged the blind community member to participate in services by having others assist him or her in attending synagogue.[11]

Most importantly, Jewish law places distinct emphasis on care for the blind. The most notable example is the biblical commandment in Leviticus, "Before the blind you shall not place a stumbling block" (Lev. 19:14). This commandment has enjoyed extensive discussion in the Talmud and later commentators, but almost exclusively limited to its extension to a wholly different sphere, that of serving as a poor influence on another. *Sifra* (*Kedoshim* 2:14), an early Midrashic work of legal exegesis on Leviticus, offers that "placing a stumbling block before the blind" need not refer to those who are literally blind, but those who are uninformed or unmindful. Thus, intentionally giving bad advice to another violates this commandment. Similarly, the Talmud frequently notes that providing indispensable assistance to another individual in sinning violates this prohibition. This latter application is the subject of numerous writings and responses aiming to ascertain the scope of when the prohibition is violated. Given the dominance of this application, some even question whether one who harms a literally blind individual violates this commandment, and not only a generic prohibition of harming others. Most commentators have concluded sharply in the affirmative: the commandment applies just as much to those who are literally blind as those who are metaphorically blind.[12] Here, in any case, we see that the Talmud emphasizes protection of the vulnerable—whether prone to bad advice or to sin—using the blind as the prototype of an individual for whom one must be especially careful not to hurt. Demonstrating concern for even the hypothetical future possibility of harming the blind, an early compilation of Jewish law, the *Tosefta*, specifically mentions that one may not throw stones on to the side of the road, since blind people are more likely to walk there and might trip (*Bava Kamma* 2:10).

In modern times, many Jews and Jewish organizations have championed this cause, forming organizations to help blind Jews integrate into the community. Such an attitude properly channels the spirit of these biblical and rabbinic sources. Even as the Talmud noted that the blind are likened to the dead, the medieval Tosafists noted that this statement, rather than suggesting any legal implications, was intended only to provoke sympathy for those who live with this disability. The rabbinic literature, replete with moral and legal imperatives to support the blind, suggests that even if there is no clear Jewish answer to the penetrating question of why God strikes people with blindness, the Jewish tradition mandates a response of compassion toward those who are most in need of the community's support.

Notes

1. Avraham Steinberg, "Jewish Outlook on the Blind" [Hebrew], *Tehumin* 3, 189.
2. See *Encyclopedia Judaica*, 2nd ed. (2007), s.v. "Blindness," which cites these and many more examples of blind individuals in Jewish tradition.
3. See Avraham Steinberg, *Encyclopedia of Jewish Medical Ethics*, Hebrew edition, s.v. "*ayin*" [Eye], 137, *125–126n*.
4. A full discussion appears in Abraham S. Abraham, *Nishmat Avraham, Orah Hayyim* 328:27.
5. These scholars include Rabbis Eliezer Waldenberg (*Tzitz Eliezer* 13:91) and Yitzhak Weiss (*Minhat Yitzhak* 5:8).
6. See *Iggerot Moshe* (*Yoreh De'ah* 2:174) and *Minhat Shlomo* (2:83).
7. See Rabbi Zvi Pesach Frank, *Har Tzvi, Yoreh De'ah* 277; Rabbi Isser Yehuda Unterman, *Shevet Me-Yehudah*, 313–322.
8. See Steinberg, *Encyclopedia of Jewish Medical Ethics*, s.v. "Blindness," *80n*.
9. However, Rama, in his glosses to *Shulhan Arukh* 139:3, notes that the prevalent Ashkenazic custom had been to allow the blind to recite the blessing before and after the reading of the Torah, since the common practice is for the person reciting the blessing to be a separate individual from the reader.
10. Rabbi Joseph Karo notes in *Shulhan Arukh* that if a blind individual already slaughtered an animal and the slaughter was found to be performed correctly, the meat may be eaten.
11. See Rabbi Yaakov Breisch, *Helkat Yaakov* 3:87.
12. See Steinberg, *Encyclopedia of Jewish Medical Ethics*, Hebrew edition, s.v. "*ivver*" ("the blind"), *129n*.

Native Stories About Vision and Impairment
Western Medicine Meets Aboriginal Mythos

ANDREW J. MCLEAN

"Vision" is a multi-faceted concept as relates to Indigenous Peoples. From vision journeys (both intentional and unintentional) to folktales of magical restoration of sight, Native mythology abounds with themes of natural and supernatural perception (or lack thereof). Certain stories are common among many tribes; other accounts are unique to individual landscapes. Parallel to these motifs are natural world illnesses and eye conditions that have disproportionately burdened Aboriginal Peoples throughout history.

This essay elucidates the "logos" and "mythos" relating to Native "vision" and is structured as such. The first section is a brief overview of actual pathologies of the eye frequently found within Indigenous groups. It also includes a discussion of contemporary/Westernized Medicine's view of perceptual changes. This is to contrast the subsequent non-linear, holistic, and culturally dynamic Indigenous experience found in the latter section. The second, a longer piece, pertains to Native legends related to blindness and vision.

It is important to remember that while terms such as "Indigenous, Aboriginal, Native peoples" and others are used, together the people they represent make up some of the most diverse ethnic groups in the world. There are estimated to be over 5000 such groups globally,[1] with more than a tenth of these formally recognized in the U.S.[2] In the States, there are multiple terms for indigenous groups, including clans, bands, tribes, pueblos and others. Here I mention only a score of individual groups, though one will find both differences and fundamental similarities across wide geographic areas. While the focus of the essay is "Native American," references to others around the globe will be noted.

I. Truth Through Logos

Diseases impacting the eye such as trachoma and smallpox were not known in the pre–Columbian Americas. At the beginning of the 20th century, it was considered that up to one fourth of all Native Americans had what was termed "Indian Sore Eyes."[3] This was trachoma, an eye infection. A leading cause of blindness around the globe, Chlamydia Trachomatis was not isolated until the late 1950s. Here, blindness occurs via granulation and scarring of the eyelid, with subsequent inversion of the eyelashes, and corneal abrasion. Another malady, diabetes mellitus, with its most common microvascular impact being retinopathy, is significantly more prevalent among American Indians and Alaska Natives than the general population. It is the same among Aboriginal and Torres Strait Islander people in Oceania. In Canada, the Alberta First Nations and the James Bay Cree peoples have the highest observed rates. The non-proliferative form (without abnormal new vascular growth) is more common than the proliferative type. Environmental, behavioral and genetic influences have impacted visual conditions among varying tribal groups.

There have been numerous studies involving geographically distant tribes across North America citing a high incidence of astigmatism, caused by an irregular shape of the cornea or lens, and refractive errors. Some of these afflictions tend to stabilize in childhood; others develop to cause complications in adulthood.

Cataracts are another cause of blindness around the world, and certain populations are more at risk. Indigenous populations living at high altitudes, such as the Andes Mountains and Tibetan Plateau have a significantly higher incidence of cataracts. A contributing factor includes higher ultra-violet exposure. Proteins in the eye's lens change in ways that cause pigments to accumulate and cloud the lens, eventually leading to failed vision.

Treatments

While not necessarily a universal approach, according to a review by Leffler et al.,[4] tribal remedies for eye inflammation often included soothing substances such as coconut or breast milk. Opacities were often treated with scraping or other harsher methods such as hot peppers. Liquid from the mesquite tree was also used in treatment of eye ailments in northern Mexico and what is now the southwestern U.S. Among certain northern Mexican tribes, healers would ceremoniously remove pus and blood from the eyes of a person suffering from trachoma, by sucking and spitting. In Canada and Alaska, it had been noted that piercing of the nose or eyebrows with a small, sharpened bone, not unlike acupuncture, was treatment for certain eye maladies. An 18th-century physician wrote of a report of a cure of near total blindness due to trauma by a Mohawk Indian using steamed witch hazel over the eyes.

While there is a stereotype within folklore of the blind sage dispensing wisdom, this should not be referred to as "fiction." Maggie Gilbert, a revered Gwich'in storyteller and historian whose recordings are in the University of Alaska Fairbanks archives, gradually lost her eyesight to cataracts and was blind during the latter part of her life.

Snow blindness (photokeratitis), essentially a "sunburn of the eyes (corneas)," often occurs in topographically flatter, colder settings. Photokeratitis is an acute insult to the eye, and while quite uncomfortable, usually leaves no permanent damage. However, chronic exposure can lead to cataracts. Many First Nations people have created ways to avoid snow blindness by utilizing goggles made from available resources (usually bone or ivory, rarely wood). The most well-known of these groups are the Inuit and Yupik.

Seva, a global foundation committed to restoring sight, launched a locally partnered American Indian Sight Initiative[5] Indigenous people have worked to improve access to linguistically/culturally appropriate eye care. As the etiologies of eye maladies have been discovered, and access to treatment has been enhanced, tribal entities have been able to effect positive change within their populations.

"Visions"

Before I begin to delve into spiritual/symbolic (mythos) aspects, I want to mention the "physiologic" (logos) components principally related to visions and changes in perception. This is not meant to "pathologize" experiences, but as a reminder of the different paradigms in which cultures view such experiences. According to the Merriam-Webster dictionary, a hallucination is a sensory perception (such as a visual image or a sound) that occurs in the absence of an actual external stimulus. (This is different from the much more common experience of an "illusion," which is a misperception of an actual external stimulus.) In fact, various studies have indicated that around 5 percent of the general population experiences hallucinations at least once in their lifetime with only a minority meeting criteria for a psychiatric disorder.[6,7] Such disorders typically associated with hallucinations include schizophrenia, schizoaffective disorder, bipolar affective disorder (manic-depression) and substance-induced psychosis.

Significantly reduced access to external stimuli (i.e., sensory deprivation) can actually lead to psychotic-like experiences. Hallucinations, particularly visual, are also quite common with extended sleep deprivation. Other manifestations of misperception related to sleep states are hypnopompic (upon awakening) and hypnogogic (upon falling asleep) hallucinations. These are known to be experienced by almost three quarters of the general population, with the most common type of hallucination being visual. Such episodes happen within the first few seconds or minutes of awakening or as one falls asleep. A more potentially frightening version of this is called the "incubus phenomenon,"[8] occurring in up to a third of the general population. This is a hypnopompic hallucination accompanied by sleep-paralysis, where an individual may feel as if they are floating, out of body, and/or in the presence of another. These are usually experienced as much more vivid and "real" than the more common type.

Hallucinations can also occur, but are much less likely, with short-term fasting. However, add severe temperature change and electrolyte/glucose imbalance, and conditions such as delirium can manifest in significant perceptual changes. Assaults to the body's homeostasis, such as severe sleep disruption, pronounced fasting, etc., can also lower the seizure threshold. It is known that temporal lobe seizures in particular are often correlated with spiritual experiences. Many individuals experience a marked religious experience in the midst of a "pilgrimage," a physical journey seeking spiritual guidance. For a few, it can become "manic/psychotic-like" (a condition described in one particular setting as "The Jerusalem Syndrome").[9] It is also recognized that many people who have had a spiritual experience, whether as part of a normal cultural revelation or a brief "condition" (i.e., fever, seizure, acute mental illness) have continued to find significant, long-standing meaning from the episode.

Hallucinogens

The federal Controlled Substances Act (CSA) was signed by Richard Nixon in 1970. Many psychedelic plant substances were placed on the Schedule I (most highly controlled) list. The most common of these are peyote, which contains the hallucinogen mescaline from the peyote cactus, and psilocybin, from the eponymous mushroom. Any cultural group wishing to utilize a Schedule I substance must prove they have a sincerely held religious belief in order to apply for an exemption. While the laws are somewhat confusing, 42 U.S. Code § 1996a ("Traditional Indian religious use of peyote") indicates that ceremonial use of peyote by American Indians has been protected by federal regulation. The largest of such groups is the Native American Church. Peyote contains the hallucinogen mescaline, and it is taken by eating the tops ("buttons") of the peyote cactus, or by drinking peyote tea.

Begged, Borrowed and Stolen

Of significant note is the renewed interest by conventional medicine around the benefit of psychedelic substances in palliative care. While part of this renewal comes from lessons garnered during the counterculture movement of the '60s, part is brought about from Native American knowledge. There are certainly other areas in which "borrowing" of ways of enlightenment has occurred. Within the mental health field, the concept of "mindfulness," borrowed from Buddhism, has been utilized in particular therapies, as well as brought forth to the general public for stress management. From the onset of the "New Age" movement to the present, there has been concern about the "commercialization" of non–Indigenous vision quests and the attempted usurping of Indigenous spirituality.

According to Stewart,[10] "Indigenous" refers to "the notion of a place-based human ethnic culture that has not migrated from its homeland and is not a settler or colonial population." As mentioned previously, despite remarkable diversity, many indigenous groups have similar themes of belief. However, it is important, particularly for an author from outside of that culture, to not define their belief system. It is defined and determined by themselves, and themselves alone. However, culture is fluid. It is not uncommon for certain peoples to have combined traditional or customary beliefs and practices with other faith traditions, such as Christianity.

Many Native people do not speak of religion or spirituality as separate entities, but as "a way of life" without division between the natural and supernatural worlds. There appear to be commonalities in one's relationship to all else. There are rites and rituals, often reflected by the particular type of community, such as hunter-gatherer or agricultural. A Maker or Great Spirit, creations stories, journeying after death, and many other elements can be seen.

Another recent area in which non–Native groups have been attending to historically Native beliefs and practices has been that of humankind's relationship to the earth. Climate change activists point to the long-standing environmental sustainability and multi-generational view of Indigenous peoples. This has afforded opportunities to partner in reaching mutual goals, but as Native Americans have frequently experienced, comes with risks of stereotyping and misapplication.

II. Truth Through Mythos

There is truth through symbolism, through indigenous people's relationships with nature—with animals, the earth, with each other. Legends are an essential part of learning. Sometimes the truth is presented, other times it is sought. An example of the former would be the gift of meaning within dreams. An example of truth being sought, an intentional journey, would be the vision quest. The term "vision quest" implies that something is lacking in "vision"—that a view, an understanding, is absent, or yet to be uncovered. The term has been associated most strongly with Native communities and experiences. Variations on the theme are legion, and while such experiences may be unique to particular populations, common elements often include isolation or solitude, fasting, sleep deprivation, a search for new meaning/insight, fostered either by the above elements or with the addition of an ingested substance, often with hallucinogenic properties.

Vision Quest

For some, indigenous vision quests are rites of passage, almost exclusively for young males entering adulthood. There are, however, stories of young females practicing similar rituals, such as Ojibwa girls fasting under the supervision of their mothers, typically at menarche.

Within these experiences, interpretation by another, such as an elder, is often necessary. In other cultures, vision journeys or quests are unique to the shamans, or shamans-to-be. A Brule Sioux story tells of a young man on a vision quest in the hopes of becoming a powerful medicine man. His quest was unsuccessful, due to his lack of humility, wisdom and patience. Some of these shamanic experiences are described as "temporary possession" by an animal or human spirit during a trance-like state. The ability to be "between worlds" allows for transmission of guidance from the spirit world to the natural world. According to Torrance,[11] this type of shamanism (i.e., possession) was more common among South American, Siberian and Northwest Coast tribes, and less so in other parts of the Americas. In far South America, the Mapuche religious practitioners were either benevolent shamans (machis) or malevolent witches (kalkus).

Many indigenous stories have been passed down relatively unchanged over generations; others change with the times, and some are begun anew. One such sun creation story is a recent one, again from the Brule Sioux; fascinatingly, evolving during a vision quest, with subsequent characters within having their own vision quests. Whether old legends or new, any change from the original language, the oral traditions that are then translated to English might be at significant risk for loss of meaning and richness.

Allegories and Legends on Blindness...

While some of the following legends were unearthed from individual sources, a number were accessed by collections such as *American Indian Myths and Legends*,[12] *First People: Native American Legends*,[13] *Native Languages of the Americas*[14] and *The Handbook of Native American Mythology*.[15]

What is striking in the literature are the rather graphic and violent tales pertaining to blindness within indigenous lore. However, this is not at all discrepant from European legends and "fairy tales." The Brothers Grimm and other purveyors of tales included gory renderings despite the fact that these were conveyed to children.

There are native stories that have been reported to be changed when translated for non-indigenous children. Here, violent themes are interestingly omitted. Indigenous legends do not always follow the "flow" of their European counterparts. At times they can be abrupt, at times without explanation of justification. They simply are truth.

The late Dr. Kenneth Jernigan, a long-time president of the National Federation of the Blind described nine themes/motifs in which blindness is presented in folklore:

As:

—compensatory or miraculous power
—total tragedy
—foolishness and helplessness
—unrelieved wickedness and evil
—perfect virtue
—punishment for sin
—abnormality or dehumanization
—purification
—symbol or parable

In indigenous legends, specific motifs are not always mutually exclusive within a story. It is not unusual to find a number of the above themes interspersed. In Maori culture there are variations on tales of blindness as punishment for transgressions, as a result of aging and other etiologies. Episodes of teasing and helplessness with subsequent miraculous healing (often from the same perpetrators, sometimes with a blind person healing another) are told. In legends of Tawhaki, a demigod, the Awara version follows the blindness themes above, with an older blind woman being the gatekeeper of the route to heaven. Tawhaki returns her vision after being granted access to the pathway to the sky. In the Ngati Porou version, Tawhaki is shown the path to heaven by a woman whose household he has violently attacked with his brother. His brother falls and dies while climbing to the sky. In this tale, Tawhaki takes his dead brother's eyes and places them in his blind grandmother, returning her sight.

Trickster Characters, Blindness and Creation Stories

One finds archetypes (recurrent symbols/motifs) in legends. One such archetype commonly occurring in tales pertaining to the theme of blindness are "tricksters." A Jicarilla Apache legend, "Two Blind Old Women," describes the two protagonists fighting amongst themselves after being "set up" by two mischievous boys. A Menominee tale relates a similar story, though with change in gender in "The Deceived Blind Men." Here a raccoon fulfills the role of the "trickster" archetype. A trickster character known to tribes of the Midwest was Wisakatchekwan. A Piankashaw tale, "How Wisakatchekwa Got Into Some Trouble," relates how this character tricked and was tricked by two blind men.

There are many stories from various tribes relating to creation themes. At times, darkness is at the beginning of all creation, until light is brought forth by the Maker. At other times, life has been present for eons, yet total darkness remains. In these legends, either the sun is created, or light is discovered in another part of the world and is stolen by an individual or an animal trickster for the tribe, with subsequent joy and celebration. A Cherokee tale, "Grandmother Spider Steals the Sun," is one such example. In another, Raven, a revered "transformer" of Pacific Northwest tribes, dashes a container of stolen daylight out of vengeance.

In an example of the symbolism of balance in nature, another Tewan (Pueblo) tale tells of the sacrifice of the moon. In this anthropomorphic legend, Moon gives up one of its eyes to allow darkness to occur to counter the impact of Sun's brightness. Another Pueblo story (Isleta), "The Man Who Married the Moon," finds the moon as a half-blind maiden prior to having gone to live in the sky. In this story, the half-blindness is not limiting, nor a driving part of the story. It seems only to be included as a description of her soon to be lunar appearance.

In many of these tales, the animal or person trying to capture the sun or the sun's light suffer hardships or harm. Some stories are full of serial failures, until a victor succeeds. The harm is usually a burn, scorched skin or hair, though at times the consequences are blindness, such as occurs in the Winnebago legend, "Little Brother Snares the Sun."

Sometimes, those with visions and special powers are lacking in their ability to "read the signs." In the tale of The Seer Who Could Not See (Pima), a seer is lacking prescience of a great flood, despite warning from an eagle. It is suspected that the great eagle may have actually caused the flood, which swept away many, including the seer. In this creation story, the son of the Maker is able to kill the eagle and make things right.

One can find trickster characters from other regions appearing in tribal lore. While as mentioned above, Raven is common to the Pacific Northwest, Coyote is common to the Plains and Southwest. However, Coyote has also appeared in "Raven's" territory and vice-versa. In a Kwakiutl tale, "Always-Living-At-The-Coast," Coyote serially heals two women of their blindness after he chances upon them and they provide him food and needed information. The Karuk (Karok) have a story in which Coyote temporarily and accidentally fastens his eyelids shut when trying to outwit other animals and the creator god, Kareya. Despite Coyote's actions, others feel pity on him and Kareya rewards him with the gift of cunning.

In Northern Cheyenne lore, the Spider trickster is Veeho (Wihio, Veho). One such story finds Veeho showing off a power he was given by a medicine man, that of being able to launch his eyeballs in and out of his sockets. He "breaks the rules" by using too many of these magical turns and loses his sight. He regains it in a rather mismatched way, through the kindness of a mouse and buffalo, each giving him one of their own eyes.

In a tale from the Tewa, poor vision is again of benefit in a contest between the visually impaired Badger, and Coyote, where the former outperforms the latter in capturing more rabbits by staying put, rather than giving chase.

For North American tribes, the loon is often believed to have particular powers. More than one legend among the Inuit describes the restoration of human sight by a loon. A blind boy treated cruelly by his mother regains sight via a loon submerging in water. Now sighted, the son hunts narwhal with his mother, and he allows her to drown. She herself becomes a narwhal. In the book, The Blind Man and the Loon: The Story of a Tale, Mishler[16] writes a fascinating treatise of variations of Inuit and Athabaskan legends. This work includes oral recitation in Native tongues as opposed to only written synopses. Here, Mishler shows a dedication to not only academic concern, but deep interest in the significance to the tellers of the tale.

A Dene (Northern Athabaskan) tale, "The Boy Who Became Strong" is rife with violence both within and outside of family. In this legend, a young man kills animals barring him from obtaining food for his sick mother. He also saves a young maiden by killing her captor. Numerous themes similar to other northern tales noted above ensue; he is then tricked and blinded by his mother, for reasons unexplained. Subsequently, the young man miraculously regains his sight, by following the example of a blind moose (submerging his head in water, a common theme of restoration). This allows his acceptance into the young maiden's tribe, in which he becomes a great chief.

Some stories of loss of visual clarity occur not in protagonists, but in witnesses. The White River Sioux version of the Rabbit Boy story has archetypal themes, such as magical creation and resurrection. In this version, the Rabbit Boy is cut into pieces by villagers. A storm and clouds cause utter blackness and an inability for witnesses to see. Upon the veil lifting, the lead character is seen rising to heaven, whole.

In this essay, we have touched on the truth through logos—of eye maladies which impact indigenous peoples to significant degrees, yet with the promise of ongoing mitigation and treatment. We have described how contemporary western society pathologizes changes in perception, "visions." We have also touched on the truth through mythos—how Native peoples have continued to teach and live through tales of sight or lack thereof; of healing; stories told by elders past, present and emerging.

So, I ask, cultivated reader; Have you experienced impairment of vision, an inability to see the truth? And if so, has this been remedied?

Notes

1. J. Foreman, S. Keel S, P. van Wijngaarden, RA Bourne et al., Prevalence and Causes of Visual Loss Among the Indigenous Peoples of the World: A Systematic Review. *JAMA Ophthalmol*. 2018 May 1; 136(5):567–580.
2. U.S. Department of the Interior; Indian Affairs.
3. R.A. Trennert, Indian Sore Eyes: The Federal Campaign to Control Trachoma in the Southwest, 1910–40. *Journal of the Southwest*. Vol. 32, No. 2, 121–149.
4. C.T. Leffler, S.G. Schwartz, R.D. Wainzstein, A. Pflugrath, E. Peterson. Ophthalmology in North America: Early Stories (1491–1801). *Ophthalmology and Eye Diseases* Vol. 9: 1–51.
5. American Indian Site Initiative. Seva.org.
6. J. van Os, R.J. Linscott, I. Myin-Germeys, P. Delespaul, L. Krabbendam, A systematic review and meta-analysis of the psychosis continuum: evidence for a psychosis proneness-persistence-impairment model of psychotic disorder. *Psychol Med*. 2009 Feb; 39(2):179–95.
7. J.J. McGrath, S. Saha, A. Al-Hamzawi, J. Alonzo, et al., Psychotic experiences in the general population: a cross-national analysis based on 31,261 respondents from 18 countries. *JAMA Psychiatry*. 2015 Jul; 72(7): 697–705.
8. M.L. Molendijk, H. Montagne, O. Bouachmir, Z. Alper, J.P. Bervoets, J.D. Blom JD, Prevalence Rates of the Incubus Phenomenon: A Systematic Review and Meta-Analysis. *Front Psychiatry*. 2017; 8: 253.
9. J. Siegel-Itzkovich, Israel prepares for "Jerusalem syndrome." *BMJ*. 1999 Feb 20; 318(7182): 484.
10. G. Stewart, What does 'indigenous' mean, for me? *Educational Philosophy and Theory*. Vol. 50 (8): 740–743.
11. R.M. Torrance, *The Spiritual Quest: Transcendence in Myth, Religion and Science*. Oct. 1997. University of California Press. Berkeley.
12. A. Ortiz, R. Erdoes, *American Indian Myths and Legends*. (New York: Pantheon Books, 1984).

13. First People. U.S. https://www.firstpeople.us/FP-Html-Legends/Legends-AB.html.
14. Native Languages of the Americas. http://www.native-languages.org/.
15. D.E. Bastian, J.K. Mitchell, *The Handbook of Native American Mythology* (New York: Oxford University Press, 2004).
16. Craig Mishler, "*The Blind Man and the Loon-The Story of a Tale*" (Lincoln, NE: University of Nebraska Press, 2013).

Blind African American Musicians
Insights from a Social Psychiatrist
H. Steven Moffic

Before I became a physician, and became known as "Dr. Moffic," I had another moniker: "Dr. Jazz," because I supplemented my studies with reviewing jazz records, especially for a publication called *Jazz Digest*. That title owed its origins to a 1926 song titled "Doctor Jazz," by Joe "King" Oliver. My study of African American musicians and blindness, and the reasons for their over-representation among musicians with visual limitations, came much later, as I can explain below. For now, it's worth considering the words of the controversial yet influential Afro-Caribbean, French-educated psychiatrist Franz Fanon, whose theories relating to race were informed by Freudian thought. According to Fanon, whites listen to blues and jazz in order to consume, from a safe distance, black "aggression."[1]

The Meaning of Music

In his poem, "I Live in Music," the African American writer Ntozak Shanke suggests many of the meanings of music. We all have individual preferences for the kinds of music that we like. Some do not even like music. Those differences can be a biological variation and/or come from music being behaviorally associated with negativity or punishment in childhood. On the other hand, it can aid overall brain development.

Music is usually considered to be man-made, but some find music in nature, in the sound of the seas, wind, birds, and wolves. Some, like the composer John Cage, claimed that music could be heard in silence, as in his silent piece of 4'33", though there are always ambient sounds when it is "played." Interestingly enough, in the Torah (Old Testament/Hebrew Bible), though God is depicted as speaking to the leaders and people, God is never depicted as singing to—or with—them. As far as the people go, Miriam, the sister of Moses, led the singing when the Jewish people left Egypt and are portrayed as having successfully crossed the Red Sea.

Music can also be used for relaxation, entertainment, or protest. A case could be made that at times music has been pivotal in history, such as its important role in the end of apartheid in South Africa or protest music here in the United States during the civil rights era.[2]

Music is often spiritual. It often has meaning that goes beyond the individual creator.[3] It can also be healing.[4] Indeed, Shamanic healers have long used song and rhythm to try to cure the sick. Now, we have a formal academic field of music therapy. Beloved songs may be preserved in memory when most else is lost in Alzheimer's Disease. Recently, the National Institutes of Health (NIH) offered twenty million dollars for research on music and neuropsychiatric diseases.

With the use of modern technology, we can make a purposeful playlist for our own benefit to encourage a change in mood or energy level, such as a lullaby for sleep because of the slow tempo and repetitive simple melody. It often encompasses such physical activity as exercise, sports, and sex.

As for African American blues and jazz, questions have deepened over the years. For instance, how did it relate to racism? What did it contribute to the wider American society? What were the healing aspects of these musics? And to address the theme of this essay collection: Why were so many of the innovators blind to one extent or another?

According to Sascha Feinstein, editor of the academic journal *Brilliant Corner* (BC), this last question "certainly hasn't been covered in BC, and I don't recall such a piece in *Down Beat, Jazz Times*, and other well-known publications." I could not find much of anything, either, so I will try to provide some answers.

To do we, we will continue on and examine the varieties of blindness, the history of racism in the USA, the development by African Americans of unique musical forms, and examples of blind African American innovators. We will conclude with examining the wondrous legacy of the intersections of these developments.

The Varieties of Blindness
"Amazing Grace
How sweet the sound
That saved a wretch like me

> I once was lost, but now am found
> T'was blind but now I see"
> —From the Christian hymn, Amazing Grace.

The term blindness is commonly used for both physical and psychological loss of sight and insight, including the less common psychological blindness formerly called hysterical blindness. Physically, blindness can differ in extent of loss of visual eyesight. Important variations also depend on the timing of eyesight loss, ranging from birth onwards.

Psychologically, blindness is often used to depict a loss of insight into the truth. All people may have "blind spots" in their insight, which often need to be explored in psychotherapy if that adversely influences functioning. All these variations are important to distinguish as applied to blind African American musicians.

Both physical and psychological blindness are combined in the Greek myth of Oedipus. The Oedipal conflict can be considered to be the essence of Freud's psychoanalytic theories. In the Greek myth, as young man Oedipus went to ask the oracle at Delphi who his parents were, he was warned that he was destined to kill his father and marry his mother. Yet, he is psychologically blind when he "mistakenly" kills his father, then marries his mother. When his country suffers as a consequence, he finds out the truth, then physically blinds himself.

For a variety of reasons, including poor nutrition and poor medical care, it seems that African Americans, especially in the South, suffered higher than usual prevalence of any kind of physical blindness in the United States. Physical blindness can be congenital, present at birth, or adventitious, occurring at a later age.[5] If sight is lost before the age of 5, visual imagery is impaired in that visual imagery rarely occurs in the dreams. One theory about why more than expected played musical instruments is that they could function as "transitional objects," particularly guitars. They could help to quell anxiety in the transition to becoming more self-reliant.

We will see representatives of the various kinds of physical blindness when we cover blind African American innovators. Often the physically blind can compensate with the development of other senses and skills, including musical.

Racism and Reconstruction

> "If you don't know what was tried and then dismantled, then your inference about why we still have these problems is, it's a problem with the people, it's a problem with their

work ethics, their family structure, their values, rather than, it's a problem of an unfinished revolution—which Reconstruction was"—Kimberlé Crenshaw.

At the time of the flowering of blind African American musicians a century ago, the effects of Reconstruction after the Civil War were diminishing. The promise of freedom under Reconstruction was limited by political disenfranchisement, punctuated by an increase in lynching, reaching a peak in the 1890s.[6]

The paradox was that out of this profound disappointment emerged the counterculture "New Negro" in a burst of intellectual and cultural creativity.[7] Hand in hand with that came a developing coalition with some prominent whites, with the founding of the NAACP in 1909.

Out of this trauma and ensuing resilience came a musical form with a fitting name, the blues. On up from the blues to Gospel, to jazz, and then rhythm n' blues, blind African Americans played a prominent role. In turn, their music helped shape the political consciousness of African Americans, especially those migrating North out of the South. Later, the so-called free jazz, meaning freedom from musical structure, of the 1960s, did something similar, emerging in the Civil Rights era and influencing the black nationalist movement.[8]

African American Musical History

Robert Johnson, who recorded "Hellhound on My Trail" in 1937, summarizes much of what is said below in a song. African American music in American history has its roots in Africa. Like much of African culture, it was suppressed in slavery, yet proved to be adaptable to many other forms of music. For example, the individual griot singers of African cultural history morph in part to the individual blues singers in the American South. A modern day sighted black blues singer, Corey Harris, explored those connections in the liner notes of his compact disc "Mississippi to Mali." As he wrote:

"Music and culture—what made us who we are—still endures to this day. Slavery killed millions of Africans, bled the continent of its riches, and left many damaged and degraded survivors in its wake, but it could not kill the spirit that makes the music. It is out of love and respect for this spirit that I traveled to Mali and Mississippi to record the sounds on the CD."

Robert Johnson, who was not blind, was known as "The King of the Delta Blues Singers" and "Hellhound" was considered to be his masterpiece. The underlying meaning of the words could be the anxiety of an attempt to run away from slavery. The low moan of the singing can feel like existential horror of the wind whistling through a graveyard. There is a story that Johnson made a pact with the devil at the crossroads of Clarksdale, Mississippi, but there were no witnesses. He then died suddenly by apparent poisoning soon after recording his classic songs.

Musically speaking, the blues emphasized notes that broke with the Western harmonic tradition, such as the use of the flatted third with major diatonic expression. The tense, slightly hoarse-sounding vocalization of the blues comes directly from the West African tradition.[9]

The blues music was a secular one. In African American life at the time, the corresponding sacred music of the Church was Gospel music. Gospel music in the church was an alternative place to release forbidden emotions from slavery in a safe place.

By the 1920s, African Americans were spearheading the development of another unique musical form, that which was generally called jazz. The blues was thought to be the basis of jazz, but most jazz was instrumental music which started in New Orleans rather than the rural South of the blues. Moreover, group improvisation became common and, in a musical way, mimicked real life conversation. Jazz also modeled the entrance and integration of White-Americans into this music. Indeed, it was one of the earliest situations where integration was possible in America. Jews were over-represented in this integration, highlighted by the "King of Swing," Benny Goodman.

Since then, there has been a continuing re-emergence of a strong African American influence that revitalizes American popular music. Rhythm n' Blues was a later urban expression of rural blues and an influence on the development of Rock n' Roll. Hip-hop and rap are the most recent innovations.

At each stage of these African American musical innovations were blind musicians. They were especially present in blues music, perhaps a reflection of how common blindness was in African Americans in the South at that time, whether that be from disease and/or limited medical care. Here is just a partial sampling: Blind Lemon Jefferson, Blind Willie Johnson, Blind Willie McTell, Blind Boy Fuller, Blind Blake, Blind Joe Taggard, Sleepy John Estes, and Sonny Terry. Though less prominent, blind African American musicians have continued to contribute up to the present.

There was even a white guitarist, John Fahey, who adopted the pseudonym of Blind Joe Death in his first album, released in 1965, with the title of *The Transfiguration of Blind Joe Death*. Though today he likely would be accused of political incorrectness, at that time it was debated whether he was being mischievous or reverent because he did not say which. Clearly, in the very least, the pseudonym was updating the music of dead blind blues musicians. In blind listening sessions, he was often thought to be an African American blues singer. In 1996, 30 years after his recording debut, he changed "transfiguration" to "legend" in *The Legend of Blind Joe Death*, to be followed in 1999 with a CD titled *The Dance of Death & Other Plantation Favorites*, which could be interpreted as a stinging parody of slavery and plantation life. Even with these blues references, he was generally labeled as a folk musician, perhaps because he was white.

The following, though, are brief biographies of some of the African American blind musicians.[10]

Blind Tom

> "Long, long ago I see Blind Tom.
> The noisy audience became calm...."
> —excerpted from the poem "Blind Tom Singing" by James D. Corrothers.

Before the blind African American blues musicians came Tom Wiggins Bethune. He was a blind piano prodigy and a savant mentally. If it were hard enough to begin integration after slavery, being disabled only added to the challenge. As in slavery, the blind were of little value for physical tasks although, perhaps paradoxically, that made them less threatening from physical and sexual standpoints.

Born in 1849, at best he seemed to be able to only distinguish light from dark. Though he seemed to be treated more like a pet to the owners at first, his unique musical talent soon emerged. By the age of 4, he may have started to play the piano without any prompting or instruction. By the age of 6, he was improvising and, at the age of 8, performing classically oriented pieces, going on to do up to 4 performances a day to make huge sums of money. He performed for the President and White House in 1860. He was said to have perfect pitch.

Both appreciated and denigrated, he fit in with the popularity of freak shows of the time. He appealed more to whites than fellow African Americans. Sometimes, his gyrations at the piano, later seeming to be mimicked by Elvis Presley, got as much attention as his music-making. He died in 1908, just as blues music was evolving. Blind Tom did have some musical followers, such as the biracial Blind Boone, who become blind at 6 months of age and went on to become a skilled ragtime pianist.

The rarity of such blind African American musical geniuses who could play so well the music of white society actually contributed to the persistence of racial denigration. They were not the norm and, hence, were the exception to the rule of racial inferiority.

Blind Lemon Jefferson and the Blindness of Blues Musicians

Though blindness was emphasized in the name of many blues singers and perhaps romanticized to some extent, it is striking that the original songs of such blues musicians were virtually bereft of content about being blind or about blindness, even though content otherwise was quite autobiographical. Instead, blindness seemed to be a public relations strategy of the record company. To the contrary, perhaps blind blues musicians had the insight that focusing on blindness would be too specific for their potential audience. In additions, the record companies first marketed these records as "race records," solely for African Americans until they generated more general popularity.

Indeed, in the songs of the well-known Blind Lemon Jefferson (1894–1929), congenitally blind from birth, were lyrics that passed for being sighted, such as his song "Got the Blues." Instead, sighted bluesmen were the ones who occasionally mentioned blindness.

Blind Lemon Jefferson could be considered the founder, at least the recorded founder, of both country blues and blind bluesmanship. The success of his 1926 recordings created the demand for county blues.

Born on a farm in Couchman, Texas, son of sharecroppers, he learned to become quite independent as an itinerate entertainer in his teens, working the streets, first in the South and then up to Chicago in the 1920s. Most blind blues musicians were accompanied by a younger "lead boy." As a later extension of that, the blind Sonny Terry partnered with the sighted Brownie McGee in a popular musical duo.

Blind Lemon had a high voice and good guitar technique. The titles of some of his songs indicated the typical content: Black Snake Moan; See That My Grave is Kept Clean; Long Lonesome Blues; Mosquito Blues; Hangman's Blues. His lyrics were ironic, humorous, sad, and poignant. Like all great blues singers, there usually was a redeeming aspect to the sadness of the blues, some suggestion of better days ahead.

Under the pseudonym of Deacon L.J. Bates, he also played gospel music, particularly on Sundays, another Africa-American style developing at the same time.

Blind Willie Johnson was another blind African American musician who played guitar and sang in a blues style, but the words where those of gospel and the church. He ended up being better known for his songs that were interpreted much later by groups like the Staple Singers as well as Peter, Paul, and Mary. His most well-known song, "Dark was the Night," was shipped to space on the spacecraft *Voyager* along with music by Chuck

Berry and Beethoven. Since his focus was on spiritual redemption, he is a direct link to gospel music.

Gospel Music and the Blind Boys of Alabama

> "And what is the mystique of blindness, from Homer to Oedipus to Blind Lemon Jefferson to Steve Wonder? What is it that the blind can see? Is it the truth?"—Lee Breuer, program notes to Gospel at Colonus.

Though evolving in tandem with the blues, gospel music, aka spirituals, was much different in content and social function. Blindness does enter the content of sin and redemption in some gospel music, as in the miraculous, such as "making the blind man see," a capability that Jesus was thought to possess.

In contrast to the male-dominated country blues, there were many blind women singer-songwriters in the African American gospel tradition.

Though some feel the best gospel group was the Blind Boys of Mississippi, the most popular were the Blind Boys of Alabama, who were destined for crossover popularity. They formed out of the Alabama School for the Negro Deaf and Blind in Talladega in 1939. They were in the original 1983 updating of the retelling of the Oedipus story as "a group of Oedipuses" in *The Gospel at Colonus*.

In the original group, only one man was sighted, whereas in later years most of them were sighted, sort of following the diminishing number of African American musicians over time. The extent of the original members' blindness and the timing of its onset are apparently unknown. In essence, this change over time emphasizes what is perhaps most important, which is the music.

The play *The Gospel at Colonus* may be the nexus where the various threads of blindness, racism, musical innovation, sexuality, and psychiatry intersect. It was adapted in 1983 from the play of the Greek playwright Sophocles, *Oedipus at Colonus*. Greek tragedy began as a religious ceremony in the 5th century BCE.

Sophocles' play follows the back story of Oedipus Rex. Even though he was warned by a blind oracle (who lived as both a man and woman), Oedipus killed a man who turned out to be his father at a crossroads, the same kind of crossroad we know from the mythical life of the King of the Blues, Robert Johnson. After killing his father, Oedipus slept with his mother. When the truth comes to life, his mother kills herself and Oedipus blinds himself and leaves in exile.

The modern *Gospel of Colonus* makes a connection between Greek tragedy and the African American Pentecostal religion. Greek plays were sung in their day; gospel singing is essential to African American church services. Both are cathartic from the pain of traumatic and inscrutable fate, as well as societal rejection. It is the blind who see the truth. It is possible to resolve the Oedipal conflict, if only both the father and son have insight about their potential and real competition about many things, but specifically for the wife and mother. As we know in psychiatry, human nature is often unsure or unaware of its own deepest desires.

In exile in *The Gospel at Colonus*, Oedipus achieves insight, love, and a promise of redemption. He is resurrected like Jesus after he dies.

To know oneself is a heroic journey but filled with painful and terrible knowledge along the way. Modern psychiatry can help with the journey. Unlike the blind Greek oracle in the play who blurts out the truth, we try to share the truth when the patient is more ready to hear it.

The Jazz of Roland Kirk, Black Protest Music and His 1968 Lyrics About "Volunteered Slavery"

Imagine, if you will, a blind African American improvising, using some invented techniques, playing three saxophones at the same time. That was Rahsaan Roland Kirk (1936–1977). Actually, you do not have to completely imagine; just look for any performance of him on YouTube.

Born Roland Theodore Kirk, he became blind at two years old, apparently from improper medical treatment. He studied at the Ohio State School for the Blind.

Already, at the age of 14, he played two horns at once. Later, he added another horn and home-made instruments, all held together by masking tape. Some thought this was too gimmicky rather than miraculous.

As his musical skills progressed, he became well-known in the early 1960s. One day, on his birthday, he had a dream and said that God told him his name now was Rahsaan, and so it was. Much of Kirk's music was based on the structure of the blues. He even added words to some songs, such as the paradoxically titled song "Volunteered Slavery" that was quoted above. His most famous song was "The Inflated Tear," with an emotional resonance akin to the title, and which seemed to integrate the history of African American music with into four minutes: old slavery spirituality, work songs, field hollers, gospel, soul, and modern jazz.

Not content to just play the music, he led movements to reduce the racism in jazz, including the Jazz People's Movement. To do so, they innovated various protests, including disrupting the TV shows of Johnny Carson, Dick Cavett, and Merv Griffin. They would attend as audience members and then disrupt the shows with whistles and signs. To avoid just such a protest, Ed Sullivan invited Kirk to appear on his show. His song "Watergate Blues" about President Nixon was on his last recording session.

Of his blindness and other abilities, Kirk once said:

"I'm a man, first. So-called blindness is secondary. I don't believe, that when I pick up an instrument, I'm blind to anybody." He called jazz "Black Classical Music."

The 2001-2003 Poet Laureate, Billy Collins, was enamored with Kirk and wrote a poem about seeing him live titled "The Five Spot 1964." Of his playing three saxophones at once with a kazoo in his mouth, he described "as a joyous impossible lesson in how to do it all at once."

Ray Charles Enters Country and Western Territory

> "Ray Charles broke down borders and showed the similarities between country music and R & B."—Willie Nelson

If there is one musical genre from which you would not expect a major contribution from blind African American musicians, it would be Country and Western. That is because African Americans have been virtually absent from the mainstream of this musical style and culture.

Then again, perhaps Ray Charles (1930-2004) came to mind. Early in his career, he was known as Blind Ray Charles, but the Blind got dropped along the way. Coming to fame as a singer and pianist, sometimes saxophonist and trombonist in rhythm and blues in the 1950s and 1960s, he made sunglasses common for a blind performer. They were a fashion statement of sorts and seemed to have a sexual attractiveness. Some white musicians wore them, too. John Fahey did so on and off, perhaps depending on the message he wanted to convey. Roy Orbison, thought not to be particularly handsome, wore them regularly in public.

He became popular with both blacks and whites, especially after the crossover song "What I'd Say." That popularity with whites helped him fuse gospel music with country and western as an alternative to mixing gospel and the blues.

Charles did not start to lose his sight from glaucoma until he was 5, and the sight was basically gone by the age of 7. He had already started to play the piano by then. Besides his skilled piano playing, vocally Charles added slurs, shrieks, wails, hollers, and other wounds to the words.

His colorful life was featured in the 2004 movie *Ray*, for which the actor Jamie Foxx won an Academy Award for Best Actor.

The Wonder of Stevie Wonder

> "I never really worried about my blindness or asked questions about it, because to me, really, blind was normal"—Stevie Wonder

Though Stevie Wonder (b. 1950, Stevland Morris) is often viewed as a child prodigy who became a genius out of nowhere, that viewpoint is more romantic than accurate. After achieving some reputation in local churches and singing on the streets of Detroit, he was signed to Motown Records at the age of 9, nurtured with that culture and that of the African American church. He got his last name when Motown founder Berry Gordy apparently said he was a "wonder" when he first heard him. This kind of wonder was different than that of the old freak show wonders. So "Little Stevie Wonder" became his nickname.

Ironically, Wonder's blindness got more attention than those children who were sighted and musical. He was educated at the Michigan State School for the Blind and had a private tutor on tours. He studied piano as his main instrument, but he also played harmonica, a popular alternative to the guitar in blues music. In addition, he learned some bass, violin, and composition.

Like most congenitally blind, Stevie Wonder did not seem to have any significant psychological distress about that. Perhaps because it is more current, the information about Wonder's blindness is clearer than most of the other blind musicians. He was born 2 months premature and spent 50 days in an incubator. He developed the most common cause of blindness in children, retrolental fibroplasia.

Wonder ends up seeming to embrace his blindness. His album *Talking Book* has the title in Braille along alongside the print. A "talking book" also harks back to African griots who talked and sang the history of their people.

As he was growing up, it was said that he had a cute, mischievous personality and that, coupled with his blindness, seemed to help his early popularity. In a later example of that, for a preview of the song "Living for the City," he surprised the journalists by having them go on a bus tour of New York blindfolded. He followed in the footsteps of Ray Charles and wore sunglasses like him, as did most blind musicians of any racial background after Ray Charles.

One of the wonders of Stevie Wonder was that he has been the last blind African American musician to emerge into great public popularity among all ethnic groups. That wonder reflects the rarity of blindness nowadays in young African Americans.

About the only prominent current one is Raul Midon, who has parents of both Argentine and African American descent. His blindness was from being born prematurely in a rural hospital in New Mexico and spending too much time in an incubator without adequate eye protection. Midon plays the guitar and sings more or less in a rhythm n' blues style. On his first recording, *State of Mind*, Stevie Wonder sang with him on the song "Expressions of Love."

The latest evolution of African American musical innovation, hip-hop and rap, has never had a known prominent blind performer. Perhaps that also reflects the availability of other societal options as adults. That reflects more of a cultural sharing of black and white youth.

Wonder communicated about how his "inner vision" compensated for his lack of "outer vision," as in the song he hoped to be remembered for, titled "Visions," which described the proverbial milk and honey land, as described in the Hebrew Bible.

This is a vision of the kind of transcendence that many blind celebrities, including Helen Keller, have conveyed. It is as if overcoming any obstacle of their blindness is evidence that peaceful coexistence among people is possible, not a naive fantasy.

The Insights, Delights, and Musical Heights of Blind African Americans

> "You shall not ... place a stumbling block before the blind."
> —Holiness Code, Leviticus 19:14, Torah (Old Testament/ Hebrew Bible)

Of course, there were so many other successful blind African American musicians not covered in this essay. One of them, the Rev. Gary Davis, was not very well known, and was also hard to characterize as to where he fit in stylistically. He lives on, though, through the covers of his songs by Bob Dylan and others.[11]

Also notable is the omission of any visually impaired African American women musicians, who were quite rare. Blind women were also rare among white musicians, with the notable exception of the jazz singer Diane Schuur. Although there do not seem to be any studies of mental health and illness in these blind musicians, most seem to have coped well.

One question is whether the blindness was essential to their success. Most of the musicians claim not, that their talent was more important. Even so, their accomplishments in view of the blindness and racism seems wondrous. Was it also magical?

There is a trope, mainly in film and fiction, of the "Magical Negro" or, to use more modern terminology, "magical black character." Created by white writers, this character type is generally disabled in some way, but ends up helping the white protagonist with their special insight, mystical powers, and wisdom. This term was even applied to President Obama, as in "Obama the Magic Negro." Is this what the psychiatrist Franz Fanon meant when he said the blues and jazz were a safe encounter with black aggression? Perhaps that fit in some way.

Racism seems to be an unfortunate contribution to the new musical forms developed by African Americans. That was especially the case with the blues. With the simple format of a musician with his guitar, it provided an avenue of success and freedom for the blind African American musicians, who were a relatively much more common street presence than the sighted blues musicians, and perhaps less threatening to a white audience, at that.

Would the history of music in the USA have been different without the blind African American musician? Likely, it would have been. The early and common blind blues musicians must have accelerated its popularity and presence, not only among African Americans, but whites who could look past the racism to embrace the music. Without Rahsaan Roland Kirk, certain innovations in jazz may have been absent, including the initial kernels of what became rap music. Moreover, music as social protest music was part of his legacy.

Even more generally, blind African American musicians were role models for productive lives with disabilities. Ray Charles and Stevie Wonder broke through musical and cultural barriers, with perhaps their blindness providing the bridge.

In trying to empathize with blind African American musicians, there are some limitations. Briefly simulating blindness by being blindfolded briefly, as Stevie Wonder did with journalists, is only a pale imitation of constant blindness and its challenges.

There is an interesting example of a bridge between the sighted and racism in regard to blindness. John Griffin experienced long periods of being blind after a brain injury from 1947 to 1957 from war trauma. With his sight back, having darkened his skin temporarily with the aid of medication, UV light, and skin paint, he lived as a black man for 6 weeks in 1959 to experience racism from that perspective.[12] However, he was never a musician.

While individual blind African American musicians may have been grateful for whatever help blindness added to their innate musical talent, most people cannot help but be grateful for the dramatic drop in blindness in African Americans. I, too, as Dr. Jazz, was grateful their music, but as a physician, so pleased that they are a disappearing phenomenon.

The Oedipal conflict in psychiatry, based more on the psychological blindness that leads to physical blindness, seems to be a part of human nature and thereby with us indefinitely. On the other hand, given the current political conflicts, some concomitant xenophobia, and the fears from the coronavirus pandemic, what we may have to worry about is any reliving of the failed Reconstruction period that could produce the need for another kind of the blues.

Notes

1. H.S. Moffic, R. Bailey, F. Clark et al., Dismantling racism in psychiatry and society. *Psychiatric Times*, 37(8): 1, 11–15, August 2020.
2. T. Gioia, *Healing Songs* (Durham, NC: *Duke University Press*, 2006).
3. T. Rowden, *The Songs of Black Folks: African American Musicians and the Cultures of Blindness* (Ann Arbor: University of Michigan, 2009).
4. T. Gioia, *A Subversive History of Music* (New York: Basic Books, 2019).
5. Goldstein J., 18-year-old blind pianist prodigy getting studied by scientists for his "remarkable" talents. People Magazine, February 24, 2020.
6. H.S. Moffic, R. Bailey, F. Clark et al., Dismantling racism in psychiatry and society. *Psychiatric Times* 37(8): 1, 11–15, August 2020.
7. Gioia T, *Healing Songs*, 2006.
8. T. Rowden, 2009.
9. T. Gioia, 2019.
10. Goldstein J: 18-year-old blind pianist prodigy getting studied by scientists for his "remarkable" talents. People Magazine, February 24, 2020.
11. John Griffen, *Black Like Me* (San Antonio, TX: Wings Press, 1964.
12. John Griffen, 1964.

Idioms and Ideas
Meanings and Metaphors[1]

Sharon Packer

As far as I can see, the English language includes innumerable idioms and metaphors referencing sight, vision, eyes or blindness. From my point of view, these idioms are rarely if ever intended to derogate the truly visually impaired—although the political purists and the anti-"oculocentrists" might say otherwise and refuse to turn a blind eye to unintended insults or innuendos. Some see these idioms as "ableist" expressions that effectively undermine persons who are visually challenged, serving as reminders of differences in people's sensory perceptions.

Regardless of the conclusions you yourself will draw, I suspect that we can all agree that these allusions are imbedded in everyday speech, as are other sensory references that bear no relationship to the sensory organ or physical function that they invoke. If you are not yet convinced, please read to the end of this section, to see for yourself.

Granted, each of us sees thing differently, and each of us has our own unique point of view, but, as far as I can see, such content usually stays strictly on the surface and carries no deep meaning. Still, I must admit that there are times when these idioms imply more than meets the eye and deserve more scrutiny. Looking at this material more closely, from a bird's eye view, instead of eyeballing it superficially, can help clarify matters—although, in the end, it becomes apparent that there are many, many ways to look at this topic. Each of us brings our own biases to the table, even before examining the evidence or looking closely at what is there.

There is no doubt in my rational mind (and not just in my more imaginative mind's eye) that some exegetes are blindsided by their pre-set conceptions when they look behind the scenes, in hopes of seeing what others cannot see. Some professionals or politicos are more likely to do this than others. For instance, psychoanalysts typically seek meaning from each syllable of every word, seeing significance where others do not. Correctly or not, they claim to have insights that are invisible to persons who are not specifically trained in psychoanalysis. And some schools of psychoanalysis believe that they have more insights than competitive schools.

Similarly, political pundits may press their particular points of view, as do the "PC police," as they are pejoratively known by those who differ with their stance. They look at words through their own lenses. Today, it is common to demand that language, signage, even sculpture be scrubbed of all hints of racism or sexism or heterosexism. We try to employ gender-neutral language whenever possible. I myself am skeptical if these endeavors will ultimately succeed, especially with respect to replacing the word "man" with more inclusive terms, given that those efforts have fallen short already, and are sometimes blocked by the biggest offenders. Still, we can choose to follow the lead of those tacticians, to see where this approach might take us, should we apply similar approaches to language alluding to vision or loss of sight.

Linguists also pursue this subject,[2] from a more neutral vantage point, although some have seen the political implications of their discoveries. In general, linguists remind us that many sense words are used "out of context," as idioms, so that references to touch and feeling or hearing and sound also appear regularly in language. "Ocularcentrism," or an emphasis on vision, is not alone, and the deaf community may very well claim that idioms related to hearing or sound are equally biased and undermine their soundless communications skills, known as sign language, which ordinarily requires vision, or very close contact with the signer to feel his or her fingers. It remains to be seen if the English language includes a disproportionate representation of eye references, compared to other languages, or if American English includes more references than other variants of English, which do not necessarily include the same idioms as Americans. The fact that "The Star Spangled Banner," America's national anthem, starts with a reference to sight—"O say can you see, by the dawn's early light"—suggestive, but not affirmative.

We might also consider the implications of "The Battle Hymn of the Republic," first penned by an abolitionist during the American Civil War, and reclaimed by civil rights activists in the 1960s, who mirrored the goals of the late Rev. Dr. Martin Luther King, Jr. Dr. King aspired to a completely colorblind society, where one is *not* judged by the color of one's skin. The hymn began: "My eyes have seen the glory of the coming of the Lord." Although the activists and the abolitionists advocated equalitarianism among Americans, one can see how their high-minded intentions might be misconstrued by equally high-minded literalists who examine all nuances of language.

146 Lenses on Blindness

Those who dabble in heuristics, be they Biblical scholars or literary analysts, typically dissect every sound, syllable and spelling of words. They also examine sentence structure. They thereby impute meaning that might otherwise go unseen. Specialists in literary criticism set their sights on some of the same material that attracts analysts and exegetes. Many see matters the same way that psychoanalysts do, especially since some schools of literary criticism borrow heavily from analytic theories. Some literary theorists favor Jacques Lacan, the French psychoanalyst who drew upon Ferdinand de Saussure's influential linguistic ideas. Although his iconoclastic psychotherapeutic techniques remain controversial to this day, Lacan was celebrated for his emphasis on language. His theories are not as well-known in the U.S. as they are in Europe. He has been called "the French Freud." Lacan is either respected or reviled by those who know of his work. Another French-speaking analyst, Jacques Derrida, was also influenced by Saussure, and went on to found deconstructionism. He became a media star as a philosopher and also had an important influence on literary criticism. The Algerian-born Derrida was a Sephardic Jew who was later educated in both France and the U.S. He was familiar with several languages and cultures, by virtue of his personal experience as well as formal education.

I see that I have gone off on a tangent, but, hopefully, you see what I mean about the nuances of languages and the ways to react to them. It would be nice if we could perform a double-blind experiment to determine the differences between sighted and unsighted people's reactions to these idioms, and to confirm that my theories are correct or to refute them as needed. However, I cannot imagine how to construct a double-blind study that meets scientific scrutiny, not now or for the foreseeable future. Just the same, there is no reason for readers to have blind faith in my suppositions. I agree that everyone should see for themselves if these ideas sound valid.

Some forgiving people can turn a blind eye to linguistic nuances that might offend others, whereas others are see negativity everywhere they look, and are blindsided by potential malevolent associations, even if they are accidental and visible only to analysts. The latter group often cannot see the forest for the trees, and focuses exclusively on nuances, taking a myopic and ultimately pessimistic view of the universe. Such persons often refuse to see the other person's point of view and do not try to look through another's lens. They fix their gaze on their own interests exclusively, with the intent to promote their own agenda. Because of their near-sightedness, they are often left in a blind rage, angry at the world, sometimes even seeing red—yet such sentiments not out of step without current sensitivities (or hypersensitivity)—and even the very concept of "seeing red" might be seen as an off-putting allusion to Native Americans.

Just because these idioms are not currently in the spotlight does not mean that they should not be in the public eye. Should someone shine a light on them, it is quite possible that they will be scrutinized, and some might demand their removal from acceptable speech, in much the same way that many statues and street names are being scrubbed as I write. However, I suspect that any endeavors to eliminate all "ocularcentrist speech" will be difficult, if not impossible, for reasons you will soon see, should you choose to read through the end of this section. The upshot of such concerns is not in sight right now, and their potential resolution remains to be seen.

Even without the advantages of scientific studies, let me continue this short monologue, to see if I can make you see my point of view. Since they say that "seeing is believing," I am obligated to show you evidence of my theories, so that you can see it with your own eyes. I promise that I will not lead you down a blind alley, even though my endeavors may admittedly appear convoluted or contrived to the untrained eye. Rather, my goal is to make each reader an eyewitness to these nuances of language, so that each can decide for himself or herself if we can circumvent unintended emphasis on vision or sight, or a lack thereof.

Before I conclude this exercise, I should mention feminist film theory and its own brand of "oculocentrism." Many feminist film theorists followed the lead of Laura Mulvey, who published influential ideas about the "male gaze," alleging that the cinematographer leads the viewer's eye by pointing the camera in one way rather than another. Filmmakers (who are mostly male) thereby "force" spectators to see what men—rather than women—supposedly see. Whether those hypotheses about "male gaze" are correct or not is immaterial here; the point is that this emphasis on "gaze" implicitly privileges vision over sound in a medium that was once called "moving pictures." The mere fact that Mulvey's theories gained so much traction since the 1970s suggests that many subsequent film critics also adopted this "oculocentrist" POV.

Having said that, let us take a look at potential pitfalls of the English language (without turning our gaze to other languages, for the time-being, lest we lose sight of the purpose of this essay). If we take a second look at the paragraphs above, where I will italicize every word that references vision or lack thereof, each of you can see for yourself what I mean. After all, seeing is believing, or is it not? In a moment you will see how many innocuous terms appear in the otherwise banal paragraphs above, and you can decide if you ever saw such a sight in your life. I doubt it. You would have to be blind as a bat not to recognize what is going on. However, I confess that I am not a linguist, and am probably overlooking any number of relevant terms, and so one might say that this exercise is simply a way for the blind to lead the blind. It is my opinion that holds most weight here, because I am the one who is editing this book about blindness. One can say that "in the land of the blind, the one-eyed man is king" (or queen, as the case may be). Even if you do not agree with me, or are totally bored by this exercise, at least the end is in sight.

Let us see if my little experiment above actually worked. Given that you have arrived at this paragraph on your own, I can see—or should I say, "infer"—that you already exerted great effort, perhaps enough to see straight through my gimmicks, which have probably grown hackneyed by now. Or maybe you did not see this coming and were totally blindsided. I can see why some may be seeing red because they are so offended by an approach that takes such a cavalier attitude toward idioms and metaphors that allude to the visually impaired or visually privileged.

Perhaps you have more insight into this matter than I and can foresee what lies ahead. For sure, some people believe themselves to be prophets or seers. Some leaders or scholars or artists or investors have an eye to the future, more than others, and can envision the next step, even if they see it only in their mind's eye, without necessarily using data or fact. Some will prove to be charlatans, while others are truly visionary. Alternatively, others habitually look backwards before responding, as if to prove that hindsight is always 20/20. Regardless of your point of view, all you need do is to read through the paragraphs below, where you can look at the italicized text, to find allusions to vision intertwined in the text (or use AI readers to make mention of italicized text). Those with an eye for detail may find even more references than I myself can see—and I envision receiving such corrections and additions, and I welcome them.

After you have engaged in this exercise, which is hopefully not too onerous, and which hopefully helped you see the light, and assess this argument better, it may be time to relax, maybe even go on a blind date or two, assuming that you have not yet set your sights on someone special, in which case there is no point in seeing someone else at this time.

Perhaps your date will be an eyeful or a real looker or, as some say, a feast for sore eyes. Or, as Bogart said to Bacall, in one of his many famous one-liners, "Here's looking at you, kid." Just do not be blinded by a glittery surface. Bear in mind that love is blind and can get just about anyone involved in a blind bargain, where one makes fatuous promises to others, simply because one cannot see clearly, especially when fleeting infatuation clouds one's view. By its very nature, going on a blind date implies that you are flying blind. But you can always see them to the door if it turns out that the two of you have little in common or do not see eye to eye on important matters. You have the option of seeing someone else in the future, even if you cannot see that far ahead at present. You can also proceed to read the rest of this book. Enjoy!

Italicized Idioms Pertaining to Vision, Sight, Blindness, Eyes, Etc.

As far as I can see, the English language includes innumerable idioms and metaphors referencing sight, vision, eyes or blindness. *From my point of view*, these idioms are rarely if ever intended to derogate the truly visually impaired—although the political purists and the anti-"oculocentrists" might say otherwise and refuse to *turn a blind eye* to unintended insults or innuendos. Some see these idioms as "ableist" expressions that effectively undermine persons who are visually challenged, serving as reminders of differences in people's sensory perceptions.

Regardless of the conclusions that you yourself will draw, I suspect that we can all agree that these allusions are imbedded in everyday speech, as are other sensory references that bear no relationship to the sensory organ or physical function that they invoke. If you are not yet convinced, please read to the end of this section, *to see for yourself.*

Granted, *each of us sees thing differently*, and each of us has our own unique *point of view*, but, *as far as I can see*, such content usually stays strictly on the surface and carries no deep meaning. Still, I must admit that there are times when these idioms imply *more than meets the eye* and deserve more scrutiny. *Looking at this material more closely*, from a *bird's eye view*, instead *of eyeballing it* superficially, can help clarify matters— although, in the end, it becomes apparent that there are many, many *ways to look at this topic.* Each of us brings our own biases to the table, even before examining the evidence or looking closely at what is there.

There is no doubt in my rational mind (and not just in my more imaginative *mind's eye*) that some exegetes are *blindsided* by their pre-set conceptions when they *look behind the scenes*, or *peek behind the curtain, to see what others cannot see.* Some professionals or politicos are more likely to do this than others. For instance, psychoanalysts typically seek meaning from each syllable of every word, seeing significance where others do not. Correctly or not, they claim to have *insights* that are *invisible to* persons who are not specifically trained in psychoanalysis. And some schools of psychoanalysis believe that they have more insights than competitive schools.

Similarly, political pundits may press their particular *points of view,* as do the "PC police," as they are pejoratively known by those who differ with their stance. *They look at* words through *their own lenses.* Today, it is common to demand that language, signage, even sculpture be scrubbed of all hints of racism or sexism or heterosexism. We try to employ gender-neutral language whenever possible. I myself am skeptical if these endeavors will ultimately succeed, especially with respect to replacing the word "man" with more inclusive terms, given that those efforts have fallen short already, and are sometimes blocked by the biggest offenders. Still, we can choose to follow the lead of those tacticians, *to see where* this approach might take us, should we apply similar approaches to language alluding to vision or loss of sight.

Linguists also pursue this subject, from a more neutral vantage point, although *some have seen* the political implications of their discoveries. In general, linguists remind us that many sense words are used "out of context," as idioms, so that references to touch and feeling or hearing and sound also appear regularly in language. "Ocularcentrism," or an emphasis on vision, is not alone, and the deaf community may very well claim that idioms related to hearing or sound are equally biased and undermine their soundless communications skills, known as sign language, which ordinarily requires vision, or very close contact with the signer to feel his or her fingers. *It remains to be seen* if the English language includes a disproportionate representation of eye references, compared to other languages, or if American English includes more references than other variants of English, which do not necessarily include the same idioms as Americans. The fact that "The Star-Spangled Banner," America's national anthem, starts with a reference to sight—"*O say can you see*, by the dawn's early light"—is suggestive, but not affirmative.

We might also consider the implications of "The Battle Hymn of the Republic," first penned by an abolitionist during the American Civil War, and reclaimed by civil rights activists in the 1960s, who *mirrored* the goals of the late Rev. Dr. Martin Luther King, Jr. Dr. King aspired to a completely *colorblind* society, where one is *not* judged by the color of one's skin. The hymn began: "*My eyes have seen the glory* of the coming of the Lord." Although the activists and the abolitionists advocated equalitarianism among Americans, *one can see how* their high-minded intentions might be misconstrued by equally high-minded literalists who examine all nuances of language.

Those who dabble in heuristics, be they Biblical scholars or literary analysts, typically dissect every sound, syllable and spelling of words. They also examine sentence structure. They thereby impute meaning that might otherwise *go unseen*. Specialists in literary criticism *set their sight*s on some of the same material that attracts analysts and exegetes. Many *see matters the same way* that psychoanalysts do, especially since some schools of literary criticism borrow heavily from analytic theories. Some literary theorists favor Jacques Lacan, the French psychoanalyst who drew upon Ferdinand de Saussure's influential linguistic ideas. Although his iconoclastic psychotherapeutic techniques remain controversial to this day, Lacan was celebrated for his emphasis on language. His theories are not as well-known in the U.S. as they are in Europe. He has been called "the French Freud." Lacan is either respected or reviled by those who know of his work. Another French-speaking analyst, Jacques Derrida, was also influenced by Saussure, and went on to found deconstructionism. He became a media star as a philosopher and also had an important influence on literary criticism. The Algerian-born Derrida was a Sephardic Jew who was later educated in both France and the U.S. He was familiar with several languages and cultures, by virtue of his personal experience as well as formal education.

I see that I have gone off on a tangent, but, hopefully, *you see what I mean* about the nuances of languages and the ways to react to them. It would be nice if we could perform a *double-blind* experiment to determine the differences between sighted and unsighted people's reactions to these idioms, and to confirm that my theories are correct or to refute them as needed. However, I cannot imagine how to construct a double-blind study that meets scientific scrutiny, not now or for the *foreseeable future*. Just the same, there is no reason for readers to have *blind faith* in my suppositions. I agree that everyone should see for themselves if these ideas sound valid.

Some forgiving people can *turn a blind eye* to linguistic nuances that might offend others, whereas others are *see* negativity everywhere they look, and are *blindsided* by potential malevolent associations, even if they are accidental *and visible* only to analysts. The latter group often *cannot see the forest for the trees*, and *focuses* exclusively on nuances, taking a *myopic* and ultimately pessimistic *view of the universe*. Such persons often refuse *to see the other person's point of view* and do not try to *look through another's lens*. They *fix their gaze* on their own interests exclusively, with the intent to promote their own agenda. Because of their *near-sightedness*, they are often left in a *blind rage*, angry at the world, sometimes even *seeing red*—yet such sentiments not out of step with our current sensitivities (or hypersensitivity)—and even the very concept of "seeing red" might be seen as an off-putting allusion to Native Americans.

Just because these idioms are not currently *in the spotlight* does not mean that they should not be *in the public eye*. Should someone *shine a light on th*em, it is quite possible that they will be scrutinized, and some might demand their removal from acceptable speech, in much the same way that many statues and street names are being scrubbed as I write. However, I suspect that any endeavors to eliminate all "ocularcentrist speech" will be difficult, if not impossible, for *reasons you will soon see*, should you choose to read through the end of this section. The upshot of such concerns is *not in sight* right now, and their potential resolution *remains to be seen*.

Even without the advantages of scientific studies, let me continue this short monologue, to *see if* I can *make you see my point of view*. Since they say that *"seeing is believing,"* I am obligated to *show you* evidence of my theories, so that you can *see it with your own eyes*. I promise that I will not lead you down a *blind alley*, even though my endeavors may admittedly *appear* convoluted or contrived to the *untrained eye*. Rather, my goal is to make each reader an *eyewitness* to these nuances of language, so that each can decide for himself or herself if we can circumvent unintended emphasis on vision or sight, or a lack thereof.

Before I conclude this exercise, I should mention feminist film theory and its own brand of "oculocentrism." Many feminist film theorists followed the lead of Laura Mulvey, who published influential ideas about the *"male gaze,"* alleging that the cinematographer leads the viewer's eye by pointing the camera in one way rather than another. Filmmakers (who are mostly male) thereby "force" *spectators* to see what men—rather than women—supposedly see. Whether those hypotheses about "male gaze" are correct or not is immaterial here; the point is that this emphasis on "gaze" implicitly privileges vision over sound in a medium that was once called "moving pictures." The mere fact that Mulvey's theories gained so much traction since the 1970s suggests that many subsequent film critics also adopted this "oculocentrist" POV.

Having said that, let us *take a look* at potential pitfalls of the English language (without *turning our gaze* to other languages, for the time-being, *lest we lose sight* of the purpose of this essay). If we *take a second look* at the paragraphs above, where I will italicize every word that references vision or lack thereof, each of you can *see for yourself* what I mean. After all, *seeing is believing*, or is it not? In a moment *you will see* how many innocuous terms appear in the otherwise banal paragraphs above, and you can tell decide *if you ever saw such a sight* in your life. I doubt it. You would have to be *blind as a bat* not to recognize what is going on. However, I confess that I am not a linguist, and am probably *overlooking* any number of relevant terms, and so one might say that this exercise is simply a way for the blind to lead the blind. It is my opinion that holds most weight here, because I am the one who is editing this book about blindness. One can say that "*in the land of the blind, the one-eyed man is king*" (or queen, as the case may be). Even if you do not agree with me, or are totally bored by this exercise, at least the *end is in sight*.

Let us see if my little experiment above actually worked. Given that you have arrived at this paragraph on your own, *I can see*—or should I say, "infer"—that you already exerted great effort, perhaps enough *to see straight through* my gimmicks, which have probably grown hackneyed by now. Or maybe you *did not see this coming* and were totally *blindsided*. *I can see why* some may be *seeing red* because they are so offended by an approach that takes such a cavalier attitude toward idioms and metaphors that allude to the visually impaired or visually privileged.

Perhaps you have more *insight* into this matter than I and can *foresee* what lies ahead. For sure, some people believe themselves to be prophets or *seers*. Some leaders or scholars or artists or investors have *an eye to the future*, more than others, and can *envision the next step*, even if they see it only in their *mind's eye*, without necessarily using data or fact. Some will prove to be charlatans, while others are truly *visionary*. Alternatively, others habitually *look backwards* before responding, as if to prove that *hindsight is always 20/20*. Regardless of your *point of view*, all you need do is to read through the paragraphs below, where you *can look* at the italicized text, to find allusions to vision intertwined in the text (or use AI readers to make mention of italicized text). Those with an *eye for detail* may find even more references than I myself can see—and I *envision* receiving such corrections and additions, and I welcome them.

After you have engaged in this exercise, which is hopefully not too onerous, and which hopefully helped you *see the light*, and assess this argument better, it may be time to relax, maybe even go on a *blind date* or two, assuming that you have not *yet set your sights* on someone special, in which case there is no point in *seeing someone else* at this time.

Perhaps your date will be *an eyeful* or *a real looker* or, as some say, *a feast for sore eyes*. Or, as Bogart said to Bacall, in one of his many famous one-liners, "*Here's looking at you*, kid." Just *do not be blinded* by a glittery surface. Bear in mind that *love is blind* and can get just about anyone involved in a *blind bargain*, where one makes fatuous promises to others, simply because *one cannot see clearly*, especially when fleeting *infatuation clouds one's view*. By its very nature, going on a *blind date* implies that you are *flying blind*. But you can *always see them to the door* if it turns out that the two of you have little in common or *do not see eye to eye* on important matters. You have the option of *seeing someone else* in the future, even if you cannot *see that far ahead* at present. You can also take detour by reading the rest of this book, which includes many intriguing topics, written by a wide array of scholars from varied fields.

Notes

1. Georgina Kleege's books about the experiences of a professor who is legally blind (but whose parents were both artists) are worth reading in their own right, plus their titles recapitulate the points made in this section: *Blind Rage; Sight Unseen; More than Meets Eye* (Oxford 2018).

2. My thanks to linguist and lawyer Debbie Felder for her insights on this subject.

Through the Eye(s) of Tiresias
From Thebes and Beyond

CALEB PUCKETT

Introduction

Numerous aspects of Western thought and culture have been shaped or informed by ancient Greek literature. Indeed, a considerable portion of the tropes, motifs, and symbols we encounter in the arts even today may be said to originate with archetypes established by the ancient Greeks. Among one of the more fascinating archetypes that we find in our cultural products—be they films, television series, novels, or comic books—is the figure who has a physical impairment while simultaneously exhibiting something akin to a special power. In a host of scenarios, this figure's impairment is directly identified as physical blindness and the power he or she holds is heightened perceptual acuity of a psychological or spiritual nature. This figure is often referred to as the blind seer.

While ancient Greek literature is rife with characters who are blind, blinded, or blind others, one of the most significant secondary characters in the mythology—one who is manifest in numerous texts—is the blind seer Tiresias. Tiresias plays a crucial role as both truth-teller and prophet in an array of Greek myths. Interestingly, Tiresias's remarkable powers of perception are the direct result of a supernatural gift—a divine compensation for the loss of his physical sight. By examining the figure of Tiresias in primary texts, as well as discussing the cultural resilience of this character and the blind seer archetype across the ages, we arrive at a better understanding as to why blindness has so often been associated with second sight in the popular imagination and products of Western culture.

Origins of the Blind Seer

Like a range of figures in ancient Greek and subsequent Roman literature, Tiresias appears in variety of texts, including a compendium, *Bibliotheca*, a renowned epic poem, the *Odyssey*, the plays *Antigone* and *Oedipus Rex*, and an influential narrative poem the *Metamorphoses*, to name but a few. While Tiresias's origin story differs from text to text, the texts tend to follow a similar formula: Tiresias unknowingly commits a transgression against a god, which leads to a punishment—the loss of his sight. As a recompense, the god in question, or another god entirely, grants Tiresias second sight. In an ironic twist, the seemingly desirable power of second sight oftentimes serves as a further punishment, as the knowledge it affords brings Tiresias further distress or pain. Alfred Schutz goes so far as to assert that the god in each of these cases may have actually "inflicted the gift of seercraft"[1] on Tiresias more than blessed him with it. Such a claim is certainly supported, for as Tiresias himself observes in *Oedipus Rex*, "A fearful thing is knowledge, when to know helpeth no end."[2]

The *Bibliotheca* contains a variety of explanations regarding the origin of Tiresias's powers, with the most common one being that the vengeful gods blinded him for sharing their secrets with humanity. In the poem "The Bathing of Pallas" by Callimachus, the goddess of wisdom, Athena, blinds Tiresias after he witnesses her bathing, but she later cleanses his ears in an act of charitable recompense. Her divine cleansing grants him the gift of augury. In some of the later literature, Tiresias receives a similar gift, but only after undergoing other trials and transformations. One notable example is Ovid's *Metamorphoses*, where we find an intriguing and rich iteration on this notion. In the work, Tiresias is a transformed into a female and back into a male before his final transformation into a blind seer.

As the *Metamorphoses* recounts it, Tiresias's transformation into a female occurs after he strikes two snakes that he discovers copulating on the side of the road. Years later, Tiresias strikes the same snakes again, thereby bringing about his return to male form. Having lived as both male and female, his perspective becomes uniquely situated in the world. Given this unique viewpoint and ostensible lack of bias, the king and queen of the gods, Zeus and Hera, call upon Tiresias to settle their debate regarding whether a male or female derives more enjoyment from sex. After Tiresias states that females derive a greater portion of the enjoyment, Hera becomes furious and proceeds to strike him blind. As a form of compensation for this punishment, and an inevitable stage of advancement in Tiresias's awareness, Zeus grants Tiresias prophetic abilities and an extended lifespan. Zeus's gift, it is worth noting, is not the power of direct revelation from the gods; rather, it is the independent ability to see well beyond normal human perception. Tiresias's power in this regard proves so great, and his lifespan proves so long, that he serves as a prophet of the god Apollo in the city of Thebes for seven generations.

Delving into the particulars of the *Metamorphoses* provides some insight into both the practical and symbolic role Tiresias oftentimes holds in the stories he inhabits, as well as illuminates the function and overall scope of his powers within an archetypal framework. One of the most notable elements in this story is the relationship between gender and seerhood. As Teresa Carp relates, Ovid frames Tiresias's experience in such a way that it makes a direct connection between androgyny and seerhood.[3] Indeed, Ovid asserts that Tiresias's broadened perspective brings with it an uncommon depth of perception. The snakes Tiresias strikes as they are intertwined in the act of coitus clearly serve as phallic symbols and operate as leitmotifs throughout his transformative journey. His attack on them suggests "a form of violation, an act with both sexual and religious connotations."[4]

In the largest sense, the snakes stand in for the notion of duality. Duality in this case provides a range of inflection points; however, it most directly points to a dichotomy between males and females, as well as further dichotomies such as danger and recovery, and death and rebirth. Breaking fee of this duality and being able to navigate its attendant sets of dichotomies positions Tiresias in a manner that allows him to serve as an agent of Apollo, for Apollo is not only the god of medicine (as represented through the symbol of the caduceus) but also the god of prophecy. Carp underscores this notion by explaining that, in Greek culture at the time, "snakes were […] specifically connected in myth with the attainment of prophetic power" and that Tiresias's story "reflect[s] a traditional concern with the duality of human existence and a preoccupation with passage from the mortal to a higher state."[5] This higher state—predicated on breaking out of binary oppositions and conventional sightedness—is a state free of the perceptual limitations most humans experience throughout their lives. As Carp maintains:

> A special few individuals, it was felt, are capable of going beyond what passes for knowledge in the temporal realm, and these persons are privileged to become seers […] the transcendence of some or all of the basic dualities of human nature is considered essential to the nature of the prophet in classical and other mythologies. Seers or wisdom figures are viewed traditionally as extraordinary individuals who have passed beyond the duality of the phenomenal world—the pairs of opposites apprehended by the rational mind—to a transcendent unity and wholeness.[6]

This framework proves crucial, particularly when viewed alongside a broader Greek view of physical beauty. As much of ancient Greek art and philosophy has demonstrated, the Greeks believed their gods could inhabit the human form and that, in such cases, those forms were ideal or perfect.

Humans, in turn, could express elements of the divine in their physical forms, but they could by no means enjoy physical perfection. This notion is in keeping with the Greek view that nature itself—however excellent—is incapable of producing anything or anyone with absolute perfection. Through these physical expressions of beauty, the Greeks believed that humans were able to convey the dimensions of their moral virtue. By connecting the body to virtue in this manner, and associating virtue with human action, the Greeks viewed the body as a vehicle to understand a person's destiny. Tiresias's blindness and accompanying gift of second sight, then, may be understood as a way of grounding him very much in the human realm while also suggesting that his virtue and the actions which correspond with his destiny all approach a point of divinity. In such a case, Tiresias holds the position of a profound intermediary between the gods and humankind.

Nature of Seeing

Tiresias's power as a seer forwards the plots and informs the themes of numerous texts in the ancient Greek world. Apprehending his power and how it is typically manifested in these texts reveals much about how the ancients framed sightedness and seerhood. As Armin Lange notes, it is critical to understand that "Greek seers [...] do not rely on divine revelations but have special ability to perceive more than normal human beings."[7] Unlike most seers, though, Tiresias's power of sight is especially strong, for he is "gifted with intuitive divination and performs it so well that he competes even with Apollon, the god of divination."[8] Tiresias is, in short, close to divine in his ability to reason and draw accurate conclusions about the affairs of humankind.

By defining the essential aspects of Tiresias's vision—particularly as it compares to that of non-visionary humans—we get a firmer sense of how this incredible reasoning is made manifest:

1. Tiresias's "visions of things to come are independent of his pre-experiences."
2. Tiresias is an "unconcerned onlooker of the future events he envisions."
3. Tiresias's "knowledge of things to come is by no means related to the knowledge other people have."[9]

The *Odyssey* provides some of the earliest insight into Tiresias as a character. Homer's presentation of Tiresias as a "prophet of contingencies"[10] also serves in some respects as a template for a character type that appears throughout some key latter day works that comprise the Western canon, including Herodotus's seminal work, *Histories*. In the *Odyssey*, Odysseus—a character known for being remarkably clever—is advised by the goddess Circe to seek out Tiresias so that he may speak with souls in the underworld and obtain advice on how to return to his home in Ithaca. Quite simply, without Tiresias, the wise and wily hero will lack the information he needs to complete his quest. One curious aspect of this meeting is that Tiresias is no longer among the living. In fact, Odysseus must travel to the underworld to consult with the seer's ghost. Despite no longer having human form, Tiresias has maintained his power as an incomparable seer and guide, which suggests that his power is not incidental or bound up in mortality, but instead an essential and transcendent aspect of his being.

Notably, Tiresias's characterization in later works, such as *Antigone* and *Oedipus Rex,* tends to suggest that he is a master of deductive reasoning more than a man with mystical insight. The Tiresias of these works may, in fact, be understood as an accomplished investigator who is able to discern past actions (however hidden they may be to others) and make logical determinations about the likelihood of future events. This difference in characterization is due, in part, to a shift from Tiresias appearing in an epic to appearing in tragedies. In an epic, like the *Odyssey*, Tiresias's prophecy is largely based on an "if ... then" statement, whereas his prophecy in *Oedipus Rex* is based on an exceptional apprehension of facts and causality.[11] When we consider these aspects of Tiresias's within the framework of a mystery, his role in the tragedy *Oedipus Rex* gains additional import.

In *Oedipus Rex*—the first detective story in Western literature—Oedipus calls upon Tiresias to reveal the person who murdered his father, the former king, and ultimately help him end a plague ravaging their city, Thebes. Even though Oedipus is an astute man—a master at solving riddles and the ostensible detective seeking to solve the mystery at hand—he remains blind to certain truths of a deeply personal nature. To get at the truth he seeks, and as an acknowledgment of his own limited abilities, Oedipus concludes that he must consult with Tiresias, for "It is Tiresias who understands all things, who knows even the secret of heaven."[12] After being confronted by Oedipus about disclosing these truths, Tiresias finally reveals that it is, in fact, Oedipus who killed his father. To make matters worse, Tiresias also reveals that Oedipus married his mother, Jocasta.

Part of what makes Tiresias's revelation significant is that it serves as clear contrast to Oedipus's ignorance, underscoring the fact that Oedipus is ill-equipped to solve the mystery and must resort to consulting the blind prophet to discover the truth. Tiresias, who is a minor character in the play, effectively serves as a powerful foil to the physically sighted Oedipus—a character whose lack of understanding and tragic actions serve as testaments to his figurative blindness. Tellingly, once Oedipus finally recognizes the truth of Tiresias's revelation, he tears out his own eyes and goes into exile. Oedipus's self-inflicted physical blindness serves as both an admission of his figurative blindness and a signifier of true self-knowledge or insight.

Modern Manifestations of the Blind Seer

The character of Tiresias and the related blind seer archetype established by the Greeks and carried forward by the Romans appears in a variety of modern cultural products. For direct uses of Tiresias as a character, one need only look to works as diverse as T.S. Eliot's classic poem *The Waste Land* to the Coen brothers' comedy-drama send-up of the *Odyssey*, *O Brother, Where Art Thou*, and to Salley Vickers's recent retelling of the Oedipus myth, *Where Three Roads Meet*, to discover but a few examples. Most often, however, modern works tend to feature less direct representations of Tiresias, offering instead imaginative iterations of the Tiresias archetype. Indeed, this archetype has appeared in an ever-expanding array of works, including Stephen King's horror novella *The Langoliers*, the popular science fiction film *The Matrix*, and the computer animated children's film *The LEGO Movie*.

In many such works, writers typically present the blind seer as a secondary character whose chief function is to assist the hero in his or her quest. However, a growing number of writers have chosen to center their narratives around the experiences of the blind seer, turned the character into a heroic protagonist in its own right, and have fleshed out the archetype in a manner that allows it to plausibly exist in worlds that many in their audiences will readily recognize. One of the interesting aspects of this reimagining and general tendency towards characterization is that writers often explicitly situate the blind seer as a guardian of secular laws—no longer a messenger of the laws or will of the gods—and, by extension, a guardian of social order. The blind seer operates in service of the law and is largely defined by his or her ability to distinguish between truths and falsehoods. Ultimately, this figure works towards justice or a restoration of balance in the communities where he or she lives. Writers often situate this function within the realm of a prevailing justice system, while also presenting the blind seer as someone who maintains something of an outsider status in said system. Owing in some cases to the character's blindness, uncommon perceptual acuity, and lack of conventionality, this version of the blind seer is an individual who is intimately familiar with the rules and conventions of such a system yet clearly advanced beyond the limitations of the system and its more ordinary, physically sighted agents.

In numerous cases, this figure serves as a detective or engages in work that is decidedly detective-like in its nature. In such cases, the character demonstrates clear conceptual connections to the most ancient versions of Tiresias, particularly the version operating within the framework of *Oedipus Rex*. Indeed, when we look at works such as the Max Carrados stories that appeared alongside the tales of Sherlock Holmes in *The Strand Magazine*, the titular character—a sightless but remarkably insightful detective—appears to be a Tiresias transformed for those times. Likewise, in both the Duncan Maclain and Naomi Blake series, the police procedural *Longstreet,* and the comics, movie, and television series that comprise Marvel's *Daredevil* franchise, we discover repeated treatments of this character type placed in modern milieus. Yet, no matter how modern the character and situations may appear, the essential functions of the character have been derived from that version of Tiresias first presented in *Oedipus Rex*. However, unlike the Tiresias of the *Oedipus Rex*, the *Odyssey*, or other ancient works, where Tiresias is a character who "does not act, does not interfere, does not hope and fear,"[13] this version of the character tends to be action-oriented and specifically designed to interfere with injustice. In the context of these works, the detached seer has been transfigured into a character who takes active measures to uphold ethical or moral precepts by utilizing a prodigious intellect. It is this form of Tiresias that has shaped the associations that so many audiences have now created between blindness and a dispensation for preternatural insight into the human mind and the messy affairs of humankind.

Notes

1. Alfred Schutz, "Tiresias, Or Our Knowledge of Future Events," *Social Research* 26, no. 1 (Spring 1959): 75.
2. Sophocles, *Oedipus, King of Thebes*, Translated by Gilbert Murray (Project Gutenberg, 2008), 18, https://www.gutenberg.org/files/27673/27673-h/27673-h.htm
3. Teresa Carp, "'Venus Utraque': A Typology of Seerhood," *The Classical World* 76, no. 5 (May–June 1983): 277.
4. Genevieve Liveley, 2003. "Tiresias/Teresa: A 'Man-made-woman' in Ovid's *Metamorphoses* 3.318–38," *Helios* 30, no. 2: 159.
5. Carp, "'Venus Utraque,'" 279, 280.
6. Carp, "'Venus Utraque,'" 283, 284.
7. Armin Lange, "Greek Seers and Israelite-Jewish Prophets," *Vetus Testamentum* 57, no. 4 (2007): 461.
8. Lange, "Greek Seers and Israelite-Jewish Prophets," 479.
9. Schutz, "Tiresias," 76.
10. Deborah MacInnes, "Jocasta, Tiresias, and the Lille Steichorus." *Quaderni Urbanati di Cultura Classica* 86, no. 2 (2007): 106.
11. Schutz, "Tiresias," 73.
12. Lange, "Greek Seers and Israelite-Jewish Prophets," 479.
13. Schutz, "Tiresias," 88.

"Close your eyes and see"
Blindness and Literature

Eric Sandberg

All readers are blind. Not literally, of course, for reading is a visual process, and thus a form of seeing.[1] But when we read, immersing ourselves in text, we stop seeing the world around us. We willingly limit our field of vision to a limited set of symbols and the spaces between them. We see black ink on white paper, and nothing more, reading precisely insofar as we resist the temptation to look away from the page at everything else that surrounds us, from our hands holding the book, to the room we sit in, or indeed the world beyond the windowpane.[2] We may look up from our reading and out of that window—as Virginia Woolf ([1932] 1965) pointed out, "How delightful to stop reading and look out!"—but we then return to the words on the page and the world they create. For at the same time as reading blinds us to almost all of the real world, it opens what William Wordsworth ([1807] 2006) described as an "inward eye" onto previously unseen and unseeable worlds. This is not, as it was for Wordsworth, the pensive and nostalgic eye of recollection, but the eye of imagination, that eye that lets us see the mud-clogged and foggy streets of Dickens' London or the empty, haunting glitter of Gatsby's parties. When we read, in other words, we become blind in order to see.

Given this intimate relationship between reading and seeing, it is perhaps unsurprising to find that not just blindness (itself a theme of no small fascination) but also the association of the inability to see with the ability to tell a story, what Argentinian writer Jorge Luis Borges ([1977] 1999) described as the "friendship of poetry and blindness," runs through literary history. Indeed, at the beginning of Western literature stands the figure of the blind poet Homer, possibly mythical, certainly unknowable, but a resonant and lasting symbol of the power of the word to evoke worlds. When he opens the *Iliad* with the invocation "[…] sing, goddess, of the ruinous wrath of Peleus' son Achilles," he is asking to be told a story so that he can see that which is not there (1.1). Now, millennia later, we open his book, blind ourselves to the busy world of the 21st century, and, in a sense simultaneously real and unreal, "see" the struggles of the Achaeans and the Trojans. Consider the overwhelming visuality, for instance, of the scene in which Hector storms the Achaeans' encampment:

> …the doors were sundered in every direction
> by the blow of the stone. Glorious Hector sprang at them,
> his face dark like the rushing night; he shone with the dreadful
> gleam of bronze that he had put about his body; in his hands
> he held two spears. No one coming against him could have restrained him
> except the gods, when he leapt through the gates; and his eyes blazed
> with fire [12.461–466].

Here we find a series of visual impressions that together create what, if we were not so familiar with the process, would be an uncanny sense of sight. Reading these lines, we do not just learn how Hector storms the fortress, but in some sense see him do it. Homer may be traditionally associated with blindness, but the poem associated with his name is signally capable of causing us to see. Literature, it seems, is the art of blind seeing.

But the association between blindness and literature is not only based on this paradoxical form of vision. The experience of a life without sight is in its own right also a powerful theme—even obsession—and as David Bolt (2014) points out "representations of blindness have always been abundant in the cultural imagination."[3] In part, this is because sight is the primary medium through which we experience the world and our place in it. While only "a very small minority will experience being blind," Shelly Kinash (2006) points out, "the rest of us will experience vision, and seeing, or not seeing, as the case may be, is a primary defining characteristic of who we are."[4] Thus blindness has often been represented as hugely important, utterly incommensurable, for instance, with an inability to smell. The loss of sight is an occasion for tragedy; consider the blinding of Gloucester in Shakespeare's *King Lear* ([1623] 2007) and Cornwall's mocking commentary: "Out, vile jelly! Where is thy lustre now?" (III.VII 88–89). Gloucester's response to his blinding (and betrayal) is attempted suicide—"This world I do renounce"—an indication of the way "the loss of sight" is frequently represented as "tantamount to a loss of life […]" (IV.V 43).[5] The loss of smell, on the other hand, is in literature the occasion for little more than cheerful humor, as in the jocular connection Salman Rushdie (1991) establishes in *Midnight's Children* between Saleem Sinai's perpetually inflamed and ineffective sinuses and his "nose-given telepathy," both of which are eventually "cured" by an operation (348). In a "visio-centric" culture, then, sight is a signifier of tremendous significance (Kinash 2006, 4).

It is thus unsurprising to find that many writers have attempted to evoke the condition of blindness in their writing, from E. L Doctorow's *Homer & Langley*, with its austere description of the "slow fade-out" of the narrator's sight as "the white ice, that last light, went gray and then altogether black and then all my sight was gone…," to Anthony Doerr's (2015) overwrought association in *All the Light We Cannot See* of blindness with a synesthetic experience of the world as "shimmering kaleidoscopes" of color and interconnection.[6]

Blindness is not, of course, a literary theme or device: it is a physiological condition, and as Moshe Barasch has indicated, "as a natural condition it knows little change."[7] Barasch's point is that while the physical state of blindness is a human constant, our understanding of its meaning and significance is culturally determined. What is important here is, first, the distinction drawn between blindness as a real condition experienced by real people, and the cultural work that the notion of blindness does; and, second, the fact that blindness is overdetermined. That is to say that it is subject to multiple interpretations and can play different roles in systems of signification. It is no more stable than any other physical reality that has been brought into symbolic currency, and perhaps less so: blindness can mean many things.

One of the most intuitive, and obvious, symbolic associations of blindness, as Kinash has pointed out, is with darkness as opposed to light, but this physical association is in turn linked to metaphysical values (4). In his valuable study on the development of the image of blindness from antiquity to the renaissance, Barasch points out that there is a fundamental split in representations of the blind: "On the one hand, he is the unfortunate creature, deprived of what is often considered man's most precious gift, the ability to see the world and to find his way without the help of others." This is the darkness of blindness. "On the other hand he is endowed, however vaguely, with an ability given to no other human being—to be in direct communication with a deity." This is the light of blindness: an uncanny ability to "see" what is invisible to those who can see.

The first of these, the traditional linkage of blindness with darkness and hence with vulnerability and weakness, can be traced deep into the Western literary tradition, and is often identified as a form of divine punishment. One might think of the Old Testament curse for disobedience: "The lord shall smite thee with madness, and blindness, and astonishment of heart. And thou shalt grope at noonday, as the blind gropeth in the darkness…" (Deut. 28: 28–29). Or consider the story of Samson, first betrayed by Delilah, and then blinded by the Philistines. Then "bound with fetters of brass" he "did grind in the prison house" until the foolishness of his captors allows him to take revenge—revenge not for his enslavement, but for the loss of his sight (Judg. 16: 21). As Julie Rodas has pointed out, "of all Samson's sufferings, it is his blindness, the memory of his absent eyes, that ushers forth his rage."[8]

The classical tradition similarly emphasizes blindness as a form punishment. Sometimes, it is inflicted by mortals, as when Homer's Odysseus takes his revenge on the Cyclops Polyphemus by blinding him with a heated stake until "the very roots of his eye crackled in the heat." At other times it is a form of divine punishment: Sophocles' Oedipus may have blinded himself out of remorse for killing his father and marrying his mother, but he was driven to do so by Apollo: "it was always Apollo / who brought each of my agonies to birth." However, in both cases, the result is weakness and dependence. Once blinded, Polyphemus is powerless to hurt the Greeks, an "embodiment of loss," and can do little more than pray to his father Poseidon for help and vengeance.[9] And as Kreon relentlessly points out to the blind Oedipus, "all the great power" he once had is now "gone / gone forever" (1988, 1976).

This equation of blindness with darkness, with punishment, and with weakness is also a prominent theme in more recent literature. In J.M. Coetzee's *Waiting for the Barbarians* (2010), the partial blinding of the "barbarian" girl by the sinister Colonel Joll, and the "worm-like sear" left by their instruments of torture, represent for the civilized if ineffectual Magistrate a sign of everything his empire is doing wrong. And of course it leaves the girl at the mercy of her captors—although Coetzee certainly does not represent her as weak or reliant. The irony in this case is that the magistrate himself is weakened by the girl's blinding, and his obsession with it, and is at the same time at least partially "blind" to his own role in the oppression of the other represented by Joll's act of pointless cruelty.

However, in the twentieth and twenty-first centuries the representation of blindness has often focused on collective rather than individual experience. An early and interesting example is H.G. Wells' short story "The Country of the Blind" (1947). The mountain climber Nunez discovers a valley inhabited entirely by people left blind at birth by an endemic disease, who have gradually lost even the concept of sight. Nunez imagines he will be their "heaven sent king and master"—as he tells himself, "In the Country of the Blind the One-eyed Man is King"—but comes to realize that despite his vision, he has no advantage over these people who navigate their world with "confidence and precision." They do not even believe that sight exists, thinking instead that Nunez is delusional, if not insane. When he eventually falls in love with a local, they only agree to the marriage on the condition that he be "cured" by blinding. He reluctantly agrees, but at the last minute, seeing the "infinite beauty" of the "sunlit ice and snow," he flees the valley into the towering and in all likelihood lethal mountains.

The original 1904 version of the story ends on this ambiguous note, representing the blind as more, rather than less, powerful than their sighted visitor. However, they are also tragically limited. In Wells' (1966) own words, the story is about "the spiritual isolation of those who see more keenly than their fellows," and the blind here are symbols of an "invincibly self-satisfied and secure" society. Wells revised the story in 1939, making the metaphorical connection between literal and metaphorical blindness even stronger. Now, as Nunez flees he notices a new fault-line in the precipice that hangs above the valley, indicating an incipient, catastrophic landslide. He attempts to warn the valley-dwellers of their danger, but of course they take this as one more example of his insanity. Inevitably, the rockslide destroys the country of the blind (allowing Nunez and his beloved to escape). The blind man is here no longer a sign of individual vulnerability, frailty and suffering, but of a broader social malaise. Given the year of republication, it is clear that the new ending is a political allegory of democratic complaisance in the face of fascist threats, but the pattern is more broadly applicable.

Indeed, other writers have used a similar conceit: John Wyndham's *Day of the Triffids* ([1951] 1979) presents a world in which most of the earth's population has gone blind due to a meteor shower of unknown, but probably military origin, and then fallen victim to the eponymous semi-sentient, mobile, and carnivorous plants. Both of these menaces are, it is implied, products of misapplied ingenuity. This post-apocalyptic nightmare thus arises directly out the actions of a civilization—ours—that has abused the environment and recklessly misused science. Blindness is a punishment for human hubris, a corrective to what the narrator describes as "one of the race's most persistent and comforting hallucinations": that "one's own time and place is beyond cataclysm." A more recent example occurs in Nobel Laureate José Saramago's *Blindness* ([1995] 2005), which details the collapse of an unnamed civilization in the face of an unexplained outbreak of the "white sickness," or blindness (41). The narrative follows a group of the blind (never named, an indication of the universal implications of the novel) who are forced into an concentration camp, where they experience a dizzying and horrifying collapse of human values, an intensified version of William Golding's 1954 novel *Lord of the Flies*, culminating in a scene of nauseating sexual violence. As the illness spreads, it becomes clear that "only in a world of the blind will things be truly what they are." Blindness here is not a textual punishment for any particular sin, but an analogue for the human condition at its bleakest.

The literary tradition is thus rich in examples of the association of blindness with punishment, vulnerability, and chaos. But the other side of the coin of blindness, its ability to confer a higher vision, is equally well represented. Often it involves the same characters or occurs in the same texts. In Saramago's *Blindness*, for example, the Doctor's wife, the only character who keeps her sight throughout the novel, wishes at points that she too could "turn blind, penetrate the visible skin of things, and pass to their inner side." However, Tiresias, the blind prophet of Thebes, probably offers the most famous example of this sort of blind vision. In the *Odyssey*, his spirit is summoned to assist the wanderer on his voyage home and is able to predict the course of not just Odysseus' adventures, but his entire life, seeing, in other words, the future. He plays a similar role in Sophocles. When he tells Oedipus that he is himself the cause of his city's travails, the king angrily mocks him: "You have no truth. You're blind. / Blind in your eyes. Blind in your ears. Blind in your mind" (507–508). But Tiresias' prophecy is accurate; he cannot be called "a prophet who cannot see" despite his blindness—in fact, he sees all too clearly. T.S. Eliot exploited this ability in his 1922 poem *The Waste Land* when Tiresias "though blind ... perceived the scene" of the ghastly, meaningless visit of the "young man carbuncular" to his lover, and thus understands something about the sterility of the times (218–231). In the literary imagination, then, blindness is not just the absence of vision; it is a higher form of vision that allows characters, and thus readers, to "see" the unseeable.

This essential bifurcation in the representation of blindness in literature arises, at least in part, out of the nature of the written word. "The blind man," as Rodas points out, "participates in a unique literary history, playing the part of inspiration incarnate ...."[10] This happens both on the level of authorship—Rodas mentions Homer alongside Milton and Borges, and the list could easily be extended—and in terms of characters like Tiresias, in whom blindness becomes a paradoxical source of illumination. But more fundamentally, if reading involves as I have argued a form of voluntary blindness which leads directly to an radical expansion of vision and understanding, this process is mirrored within our literature. Blind characters are represented as tragic figures, but also as able to perceive that which other cannot. Similarly, the state of blindness has often been used to represent a more systematic, widespread social weakness or vulnerability, but also as a way of making visible to readers a truth that would otherwise remain imperceptible; metaphorical blindness allows us to see ourselves more clearly.

The last word here will be left to another major figure in world literature, who for much of his life suffered from partial blindness, James Joyce. Like Borges ([1977] 1999), who claimed that "blindness is a gift," Joyce refused to mourn his loss of vision. He is reported to have said that "of all the things that have happened to me, I think the least important was having been blind" (qtd. in Borges 1999, 481). Joyce also associated a lack of vision with a higher form of sight. In his masterpiece *Ulysses* (1922), Stephen Dedalus walks on the beach while contemplating the world as a text legible through "the ineluctable modality of the visible," through, in other words, sight. But this is not enough for Stephen, whose instruction to himself applies, the literary tradition examined here suggests, to all of us: "Shut your eyes and see."

Notes

1. With the obvious exceptions of audiobooks and Braille.
2. Technological changes in reading—ereaders, tablets, mobile phones, and so on—affect this only in terms of terminology, and the additional potential for distraction inherent in their multiple functions.
3. David Bolt, "The Supremacy of Sight: Aesthetics, Representations, and Attitudes." In *Changing Social Attitudes Toward Disability: Perspectives From Historical, Cultural, and Educational Studies*, edited by David Bolt, 109–117. Hoboken: Routledge; 2014.
4. Kinash, Shelley, *Seeing Beyond Blindness*. Greenwich, Conn: Information Age Publishing; 2006.
5. Georgina Kleege, "Introduction: Blindness and Literature." *Journal of Literary & Cultural Disability Studies* 1.2: 2009: 113–114. *Project MUSE*. https://muse.jhu.edu/article/270153/pdf.
6. Anthony Doerr, *All the Light We Cannot See* (London: Fourth Estate, 2015).
7. Moishe Barasch. *Blindness: The History of a Mental Image in Western Thought* (New York: Routledge, 2001).
8. Julia Miele Rodas, "On Blindness." *Journal of Literary & Cultural Disability Studies*; 2009. 1.2: 115–130. *Project MUSE*. https://muse.jhu.edu/article/270154/pdf.
9. Rodas, 124.
10. Rodas, 116–117.

Blindness as Holocaust Metaphor
Elie Wiesel's A Beggar in Jerusalem *and* The Forgotten

Eric J. Sterling

I. Introduction

Elie Wiesel's novels *A Beggar in Jerusalem* (1969—winner of the prestigious French Prix Médicis)[1]—and *The Forgotten* (1992) focus on the Holocaust, remembrance of suffering and atrocities, loss, and blindness. Both novels, in fact, contain an old blind madman who is seemingly human and insane but perhaps is actually a mystical seer who serves as the caretaker and preserver of knowledge of past anti–Semitic tragedies for the enlightenment of current and future generations. Influenced by Hasidic tales of mysticism, Wiesel shows that even—or particularly—blind people may serve as witnesses of the past. Shlomo in *A Beggar in Jerusalem*, set during and shortly after the Six-Day War of June 5–10, 1967, remembers being present during the crucifixion of Jesus Christ and informing the great martyr that His death would result in tremendous suffering (primarily the Holocaust) for the Jewish people at the hands of His followers. In *The Forgotten*, Ephraim cries so hard about the destruction and mass murders in his village during the Holocaust that his tears literally and permanently blind him. Like the ancient Greek mythological character Tiresias, the ocular blindness of Shlomo and Ephraim renders them capable of supernatural visions and superhuman powers. One form of vision is shut down yet replaced by another. In the Hasidic tradition, Shlomo and Ephraim become receptacles, maintainers, and storytellers of Jewish history—envisioning and preserving the past at the expense of their eyesight while teaching moral lessons to other characters and the readers. Wiesel's focus on blindness serves as a metaphor of the moral blindness of passive bystanders who did nothing to save the innocent victims and the moral blindness of the remorseless perpetrators. The Jews suffering from physical blindness function as human receptacles that store information so horrifying that it literally blinds them, while perhaps even paying homage to the memory of the horrific suffering of victims of Nazi doctor Josef Mengele's heterochromia iridis experiments in Auschwitz, which often led to permanent physical blindness.

II. A Beggar in Jerusalem

In *A Beggar in Jerusalem*, one of the first characters to whom the narrator, David, introduces the reader is the old Hasid Shlomo, a blind seer and visionary who, along with other beggars and madmen, haunts the historic Western (Wailing) Wall (*Kotel HaMaaravi*) in Jerusalem daily after Israel's magnificent triumph over their enemies in the Six-Day War. The desire never to experience the horrors and displacement of the Holocaust again renders the Israeli armed forces determined to emerge victorious in this war; the failure and suffering of the past leads, in part, to the success of the present. Jerusalem and the Western Wall obviously hold great significance to the Jewish people, for they represent the people's devotion to God and God's presence and to the Lord's covenant with them. Shlomo sits daily at the Western Wall, a "symbol of the past, present, and future ... where all aspects of creation are gathered together, and where at midnight the *Shehina* [*Shechinah*], the female aspect of the Godhead representing God's presence, comes to mourn, along with the beggars, mystics, and madmen, who sit before it, the destruction of the Temple."[2] Writing about the mystical effect that Jerusalem has upon him, Wiesel said:

> I love to linger in this city where I feel close to my ancestors, and, through them, to all beings who share my faith in mankind ... the Old City where, since the destruction of the Temple, there has always been a man, or a child, to lament the tragedies of the Jewish people, and when there was no one, the Shekhina—the devine [sic] presence—herself would appear among the ruins to repel forgetfulness with her tears.... So we do not inhabit Jerusalem: Jerusalem inhabits us.[3]

Additionally, in *A Beggar in Jerusalem*, the rabbi who taught David's mother mentions that his father reminded him that as a holy man, he represents "the Wailing Wall, which, according to our sages, protects the gate of heaven."[4] Therefore, Jerusalem is not merely the setting of Wiesel's novel. Jerusalem exists in the present but has an enormously rich historical past. It is more like a mystical, spiritual essence within the soul of the characters, particularly the beggars like Shlomo. As the blind beggar sits by the Wailing Wall, the spirits of "all the dead of the town, all the dead towns of the cemetery that was Europe" sit next to him, and "their eyes are eternity and its night."⁵ Wiesel suggests that the souls of the six million Jews who died during the Holocaust live on by the Wall, and they can see through the dead eyes of Shlomo.

Historically, after the Six-Day War, Wiesel himself, like his character Shlomo, felt the instinctive need to venture to the Western Wall in order to be closer to God and embrace his faith and the rich Jewish history the wall represents. Shlomo, the blind beggar, resembles Wiesel himself in being a storyteller, who shares his wisdom with his audience. Shlomo seems to possess a mystical quality because he lives in the present and the distant historical past: Focusing on Shlomo's blindness, the narrator asks the reader, "Do his eyes disturb you? They are not his, and he doesn't know it.... [He] lived a day before, a century before: he no longer remembers. For him, you see, time has no meaning."⁶ God took his eyes but provided him with memory. Shlomo claims to the other beggars that he remembers meeting and speaking with Jesus Christ almost two thousand years before on the day in which the latter was crucified. Shlomo was not always a blind man and served as an eyewitness to the crucifixion. As the crucifixion began, the blind visionary, who has searched at least two thousand years for the Messiah (*Mashiach*), saw Jesus with his own eyes and told the dying priest he was disappointed in him: "Poor man. I saw him the day he was crucified. 'It is not you I shall be waiting for....'"⁷ After seeing Christ, Shlomo determines that this great man of peace is in fact not the Messiah. The blind seer expects the *Mashiach* to lead the Israelites into the Promised Land permanently as Hebrew prayer and rituals are reestablished, as the Old Testament (*Nevi'im*) prophesizes. God promises Jeremiah that the days are coming ... when I will restore the fortunes of My people Israel and Judah.... I will bring them back to the land that I gave their fathers, and they shall possess it.... I will raise up a true branch of David's line, and he shall do what is just and right in the land.... Nor shall there ever be an end to the line of the Levitical priests before Me, of those who present burnt offerings and turn the meal offering to smoke and perform sacrifices.⁸

All the beggars are excited when Israel retakes the Old City of Jerusalem during the Six-Day War, except for Shlomo because the Messiah is still nowhere to be seen (or found, since Shlomo is now blind).

Finding the Messiah is the blind man's goal because the *Mashiach* functions as the caretaker of collective Jewish pain and memory and a bridge to a promised, spiritual, and holy covenant with God in Jerusalem. Twenty centuries after meeting Christ and watching Him die, the seer still searches every day for the Messiah. In the Book of Isaiah, God describes the Messiah as:

> My servant, whom I uphold,
> My chosen one, in whom I delight.
> I have put My spirit upon him,
> He shall teach the true way to the nations.⁹

The blind man can still use his other senses, which have been heightened upon the loss of his eyesight, to find the Messiah. Yet he cannot rest or die until he finds Him, when he will no longer endure the burden of preserving the history of inhumane atrocities committed against Jews since the death of Christ. The Messiah will "teach the true way to the nations" so that Shlomo will no longer be needed and the blind seer can, after two thousand years, finally be at peace.

Shlomo informs Jesus, whom he considers a noble but misguided man, that He is not dying for a worthwhile purpose because "no death is worthy of being invoked or sanctified. All life is sacred, irreplaceable."¹⁰ Because all life is precious, Shlomo cannot understand why the prophet willingly dies. Shlomo laments future pogroms, the Holocaust, and other bloody atrocities occurring centuries after Jesus' death, resulting in the loss of millions of Jewish lives—horrific murders committed because of anti–Semitic hatred deriving from the crucifixion and the subsequent false narrative of Jews as Christ-killers. Jewish enemies employed (and still use) as an excuse to slay Jews. Shlomo informs Jesus that the martyr is blind to the suffering that will ensue from His crucifixion: "'You think you are suffering for my sake and for my brothers, yet we [Jews] are the ones who will be made to suffer for you, because of you."¹¹ Initially, Jesus blindly refuses to accept Shlomo's words because He intends for his crucifixion to lead to redemption, not genocide. The blind Hasid then informs the other beggars sitting by the Western Wall that he created a visual picture for Christ because although Jesus lacked the vision to see into the future, he possessed physical sight: "I painted a *picture* of the future which made him *see* the innumerable victims persecuted and crushed under the sign of his law. Thereupon he burst into *tears* of despair. 'No, no! ... This is not how I *foresee* the reign of my spirit! I want my heritage to be a gift of compassion and hope, not a punishment in blood...!'"¹² Shlomo emphasizes words that allude to ocular vision and the eyes to show, by contrast, that Jesus lacks vision into the future and thus must be told of the bloody consequences of His death. Shlomo focuses on Christ's visual sense because the martyr is actually blind to the ramifications of the crucifixion, being unable to envision that prejudiced opportunists will subsequently exploit His death as an excuse for their bigotry and senseless violence.

Shortly after Shlomo sees into the future and describes it to Jesus, he loses his eyesight and becomes a true visionary who will serve as a blind witness to Jewish suffering and mass murder. Wiesel's focus on words pertaining to the eyes emphasizes his belief in his novels that human beings can have ocular sight but be blind in other ways. Contrariwise, during the course of Wiesel's novel, Shlomo is blind but is a mystical seer who sees into the past, present, and future. He also seems to be immortal because he has lived for centuries and cannot die until he finds the Messiah. Shlomo will have to locate Him without physical sight because he is a visionary.

Like Wiesel himself, Shlomo is also a storyteller. In fact, the novel is very much about the art of storytelling. Wiesel considers *A Beggar in Jerusalem* to be not a book but rather "a *récit*, a multilevel, complicated text founded upon shrift, stories, and parables."[13] Storytelling is integral to the Hasidic tradition, and Shlomo embodies it with his relation of historical events. Each chapter, told by David, brings together the past and the present while serving as a witness to Jewish victimization from Masada to the Holocaust and showing how such suffering affected Jewish attitudes toward the current struggle, the Six-Day War. David, the narrator and protagonist, is a Holocaust survivor who goes mad from survivor guilt (rendering him suicidal) but still fights in the Six-Day War. David tells the reader of his meeting with a madman in a mental institution who thinks he is insane because he has gone blind. After the Holocaust, the man thought he had lost his eyesight because he no longer could see the inhabitants of his village. It was easier for him to convince himself that he had gone blind and insane than to accept that the Nazis had murdered all his friends, relatives, and acquaintances. David also tells blind Shlomo's visions of past Jewish suffering to the reader. Wiesel stresses in *Beggar in Jerusalem* that the past is never truly gone, and that Jews cannot comprehend the impact of the Six-Day War without the underlying memory of the Holocaust and the six million Jews who perished. Wiesel's mystical visionaries are often blind, blinded by the pain and suffering they have witnessed and must convey to the present generation. The novelist indicates that even blind Hasidic beggars can serve as eyewitnesses because they are divinely inspired.

III. The Forgotten

In his novels, Wiesel employs Hasidic mysticism to convey the supernatural concept that blindness is actually a form of sight but in a spiritual and visionary way, as opposed to in a physical manner. In *The Forgotten*, the character Ephraim resembles Shlomo from *A Beggar in Jerusalem* in being a blind visionary who serves as a divinely inspired witness to the Holocaust. The elderly Ephraim and his roommate Herschel the gravedigger are the last two remaining Jews in the Romanian town of Feherfalu that was liquated by the Nazis during the Shoah.[14] Herschel the gravedigger informs Malkiel that Ephraim began crying when the war began in 1939 and wept incessantly until the Nazis arrived in their village in 1944. When Herschel asked Ephraim how it was possible for a human being to cry for five consecutive years, the caretaker answered that even when the gates to Heaven are closed, "'the gate of tears remains open.... [Consequently, Ephraim's eyesight] disappeared altogether the day the Germans arrived.'"[15]

Ephraim compares himself to Hasidic rabbi Yaakov Yitzchak HaLevi Horowitz, the Seer of Lublin, who also had supernatural visionary skills. Ephraim prays to God that although He took his sight, as he did that of Horowitz, "do not touch my memory.... I cling to my memory because it is my life."[16] When Malkiel ventures to his grandfather's grave in the old Jewish cemetery to pay his respects and then visits Herschel's room, "Ephraim raised his dead eyes to the visitor."[17] Ephraim demands to see Malkiel (whose father survived the Shoah but whose grandfather was the Feherfalu ghetto leader martyred during the Holocaust), even though the visionary clearly has no sight. Ephraim explains to Malkiel, "'Men are wrong to think that the blind cannot see. The truth is that they see, but differently.'"[18] The blind visionary's touch of the contours of Malkiel's face enables him to visualize him and determine correctly that his father and grandfather lived in Feherfalu; the touch is not physical but rather mystical, with supernatural help. He touches Malkiel's face with hands and informs him, "'I see with my hands. In your face I find your father again. And his father again. One must know how to read a face. Only a blind man truly knows.'"[19] He confirms that Malkiel is indeed related to the Holocaust victims whose fate he maintains in his memory. Ephraim admits to Malkiel that he had witnessed all of the atrocities that his eyes and mind could handle: "'I knew I'd witness more bloody events. I knew my memory would not be able to hold them all. So to recall all that I saw and heard in Poland, I had to cease seeing.'"[20] Ephraim's spiritual vision and need to store the memory of atrocities costs him his eyesight but allows him to bear witness to Malkiel and anyone else whom he encounters.

Malkiel likes Ephraim because the young visitor "had always been fond of old men and blind men,"[21] but also because Ephraim remembers Malkiel's father and grandfather. Malkiel is still nonplussed that Ephraim is a blind caretaker, not comprehending fully that the old man is a mystical caretaker of memory, which occurred as he became blind. In his capacity as a blind seer, Ephraim serves as a caretaker of "'what history rejects, what memory denies. The smile of a starving child, the tears of its dying mother, the silent prayers of the condemned man and the cries of his friend: I ...

preserve them. In this city, I am memory.'"²² Herschel personally dug the graves of all the Holocaust victims in Feherfalu, and the very rare visitors can see the headstones, but the headstones cannot tell the story of the horrors and bloodshed that occurred. Only Ephraim can do that. God has taken away his sight but compensated by giving his life more meaning as he stores up the past so that the Holocaust victims murdered by the Nazi soldiers in Feherfalu do not die in vain and fade forever into oblivion. He serves a function similar to that of Shlomo in *A Beggar in Jerusalem*.

IV. Josef Mengele and Heterochromia Iris Experiments

There were many Jews in Auschwitz-Birkenau who, like Shlomo the beggar and Ephraim the seer, were physically blind. However, these Jews became blind at the hands of sadistic Nazi medical doctors such as Josef Mengele. The Nazis themselves were blind to the suffering that they inflicted upon their Jewish victims because they dehumanized them. Nazi propagandist Ernst Hiemer, for instance, wrote in a popular children's book, "Tapeworm and Jew are parasites of the worst kind. We want their elimination. We want to become healthy and strong again. Then only one thing will help: Their extermination."²³ It was easier to experiment on and murder victims when they did not consider them human beings, for they could commit evil without experiencing pangs of conscience or remorse. Auschwitz survivor Vera Kriegel remembers Mengele "sending people with a flick of his finger either in one direction, to instant death in the crematorium, or in the other, to the labour camp. 'Children were having their heads beaten in like poultry by SS men with their gun butts,' she recalled, 'and some were being thrown into a smoking pit…. I thought that this was some sort of animal kingdom or perhaps I was already in Hell.'"²⁴ Kriegel's words are significant because Mengele's ability to decide the fate of countless thousands of human lives with a mere and arbitrary "flick of his finger" demonstrated his sadistic tendencies and undeniable indifference to people's lives and suffering. Kriegel's comparison of the Nazis beating up Jews before killing them to clubbing poultry and an animal kingdom is apropos because it reflects Nazi cruelty and dehumanization of their victims, as if they are mere disposable farm animals, before slaying them. Robert Jay Lifton and Eric Markusen contend that in order to commit and justify their atrocities against Jews, Nazi doctors and guards had to engage in dissociation (separating from one's own sense of identity), doubling (separating one's self into two selves), and disavowal (denying responsibility) in order to act cruelly, murdering Jews and experimenting on them during the day but returning to their families and acting kindly at night:

Through an extraordinary "dissociation," a Nazi doctor could live simultaneously as a man active in mass killing and an ordinary human being.... The doubling process was enhanced by ... a doctor's sense of being able to make 'humane' contributions in a difficult situation, and his feeling that what one did in Auschwitz as 'a separate planet' did not count."[25] The dissociation, doubling, and disavowal are significant to this essay's argument partly because the perpetrators had to blind themselves to their actions. They blinded or shielded their actions from themselves psychologically, as if someone outside of themselves had committed them.

Scientists conduct vivisectionist experiments on lab rats and vermin because they fail to consider the feelings of—or value—their subjects; they do not concern themselves with the pain and fate of the lab animals because they recognize that the subjects are clearly of an inferior, subhuman species. During the Holocaust, Nazi scientists similarly chose not to distinguish between Jews and lab animals. It is noteworthy that IG Farben/Degesch's Zyklon B hydrogen cyanide that the Nazis employed in the gas chambers to kill their Jewish victims was invented not to murder innocent people but rather as a pesticide to kill rats, vermin, and bugs. Furthermore, IG Farben/Degesch added the eye irritants chloropicrin and cyanogen chloride to the Zyklon B they sent to the Nazi death camps, which blinded the Jewish victims as they died from the poisonous gas.[26] It was not enough for the Nazis to murder their victims in Auschwitz-Birkenau: they wanted to blind them in the process.

In addition to the eye irritants that blinded victims as they perished in the gas chambers. Josef Mengele conducted many heterochromia iridis experiments in Auschwitz on Jewish children. Heterochromia involves a person who has two eyes that are not the same color. Mengele and countless other Nazis were morally and psychologically blind to the suffering of the Jews they destroyed violently and remorselessly. Such Nazis suffered, perhaps, from deindividuation and what the American Psychological Association calls Antisocial Personality Disorder. Their behavior exhibited a blindness "for and violation of the rights of others... [and a] [l]ack of remorse, as indicated by being indifferent to or rationalizing having hurt, mistreated, or stolen from another."[27]

After examining the eyes of prisoners with heterochromia iridis, Mengele "killed [them] by phenol injection."[28] Robert Jay Lifton notes that Mengele continually sent eyes of inmates with heterochromia to the Berlin Institute, especially if the prisoners had one blue eye and one brown eye Mengele conducted "experiments" on Jewish children and injured their eyes in a futile but sadistic attempt to change eye color. Noticing that some Jewish children had blond hair, which was considered desirable by "Aryan" standards, but had brown eyes, he attempted to make their eyes blue, conforming to the "Aryan" myth of ideal looks. Mengele was apparently willing to blind these prisoners in an effort to transform not only their physical appearance but also, perhaps, their genetic characteristics from being inherited to being acquired through phenol injections. Martin Gilbert writes that Vera Kriegel and her twin sister Olga survived Birkenau because they were twins, and Mengele was fascinated that they had brown eyes, yet their mother's eyes were blue. Mengele "'injected our eyes with liquid that burnt.'"[29] The doctor obviously was trying to supersede genetics by transforming their eye color to blue, even if it meant blinding them in the process. While in an experimentation room in Auschwitz, Vera noticed a large "collection of human eyes being used in experiments,"[30] which must have been the same heterochromia iridis experiments involving her, her mother, and her sister. This terrified Vera, who still remembered the horrific sight in 1985, forty years later, even though she was only five years old at the time. Dr. Abraham C., who worked in Auschwitz, noted that "Mengele actually injected methylene blue into their eyes, causing severe pain and inflammation, but 'their eyes of course did not change.'"[31] Any doctor or medical student with training would know that the injections would blind or at least seriously inflame the eyes of the prisoners but could not, of course, alter someone's genetic makeup. Therefore, one has to wonder if Mengele blinded and tortured his "patients" in a futile and misguided pursuit for scientific knowledge to benefit the Fatherland or rather for sadistic pleasure. Robert Jay Lifton's feelings are ambivalent, for "the methylene blue injections are of a different order, not in their cruelty (which was usual), but in their extraordinary scientific naïveté— or, one might more accurately say, their scientific corruption."[32] Helena Kubicka notes that evidence clearly supports the fact "that Mengele performed ghastly experiments on children for no medical purpose."[33] It is worth noting that when Mengele informed Dr. Alexander O. that he was missing the two eyes from a dead heterochromia iridis prisoner and the doctor was scared that Mengele would punish him for not locating them, he simply extracted one blue eye from a dead prisoner and one brown eye from a different deceased man and placed them in a jar with preservatives for Mengele. Mengele never noticed the difference.[34] This example supports Kubicka's statement.

V. Conclusion

Shlomo and Ephraim are madmen. As Wiesel emphasizes in both books, madmen hold a highly respected place in Hasidic tradition. Colin Davis notes that Wiesel's blind madmen are mad in a mystical, not a clinical, sense, and their "madness may be holy . . [and] may represent an access to truth beyond the constraints of ordinary discourse."[35] Blind madmen such as Shlomo and Ephraim are unique because the horrors they have witnessed have altered them forever since "truth is not to be found in the sanities of the rational world; more bleakly, Wiesel frequently implies that our rationality is itself insane, so that madness is a sane reaction to a world in which all decency has been overturned."[36] As Wiesel stresses in both novels, madness is inevitable after witnessing the Holocaust, a horrific event that extends beyond the realm of reality and sense. After having witnessed so much genocide, perhaps it is better not to have sight. How can human beings act so cruelly and commit unspeakable and incomprehensible atrocities, such as the ones endured by the victims of Josef Mengele? Considering the torture inflicted upon innocent children to which Shlomo and Ephraim serve as eyewitnesses, is it any wonder that they become madmen? Mengele took away the eyesight of some of his victims, but blind witnesses such as Shlomo and Ephraim bear witness of these atrocities for future generations, at the expense of their sanity, so that their pain will never be forgotten.

Notes

1. First published in French as *Le mendicant de Jérusalem* in 1968.
2. Simon P. Sibelman, *Silence in the Novels of Elie Wiesel* (New York: St. Martin's Press, 1995), 106.
3. Elie Wiesel, "The Jerusalem of David," *The New York Times*, April 18, 1982, accessed June 1, 2020, https://www.nytimes.com/1982/04/18/travel/the-jerusalem-of-david.html.
4. Elie Wiesel, *A Beggar in Jerusalem*, trans. Lily Edelman and Elie Wiesel (New York: Schocken Books, 1970), 68.
5. Wiesel, *Beggar in Jerusalem*, 201.
6. Wiesel, *Beggar in Jerusalem*, 4.
7. Wiesel, *Beggar in Jerusalem*, 56.
8. Adele Berlin and Marc Zvi Brettler, eds., *The Jewish Study Bible*, 2nd ed. (Oxford: Oxford University Press, 2014), Jeremiah 30: 2–3, 33:15, 33:18. According to the New Testament, Jesus is a descendant of David, but Shlomo believes that He is not the Messiah.
9. Berlin and Brettler, eds., *The Jewish Study Bible*, Isaiah 42:1.
10. Wiesel, *Beggar in Jerusalem*, 56.
11. Wiesel, *Beggar in Jerusalem*, 56.
12. Wiesel, *Beggar in Jerusalem*, 56–57, my italics.
13. Sibelman, *Silence in the Novels of Elie Wiesel*, 104.
14. Feherfalu is an actual city, currently located in Hungary but inside Romania in the novel. This peaceful village in the Carpathian Mountains should remind readers of Wiesel's hometown of Sighet, Romania, also located in the Carpathian Mountains. Many of Wiesel's novels, including both *A Beggar in Jerusalem* and *The Forgotten*, contain autobiographical elements. For example, in *The Forgotten*, the lovely village of Feherfalu and its heartbreaking destruction at the hands of the Nazis allow Wiesel to reflect upon and teach his readers about the peaceful, charming, and idyllic village and childhood that was destroyed forever. One example of the autobiographical nature of *A Beggar in Jerusalem* occurs when David, shortly before the Nazis invade their village, begs his father to leave

the town and emigrate to Palestine, but his father refuses, leading to tragedy. A strikingly similar conversation occurs in Wiesel's memoir, *Night*.

15. Elie Wiesel, *The Forgotten*, trans. Stephen Becker (New York: Schocken Books, 1992), 256.
16. Wiesel, *Forgotten*, 254.
17. Wiesel, *Forgotten*, 256
18. Wiesel, *Forgotten*, 255.
19. Wiesel, *Forgotten*, 255.
20. Wiesel, *Forgotten*, 255.
21. Wiesel, *Forgotten*, 255.
22. Wiesel, *Forgotten*, 255.
23. Ernst Hiemer, *Der Pudelmopsdackelpinscher und andere besinnliche Erzahlungen* (*The Poodle-Pug-Dachshund-Pinscher and other contemplative stories*) (Nuremberg: Der Stürmer-Buchverlag,1940), quoted in Lisa Pine, *Education in Nazi Germany* (Oxford: Berg, 2010), 58.
24. Martin Gilbert, *The Holocaust: A History of the Jews of Europe during the Second World War* (New York: Henry Holt, 1987), 687.
25. Robert Jay Lifton and Eric Markusen, *The Genocidal Mentality: Nazi Holocaust and Nuclear Threat* (New York: Basic Books, 1990), 196–97.
26. Scott Christianson, *The Last Gasp: The Rise and Fall of the American Gas Chamber* (Berkeley: University of California Press, 2010), 95.
27. American Psychiatric Association, *Diagnostic and Statistical Manual of Mental Disorders (DSM-5)*, 5th ed (Washington, DC: American Psychiatric Publishing, 2013), 659.
28. Robert Jay Lifton, *The Nazi Doctors: Medical Killing and the Psychology of Genocide* (New York: Basic Books, 1986), 361.
29. Gilbert, *The Holocaust* 687.
30. Gilbert, *The Holocaust* 687.
31. Gilbert, *The Holocaust* 362
32. Gilbert, *The Holocaust* 362–63.
33. Helena Kubicka, "The Crimes of Josef Mengele," in *Anatomy of the Auschwitz Death Camp*, eds. Yisrael Gutman and Michael Berenbaum (Bloomington: Indiana University Press; Washington, D.C.: United States Holocaust Memorial Museum, 1994), 324.
34. Kubicka, "The Crimes of Josef Mengele," 362.
35. Colin Davis, *Elie Wiesel's Secretive Texts* (Gainesville: University Press of Florida, 1994), 104.
36. Colin Davis, *Elie Wiesel's Secretive Texts*, 104.

In Darkness and Light
The Meanings of Blindness in the West
Brenda S. Gardenour Walter

Blindness and sightedness, darkness and light, are two sides of a single coin, both of which are central to human experience. This essay serves as a brief introduction to the multivalent meanings of blindness in western history from the first human civilizations through postmodernity. In ancient Egyptian and Mesopotamian texts, as well as in the Hebrew Bible, blindness is associated with corporal punishment and ritual impurity. Ancient Greek literature such as Sophocles' *Oedipus Rex* reveals a belief that some cases of blindness are a form of divine punishment entailing the gift of second sight. While ancient texts depict blindness as a cultural marker for alterity, they do not speak to the lived experiences of blind individuals during these periods. Medieval Christian sources elaborate on the complex and often contradictory meanings of blindness. In miracle tales, the inability to see out of one or both eyes is correlated with disbelief and sinfulness; in the Christian mystical tradition, however, the loss of carnal sight facilitates divine illumination. Beyond metaphor, the itinerant blind in medieval society were both derided and seen as worthy of charity, the latter made manifest in the founding of the first hospital for the blind by King Louis IX.

The secular debates of the Enlightenment further complicated cultural perceptions of blindness. Rationalists such as Descartes argued that vision was imprinted on the mind at birth, therefore the blind could still "see" through reason. Empiricists such as Diderot, on the other hand, argued that the idea of innate knowledge was fantasy and that humans learned about the world through sensory input, of which sight was only one option. Diderot held that the blind were equal to the sighted in their ability to learn about the physical world and function in society. Throughout the early modern and modern periods, the demystification of blindness and increasing secularization facilitated the founding of schools for the blind. As blind culture developed its own identity, sighted culture continued in its ocularcentrism, which privileges vision over other senses as a primary epistemology. This hegemony of the eye has been countered by postmodernist thinkers, who argue that the sighted and the very act of seeing should not be privileged, nor should blindness be defined or controlled by the sighted. Through a postmodernist lens, blindness is neither a disability nor a medical condition, but an existential experience—a unique way of being and knowing—different from but as valuable as that of the sighted.

First Civilizations: Corruption and Punishment

In Ancient Egypt, blindness was equated with corruption, while sightedness was associated with wholeness. For example, the god Horus was blinded in one eye by his brother Seth in the form of a pig. Thoth restored Horus' corrupted vision by reassembling his eye, piece by piece. Horus' restored eye then became a symbol for wholeness, "luminous and sound," and its discrete parts became a shorthand for doctors measuring the fractions of a whole.[1,2]

In Ancient Egypt, human blindness might be caused by human agency, such as a curse sent by an enemy, or divine wrath, a form of punishment for some transgression. These forms of blindness required the ministrations of a priest-healer who could perform the appropriate rituals, prescribe magical formulae, and construct appropriate amulets for redemption and future protection.[3] Blindness was also the result of natural causes including wounding, cataracts due to over-exposure to the sun, and ophthalmia, all of which are mentioned in the *Ebers Papyrus*, a medical text dating from the 16th century BCE. Doctors treated blindness with a mixture of incantations and salves, many of which included honey and garlic, both of which have anti-bacterial properties.[4] Beyond the rituals and recipes recorded on temple walls and in medical papyri, we have little evidence of the efficacy of priests and doctors—who were often the same individuals—in bringing their patients out of the corruption of darkness and into the wholeness of light.

The equation of blindness with corruption and punishment is likewise threaded through the cultures of Ancient Mesopotamia. In Sumerian mythology, Enki, the god of water, creates perfect human beings out of clay. The goddess Nimnah challenges him to a contest by creating deformed or incomplete human beings that Enki must find a purpose for in human society. When Nimnah creates a blind man, Enki gives him inner sight and makes him a musician in service to the king.[5,6]

While this myth depicts the blind as possessing divine talents, more quotidian sources depict the blind as imperfect and impure. The blind, for example, were not allowed to participate in the ritual sacrifices inherent to Mesopotamian culture. Because blindness carried the stigma of exclusion, blinding became an effective form of retribution. In Sumeria and Babylon, blinding was a form of corporal punishment meted out by the law. The Law Code of Hammurabi operates on the idea of *lex talionis*, or an eye for an eye. Code 218 stipulates that a physician who blinds the eye of a free man during surgery will have his hands cut off. Code 220 states that if a physician operates on a slave and blinds him in one eye, he must compensate the owner for half of the slave's value. These codes reflect the value of sightedness and its correlation with one's worth in Mesopotamian society. In the case of a child who dishonors his parents or covets their property, the code stipulates that he or she be blinded completely, a punishment that would render the convict as worthless and excluded from civic life. Whether blinded intentionally or accidentally through divine, natural, or human agency, the blind were not without recourse. They might seek out the help of a priest-healer, or *ashipu*, who could perform rituals; they might also consult physicians, or *asu*, who could recommend regimens and prescribe medicinal ointments to ease their suffering.[7] The state provided them with grain rations for their survival and in some regions such as Sumeria there existed charitable institutions for destitute women, children, and the blind—three demographics often bound together.[8]

Emerging from within Mesopotamian culture, the ancient Hebrews shared the construction of blindness is a sign of punishment and exclusion. As in Egypt and Mesopotamia, blindness might come from divine sources. In the Hebrew Bible, Genesis recounts the rescue of Lot from the Sodomites. When an angry mob demands an audience with the angels that Lot is protecting, they are "struck with blindness" so that Lot and his family might escape (Genesis 19:11). Similarly, the Prophet Elisha calls on God for protection from his Syrian assailants: "Smite this people, I pray thee, with blindness. And He [God] smote them with blindness according to the world of Elisha" (2 Kings 6:18). Just as God and his messengers blinded those who threatened his chosen ones, so too did warriors blind their enemies after victory in battle. When the Philistines finally captured Samson, for example, they "gouged out his eyes" and "bound him with bronze fetters." To be blinded by your victor was the "the lowest, most offensive degradation that could be inflicted upon man" (Barasch 2001, 14). Hebrew Bible associates blindness not only with defeat, but also with ritual impurity and exclusion. As in Mesopotamian culture, the blind were seen as blemished and therefore banned from participating in ritual sacrifices at temple. That which came before the presence of God was expected to be perfect, a reflection of the divine (Barasch 2001, 16). This imperfection, however, did not mean that that blind were abandoned by God. Consider Samson who, though blind, regrew his hair, regained his strength, and exacted revenge on the Philistines. Or Leviticus, which warns that no one should "put a stumbling block before the blind, but shalt fear thy God." While blindness was a mark of exclusion, the blind themselves were also deserving of compassion. In their perceived incompleteness, the blind were living testaments to the power of a God—imagined as sighted and therefore whole—who created both light and darkness at the beginning of time.

Ancient Greece

In Ancient Greece, the multivalent causes and meanings of blindness were guided by a bifurcated cosmology, one that placed earthly and human imperfection below the moon and divine perfection in the ethereal realms above it. In the earthly realm, acute causes of blindness included accidental injury, wounding in war, and corporal punishment. Blindness might likewise be caused by medical conditions. For example, in Aphorism 56, Hippocrates claims that those with an abundance of black bile, or "melancholic affections," were prone to "apoplexy," "convulsions," or "blindness." The ancient Greeks understood that blindness was sometimes hereditary, and that the son of a blind man ran an increased risk of losing his sight. In all of these contexts, physicians recognized blindness as incurable and, as such, beyond the purview of rational medicine. This did not stop sufferers from seeking cure at Asclepian temples, where ritual offerings, incubation, and the presence of sacred snakes might facilitate divine healing.[9,10]

Divine causes for blindness centered on punishment for the transgression of boundaries, including incest and intrusion on the secrets of the gods. The most famous examples of blindness as divine retribution come from Sophocles' play, *Oedipus the King*. Oedipus is guided by divine fate to marry his own mother and have children by her. Oedipus is blind to his transgression; early on, he consults the blind seer, Teiresias, who informs him that "you have sight but cannot see what trouble you are in" (Lines 412–13). When his eyes are finally opened and the truth of his marriage is revealed, he blinds himself. In Teiresias, we have another example of blindness caused by divine agency. He not only glimpsed the naked body of the goddess, Athena, but also threatened to expose her secrets to other humans. In retaliation, Athena blinded him, cursing him to perpetual darkness. As compensation, she later "cleansed his ears" and gave him the gift of augury by birdsong as well as that of inner vision, or second sight.[11,12]

In his blindness, Teiresias could see what the sighted could not. The curse of blindness and the gift of second sight were passed down through Teiresias to his granddaughter Mopsus, who was sired by Apollo.

In Ancient Greece, the correlations between physical blindness and spiritual "insight into supernatural secrets" coalesced in the trope of the blind oracle.[13] The cultural belief that the blind have enhanced intellectual capacities is attested to by Aristotle. In *On Sense and the Sensible*, he writes that "rational discourse" is verbal and "each word is a thought symbol." Since the blind can hear, "they are more intelligent than the deaf and dumb" (Book 1:1). Aristotle's *Eudemian Ethics* states that "the blind remember better, being released from having their faculty of memory engaged with objects of sight" (1248b:1). Sanctioned by divine authority, this already heightened ability to conceptualize abstract truths beyond the corrupt earthly realm made the blind seer a powerful character, one who could bridge the cosmic gulf between humans and gods. Much like Plato's Philosopher King, the blind seer was not bound to a cave of shadows but saw the pure light of eternal truth emanating from far beyond the moon.

The Medieval Christian West

The early medieval West inherited the bifurcated cosmology of the Greeks. It was first transmitted through textual remnants of Roman natural philosophy, including Pliny's *Natural History*, as well as through the Hellenized writings of the Church Fathers.[14] In the 12th century, the translation movement introduced medieval intellectuals to a broader selection of ancient scientific texts. Scholars were most interested in treatises of natural philosophy, astronomy, and medicine—all of which focused on the earthly world below the moon. These texts fueled the growth of burgeoning universities and facilitated the development of Europe's first medical schools. In theory and practice, medieval physicians focused on the physical causes of blindness, or *caecitate*. These included injury, cataracts, humoral imbalance, and conditions such as leprosy. While some conditions might be improved through surgical or therapeutic intervention, most cases of complete blindness—especially blindness from birth—remained incurable.[15]

In medieval society, blindness was not only a medical condition grounded in natural causes, but also a cultural construct with spiritual and religious implications. Blindness was often associated with disbelief. Take for example the New Testament story of Saul, a Jew sent to persecute Christians. While on the road to Damascus, Saul was blinded by the Christian God (Acts 9: 1–19). Sighted, Saul was blind to Christian truth;

blinded, he was illuminated by divine authority and converted to Christianity. Medieval Christian sources often ascribed spiritual blindness to heresy and, more frequently, Judaism.[16] From the late-Carolingian period forward, churches often included the statues of *Synagoga* and *Ecclesia*. The female embodiment of Judaism, *Synagoga* wears a blindfold; her counterpart *Ecclesia*, however, is fully sighted.[17] In miracle tales, the blindness of disbelief was often intertwined with sinfulness. For example, Saint Foy blinded a knight named Reinfroi for stealing from the Church, then restored his sight after he repented and made pilgrimage to her shrine.[18] In another tale, a man named Guibert had his eyes gouged out by a priest "as treasonous as a Jew."[19] Taking pity on Guibert, Saint Foy restored his eyes while he incubated near her relics. When Guibert fell into sin after his miraculous healing, Foy punished him with blindness; after his repentance, he was once again made whole. Miracles featuring the restoration of sight to the incurable blind reinforced the redemptive power of Christianity. The blind beggar served a similar didactic purpose. Wandering the streets and subsisting on alms, the itinerant blind were at once stigmatized and glorified.[20] In the context of Christian theology, the blind beggar not only contributed to the collective penance of the Christian body as a whole, but also provided an opportunity for individual Christians to give to them in charity, thus reducing their debt of sins.[21] That the blind were deserving of charity is evidenced in the founding of the Quinze-Vingts hospital for the blind by King Louis in 1260.[22,23]

Medieval meanings of blindness were multivalent and often contradictory. Drawing from Greek tradition through Pseudo-Dionysus, medieval mystics saw blindness not as a source of corruption but as a path to inner vision and ecstatic union. The physical body and the five outer senses, including sight, were believed to be subordinate to the immaterial body—the mind and soul—and the five inner senses. Through prayer and asceticism, the mystic deadened the body and relinquished lust and other visual distractions associated with the outer senses. In becoming blind to the carnal world, the mystic focused their inner sight on the divine realms beyond the moon. Through God's grace, the mystic might see Christ through a "spiritual vision, a 'vision' autonomous of the physical senses."[24] For mystics, then, the eyes of the head were far less important than the eyes of the heart.

Toward Modernity and Beyond

Tension between the inner senses and the outer, between knowing and seeing, and the ability of each to discern truth persisted throughout the early modern period. In the 16th century, artists such as Carracci continued to paint the blind as representations of the *vita contemplativa*, a life of inner knowledge and revelation that privileged the inner senses. By the 17th century, philosophers began to wonder just what the inner life of the blind was like. In 1690, William Molyneaux proposed a problem to John Locke; should a man blind from birth suddenly recover his sight, would he recognize the world around him? Molyneaux's letter touched off an enduring debate on the nature of vision and its relationship to knowledge of the physical world.[25] For Rene Descartes, physical sensation was subordinated to reason, which was the highest faculty. He argued that humans are born with innate images, imprinted at birth; therefore, all thought was visual and could lead to rational truth. Diderot countered Descartes' rationalism, supporting instead a materialist and empiric stance. For Diderot, the human mind was a blank slate, and all knowledge came through sensory input. He did not privilege vision in cognition and argued that the blind could know the world through touch as well as the sighted. In his "Letter on the Blind for the Use of Those Who Can See," Diderot introduces the reader to two men, a vintner and a Cambridge-educated mathematician, both blind since birth, who are intelligent, self-sufficient, and "lacking" in nothing.[26] In his desire to "map and understand the world and the experience of the blind as blind," Diderot represents a shift towards blindness as a culture valid in its own right.[27,28] The long process of secularization and the concomitant disenchantment of blindness hinted at in Diderot ultimately facilitated the establishment of schools for the blind such as the Insitut National des Jeunes Aveugles, which was founded by Valentin Haüy in 1784. Haüy used raised dots to help his students read and write; this system was later modified by one of the Institute's alumni, Louis Braille, and is an international standard in blind education and communication to this day.

As blindness became a cultural identity—developed by the blind for the blind—the sighted continued in their ocularcentrism. For the sighted, "making the world visible" remained a "means to capture it as objects."[29] To see was to know, and to know was to own. This hegemony of the eye has persisted through modernity and dominated much of western culture, from science and consumerism to the visual arts. Juhani Pallasmaa discusses this phenomenon in his architectural treatise, *The Eyes of the Skin*.[30] Pallasmaa argues that modern architects have fallen out of touch with what it means to be fully human. Modern buildings cater strictly to visual aesthetics; as such, they are slaves to the eye. Walking through these structures with our eyes closed, as if blind, we feel nothing at best and alienated at worst. As a corrective, Pallasmaa advocates for an architecture that speaks to all of the human senses, both physical and spiritual. The eye, after all, is only one way to understand, to truly know the world. Pallasmaa is only one among many modern scholars, inspired in part by the work of postmodernists such as Foucault and Derrida, who reject the binaries of blind and sighted, darkness and light, which have dominated western discourse on the blind since antiquity. In recent decades, the discipline of Disability Studies has emerged as a voice for those once marked by alterity. Moving beyond categories and labels, these scholars express the multivalent meanings of blindness through the words and experiences of the visually impaired themselves—thus liberating a discourse long held captive by the sighted.

NOTES

1. Robert K. Ritner, "Daily Ritual of the Temple of Amun-Re at Karnak." In *Context of Scripture: Volume One*, edited by William W. Hallo (Leiden: Brill, 1997), 55.
2. J. Worth Estes, *The Medical Skills of Ancient Egypt* (Canton, MA: Science History Publications, 1993), 95–6.
3. John Nunn, *Ancient Egyptian Medicine* (Norman, OK: University of Oklahoma Press, 2002).
4. S. Ry. Andersen, "The Eye and Its Diseases in Ancient Egypt," *Acta Opthalmologica Scandinavica* 2009. 75: 338–344.
5. Jacob Klein, "Enki and Ninmah." In *Context of Scripture: Volume One*, edited by William W. Hallo (Leiden: Brill, 1989), 5–16-22.
6. Samuel Noah Kramer and John Maier. *Myths of Enki: The Crafty God* (New York: Oxford University Press, 1989).
7. Robert Biggs, "Medicine, Surgery, and Public Health in Ancient Mesopotamia." In *Civilizations of the Ancient Near East*, edited by Jack Sasson (New York: Charles Scribner's Sons, 1995).
8. Ray W. McAllister, *Theology of Blindness in the Hebrew Scriptures*. Dissertation. http://digitalcommons.andrews.edu/cgi/viewcontent.cgi?article=1088&context=dissertations; 2010, 41–2.
9. Emma Edelstein and Ludwig Edelstein, *Asclepius: Collection and Interpretation of the Testimonies* (Baltimore: Johns Hopkins Press, 1998).
10. Gerald Hart, *Asclepius, The God of Medicine* (London: Royal Society of Medicine Press, 2000).
11. Moishe Barasch, *Blindness: The History of a Mental Image in Western Thought*. (London: Routledge, 2001), 39.
12. Chad Hartsock, *Sight and Blindness in Luke-Acts: The Use of Physical Features in Characterization* (Leiden: Brill, 2008), 77–81.
13. Barasch, 31.
14. Edward Grant, *Planets, Stars, and Orbs: The Medieval Cosmos, 1200–1687* (Washington, D.C.: Catholic University Press, 1996).
15. Edward Wheatley, *Stumbling Blocks Before the Blind: Medieval Constructions of a Disability* (Ann Arbor: University of Michigan Press, 2010), 189.
16. Miri Rubin, *Gentile Tales: The Narrative Assault on Medieval Jews* (Philadelphia: University of Pennsylvania Press, 2004), 9–11.
17. Barasch, 81–2.
18. Sheingorn, 163–64.
19. Sheingorn, 44.
20. Zina Weygand, *The Blind in French Society from the Middle Ages to the Century of Louis Braille* (Stanford: Stanford University Press, 2009), 16.

21. James Brodman, *Charity and Religion in Medieval Europe* (Washington, DC: Catholic University of America, 2009).

22. Mark P. O'Toole, "Disability and the Suppression of Historical Identity: Rediscovering the Professional Backgrounds of the Blind Residents of the Hôpital des Quinze-Vingts." In *Disability in the Middle Ages: Reconsiderations and Reverberations*, edited by Joshua R. Eyler (New York: Routledge, 2016), 11–24.

23. Wheatley, 52–4.

24. Tarjei Park, "Reflecting Christ: The Role of the Flesh in Walter Hilton and Julian of Norwich." In *The Medieval Mystical Tradition in England: Exeter Symposium V*, edited by Marion Glasscoe (Suffolk: Boydell and Brewer, 1992), 17–38.

25. Mark Paterson, *Seeing with the Hands: Blindness, Vision and Touch After Descartes* (Edinburgh: Edinburgh University Press, 2016).

26. Curtis Margo, M.D., "Blindness and the Age of Enlightenment: Diderot's Letter on the Blind," *JAMA Ophthalmology* 2013. 131:1 98–102.

27. Barasch, 151.

28. Kate Tunstall, *Blindness and Enlightenment: An Essay* (London: Bloomsbury, 2011).

29. Bronwen Wilson, "Visual Knowledge / Facing Blindness." In *Seeing Across Cultures in the Early Modern World*, edited by Dana Leibsohn and Jeanette Favrot Peterson (Burlington: Ashgate Press, 2012), 97–124.

30. Juhani Pallasmaa, *The Eyes of the Skin: Architecture and the Senses* (New York: Wiley and Sons, 2012).

Out of Sight
Body and Building from Medical Architecture to Post-Modern Haptic Space

BRENDA S. GARDENOUR WALTER

Architecture and the human body are engaged in a reciprocal process of creation. A close reading of architectural structures can reveal deep cultural assumptions about the body, the form and function of which have been projected onto the built environment. In the west, the human body is constructed as a Cartesian "bete-machine" with myriad gears and mechanisms whirring together, much like an animated automaton.[1] The fundamental belief that that human body is a machine with parts that can be replicated and modified through routine maintenance is inscribed on the buildings designed to both house and repair it. Domestic architecture, for example, functions in accordance with human anatomy and physiology, with timber framing that serves as skeletal structure, HVAC ducts that work like a mechanical respiratory system, plumbing that operates like intestines, all within a skin-like facade that protects the body-building from external invasion and corruption.[2] Medical architecture, in particular that of the hospital, not only reflects the Cartesian human body but also acts as a body-factory focused on the production of health through machine mediation and the medical gaze. In both domestic and medical architecture, vision is a manifestation of power, while visibility is a form of submission.[3] Sightlines in domestic settings control the movement of people between public and private areas, while access panels and camera probes are used to identify and repair hidden structural malfunctions. In the hospital, the bodies of patients are closely monitored by medical authorities who use medical imaging technologies and surgical methods to see into and repair the body's hidden mechanisms. While both utilitarian and efficient, mechanistic architectures are not only reductive, but also disempowering in their subjection of humans to the tyranny of the eye.

Postmodern architectural theory offers a corrective to the mechanistic construction of standardized bodies and buildings by promoting structural designs that are reliant on the inner senses rather than physical sight alone. Out of sight, postmodern structures reflect a holistic construction of the human body that is individual, multi-abled, and fluid. Theorists Juhani Pallasmaa and Sarah Robinson have suggested powerful pathways to postmodern architectural embodiment, including the construction of digitally-mediated, disembodied, and organic nesting spaces that reflect and nurture bodies of all shapes and abilities.[4] Beyond vision and visibility, and therefore beyond external power and control, postmodern spaces are shaped by their inhabitants through embodied knowledge, including the olfactory, auditory, and haptic experiences that are so often left out of the mechanical architectures. Just as embodied knowledge has the power to shape domestic architecture from within, like a bird creating a nest, so too might it have the ability to reshape medical architectures, including clinical relationships, healing spaces, and the construction of wholeness beyond the machine.

Building the Machine: Body, House, Hospital

Architectural structures are projections and reflections of the human body, the shape and meaning of which shift according to historical and cultural context. In the patriarchal worlds of Ancient Greece and Rome, male architects created spaces that echoed their own embodiment, a pattern that would be replicated across millennia. The father of architecture, Vitruvius, argued that the design of buildings should be founded on the proportions and symmetry of the perfect human form, the male body.[5] Balanced in the composition of its humors and members, the male body was constructed as orderly and rational, the paradigm of creation. Grounded in the textual authority of the Vitruvian school, Renaissance architects such as Filarete argued that "the edifice is exactly like a live man," even as Michelangelo wrote that "the members or architecture derive from the members of man."[6] At the intersection of architecture and anatomy, Italian scholars such as Stratico and Rusconi described buildings as bodies, with plaster skin and structural bones.[7] In keeping with the interests of their contemporary, the anatomist Anton Vesalius, these architects drew artistic cross-sections of buildings, their parts rendered in painstaking detail, revealing the hidden organs and internal systems vital to their survival.[8] Seeing the inside of architectural structures, holding them in the gaze, became the primary means of knowing and possessing them.

In the twentieth and twenty-first centuries, much of modern western architecture remains grounded in patriarchal anatomical forms, now couched in terms of mechanism and dualism. Through a Cartesian lens, the body is "nothing but a statue or machine made of earth," its anatomy and physiology comprising a "functional unity" that operates according to the laws of physics.[9] Within this anatomical structure, the mind-spirit or "thinking stuff" wafts about like a ghost in a haunted house, ethereal and disconnected. The mechanical building-body's exterior serves as a skin-like barrier to protect vulnerable internal systems, while its façade gazes out at the street, its windows like eyes, its front door like a mouth.[10] Beneath the skin, the building's furnace, fan, and ventilation ducts serve as a cardio-pulmonary system, inhaling and exhaling air while circulating warmth. Electrical wiring acts as a network of nerves, sending communicative impulses to different areas of the structure. Kitchens are digestive spaces associated with the mouth and stomach, while bathrooms and basements represent the lower digestive tract, their gurgling drains and intestinal pipes carrying waste into the cellar-bowels of the building and ultimately discharging it into sewer lines buried deep in the soil. In multilevel structures, the central staircase serves as a backbone, the core that connects specialized areas into a single building-body.[11] In keeping with Cartesian paradigms, modern architecture is constructed as a rational male domain that privileges the physical and quantifiable over the ethereal—the visible over the invisible—the machine over the ghost.

Architectural and anatomical mechanism, the form of the building, dictates the function of the structure by shaping the behaviors of those dwelling within it. For example, agnatic buildings such as the cisgender and heterosexual (cis-het) nuclear family home are tightly inscribed domains designed to facilitate the regulation of the bodies and activities of family members.[12] Whether a detached single-family house, trailer home, or apartment, the patriarchal *domus* is organized into public and private spaces. Public areas include the front foyer, living room, and kitchen, with many 21st-century homes featuring a kitchen integrated into a great room. These areas are designated for receiving guests and for communal family activities. Private spaces include full bathrooms—as opposed to the half-bathroom designed for guests near public areas—and bedrooms. Both of these private spaces are associated with bodily acts involving exposure, including excretion, bathing, and sexual activity, and are therefore located at the back of the structure or in upstairs areas, hidden from public view.[13] The most private of rooms is the paternal or master bedroom, the sanctified cite of cis-het reproduction in a domestic structure where "fertility and fulfillment are identical."[14] Collectively, the formal design of the family home promotes utilitarianism and productivity. Kitchens facilitate the production and consumption of food, kitchen islands and office areas function as spaces for learning and home industry, laundry rooms act as processing centers that receive dirty clothes and produce clean ones, while basements and storage areas serve as warehouses where goods are received and distributed. Here, the form and function of domestic architecture join together to become a patriarchal factory, a projection of the efficient and fully functional male body-machine.

In this paradigm, the functioning of the obsessively-ordered family home is predicated on vision—and by extension, visibility—as a form of control. Within the home, sightlines are used to monitor the movement of people between public and private spaces, to restrict the introduction of substances or items determined to be contraband, and to detect potential sources of danger before they can do damage to the building-body and its inhabitants. These sightlines can be human, such as the mother who sees her children playing in the family room from the kitchen, or the father who can watch the front door from his seat in the family room. In the 21st century, sightlines are increasingly digital, with surveillance cameras monitoring activity within the home and around its perimeter. Vision and visibility are critical not only to protecting the house-body, but also to maintaining its physical health. In order to ensure orderly operation, houses contain various access panels through which vital systems and structures, from leaky pipes and faulty wiring to damaged studs, might be observed, tested, and repaired. In areas where access panels do not allow for clear sight, such as deep wall cavities, chimneys, and sewer pipes, incisions can be made, and endoscopic cameras introduced to reveal hidden disorders contributing to systemic inefficiency. In the modern house-body, every part can be rendered visible and accessible, as well as reparable or replaceable.

The modern hospital, which replicates the symbolic order of the patriarchal domus, is an architectural projection of mechanized embodiment.[15] In *Medicine by Design: The Architect and the Modern Hospital 1893–1945*, Annmarie Adams traces the history of hospital architecture in Canada, from the pavilion plan to the block plan. Popular during the late 19th century, the pavilion plan featured open wards with numerous large windows and high ceilings to facilitate an "abundance of light" and the free circulation of air to prevent miasmatic infection.[16] At the center of each ward was a nursing station, from which every patient was visible by matronly nurses and paternal physicians. This model allowed for continual monitoring of patients, and timely attendance to their needs. The first quarter of the 20th century saw the introduction of the block plan, which featured "functional zoning," "factory-inspired kitchens and laundries, suites of rooms for surgery, and a new emphasis on individual patient rooms" influenced by domestic and hotel architecture, all supported by a steel skeleton and encased in a concrete skin.[17] Mechanized and designed for efficiency, patients arrived by automobile and were ferried from room to room in wheelchairs or gurneys. The increased number of walls required a larger nursing and medical staff as well as machine-mediated vision in the form of internal communication technologies such as monitors augmented by intercoms and call systems. Self-contained and frenetic with activity, the block plan would serve as the foundation for the general hospitals of the twentieth and twenty-first centuries.

In both form and function, modern hospitals operate much like factories, with specialized spaces carefully organized for optimal workflow and efficiency.[18] The mechanized hospital is designed to diagnose and repair malfunctioning human bodies and return them to a standardized state of health as determined by clinical algorithms.[19] From admission to discharge, patients are conveyed to different areas of the building, many of which contain technological devices designed to see the hidden mechanisms of the human body. This movement from space to space is determined by a clinical feedback loop involving the collection and interpretation of health information by medical authorities. For example, outpatients are checked in at computer kiosks, where their personal data is collected and entered into the system. After a period in a waiting area, they are admitted into another room where vital metrics such as blood pressure, height, and weight are recorded onto a digital chart. They might then be directed to another waiting room outside of a different testing area, such as hematology or radiology, until sufficient diagnostic information is collected. At each step, data is gathered for use by the attending physician, who logs results into the evidence-based medicine algorithm, and through this determines a diagnosis and the most promising path to cure, known as a best practice.[20] The outpatient may be given a prescription, such as an antibiotic, or referred to a surgeon. Whether chemical or manual, the goal of each therapy is the same—to repair the broken human mechanism and to restore it to order. Be it a hip, heart valve, or missing limb, that which cannot be repaired is often replaced with a mechanical device to bring the flesh-machine into compliance with anatomical and physiological baselines and paradigms.

As they move through the specialized areas of the hospital-factory, patients are subject to vision and visibility—seeing and being seen—as forms of control. As in domestic architecture, sightlines in the hospital are mediated by both mechanical and human eyes, often simultaneously. Mechanical eyes monitor vital signs, heart rhythms, brain waves, and the flow of substances into the body, rendering invisible processes visible through digital readouts. Under the watchful eye of technicians, biological samples, such as blood and urine, are subjected to machine-mediated testing and transformed into visible data. Technologies associated with medical imaging, including x-ray radiography, ultrasonography, and magnetic resonance imaging, painlessly penetrate the body's surface to reveal pictures of hidden organs and structures. More invasive forms of seeing beneath the skin include nuclear imaging, which involves the oral or subcutaneous introduction of radioactive substances that highlight specific systems when viewed through a mechanical interface. In endoscopy and laparoscopy, a camera penetrates the body through the natural openings of the digestive tract or through a surgical incision in the skin, producing living images of internal systems. All of these technologies use vision to render invisible organs and biological processes visible to medical authorities and patients, resulting a trebling of sight. Mechanical and human sight are fundamental not only to diagnosis but also to surgical repair. In medical school, students practice surgical techniques and procedures on simulation machines that act as visual mediaries between the human eye and the digital body, all under the watchful eye of preceptor.[21] In medical practice, surgeons cut access panels into the human body, much like those found in modern architecture, and use mechanical interventions to facilitate repair.

Across all of these categories, medical authority over the body is grounded in the very power of sight. Through the penetrating power of the medical gaze, the body is held fast, acted upon, opened up, and possessed by the viewer.[22] Objectified, the patient as a whole person becomes little more than a blurry field surrounding a narrowly focused image of disease or dysfunction within their mechanical body. The discursive regime of the clinical gaze is inscribed in the form and function of the hospital and the bodies within them, machines within machines, projections of Cartesian embodiment in a continual feedback loop. The cessation of sight disrupts the algorithm, disempowers medical authority, shifts the narrative of hospital space. In modern medicine, where seeing is knowing, and knowing is control, vision loss is seen as a mechanical failure and a disability. Yet surrendering vision as a mechanism of architectural, bodily, and medical authority allows for a new means of understanding space and embodiment as a holistic and haptic experience beyond hegemonic constructs of mechanism and standardization.

Beyond the Machine: Haptic Nests and Healing Spaces

Postmodern architecture contests ocular-centrism and the Cartesian construction of the human body as a standardized machine and offers new pathways to architectural embodiment that are at once haptic, imbued with spirit, and inclusive. Juhani Pallasmaa argues that architects have traditionally been both leaders and followers in the aesthetic cult of the eye.[23] The form and function of modern buildings are predicated on vision, from the placement of doorways and the configuration of rooms to the folds of shadow and projection of light through windows—openings that expose the interior of the structure to public view.[24] This obsession with vision and visibility, according to Pallasmaa, obscures the multisensory ways in which humans, as embodied beings, experience architectural structures. Entering into a space, the human body is enveloped by an architectural body, within which it "spreads out and connects with the environment like an invisible network."[25] Information flows from body to building and back again in a continuous feedback loop, creating a "singularity of self and world."[26] This embodied knowledge of architectural space encompasses all human senses, both physical and spiritual, without according privilege to any single one.[27] For example, our experience of home is an intense form of multi-sensory embodied knowledge beyond the visual. With eyes closed, other dimensions of domestic space move to the foreground: the smell and warmth of wood on the fire, the smell and taste of fresh coffee and pastries, the sounds of radiators clicking and the rattling of windows in the wind, the feel of soft blankets and cold tile. Our embodied knowledge of home is deeply haptic, from the movement of hands-on walls and feet on floors, like skin on skin, to the repeated handling of the artifacts of everyday life. Pallasmaa argues that architectural design should embrace such invisible dimensions of space—multisensory and haptic—in order to create meaningful human environments beyond the mechanical and utilitarian regime of the eye.[28]

Embodied knowledge is not only shaped by but also shapes architectural structures from within, with human actors continually recreating built space according to their own sense of embodiment. According to architectural theorist, Sarah Robinson, body and building are engaged in a reciprocal process of imprinting.[29] She argues that living in domestic architecture is an act of physical intimacy. Our bodies brush against walls, press into furniture, and wear pathways onto floors as we inscribe patterns onto a home's surfaces. Like a bird in its nest, we nestle into domestic structures, shaping them with our bodies and making them our own.[30] Homes designed in keeping with patriarchal structures and mechanical constructions of the body, therefore, can be modified from the inside out in order to reflect the unique bodies and embodied knowledge of their inhabitants. This reconstruction of space, or what Colomina calls "changing position," is particularly empowering for those who do not conform to hegemonic frameworks, including individuals whose minds and bodies do not fit the model of mechanistic wholeness ascribed by the symbolic order of modern medicine.[31] For example, those with acute anxiety disorders and /or the neurodiverse may construct womb-like safe spaces in spare rooms or closets, places where sensory input can be carefully controlled and the outside world shut out completely. Domestic spaces may likewise be reconfigured to accommodate bodies labeled as disabled by medical and able-ist cultures. The result is a nurturing space that functions as an extension of the body, provides a refuge from the able-ist world, and becomes a place to "dream" and nestle in safety.[32] Shaped from within, the haptic nest becomes at once a container for identity and memory as well as an act of resistance, one that counters the biomedical view of disabilities as a "malfunction of a biophysical mechanism," insisting instead that disability is the "unique experience of a meaning-making and embodied cultural being."[33]

The malleable nature of postmodern architecture is informed by the digital revolution, in which invisible webs of internet connectivity have enveloped the world and permeated our architectural domains.[34] Digital technologies, most notably computers and smartphones, have changed the ways that we inhabit built space. Juhani Pallasmaa argues that postmodern architecture is increasingly designed for humans whose bodies may rest in a physical place, but whose intellectual and spiritual experiences unfold in a disembodied digital realm. Gatherings of friends, for example, as well as networking, office functions, family exchanges, and shopping now unfold online, sometimes simultaneously, from a dining room chair, couch, or bed. Beyond personal comfort, the physical location of the participant is irrelevant. For Pallasmaa, "lived space is always a combination of external space and inner mental space," representing a simultaneous collapse of "actuality and mental projection."[35] The "modes of experiencing architecture" and digital media "become identical in this mental space, which meanders without fixed boundaries."[36] The disembodied architecture of the digital world exists beyond the constraints of the physical body; accessible through a multitude of interfaces, it is multimodal and multisensory, and therefore inclusive. Somewhat ironically, machine language has offered a pathway toward liberating the body from mechanistic constructs that privilege vision and standardization. This shift is likewise reflected in the creation of digital nests to accommodate disembodied humans.[37] Interactive digital technologies can create dynamic environments that enable humans of all abilities to live more independent and meaningful lives.[38] Digital interfaces have likewise created spaces of increased freedom. In many homes, rooms have lost their once-specialized functions, with private and public spaces often conflated, the connections between them fluid. For example, an individual might participate on social media while using the bathroom, then carry that conversation into the living room. Digital banking might be done in the bedroom, while online learning takes place in the kitchen, or even outdoors. This fluidity is a hallmark of queer ecology, in which "all life-forms, along with the environments they compose and inhabit, defy boundaries between inside and outside at every level."[39] The organic openness of the digital nest contests not only the standardized and mechanistic construction of the body, but also the patriarchal ordering of space and mechanisms of control within the home, with digital relationships and ideas flowing in and out of domestic space beyond the watchful eye of gatekeepers.

The postmodern movement toward a fluid, organic, and digital embodiment has not only begun to reshape domestic architecture, but also promises to change clinical practices and spaces. As spaces of safety and growth, digital and haptic nests empower those who shape them to own their identities and experiences, and to be accountable for their own well-being, both physical and spiritual, visible and invisible. These same values are shaping clinical care in the digital age. Patients at home now access their personal records through E-health interfaces and engage with healthcare professionals via digital appointments. Rather than being acted upon by medical authorities in a mechanized clinical environment, patients are agents in their own health as they make informed decisions from within their nests. Colomina argues that, because "architectural discourse has from its beginning associated building and body" and "the body that it describes is the medical body," both can be "reconstructed by each new theory of health."[40] Through this lens, it is possible to imagine a greater emphasis on individualized care that takes place in architectural environments that are holistic, that honor the invisible and visible elements of a human life, and that embrace difference as a unique form of embodied knowledge rather than a mechanical malfunction to be fixed. In learning to un-see the body as a locus of power and control, we might collectively redefine health and encounter embodiment as a form of living architecture—nests within nests, gardens within the biophysical machine—deserving of wholeness beyond the medical gaze and the tyranny of the authoritative eye.[41]

Notes

1. Dennis Des Chene, *Spirits and Clocks: Machine and Organism in Descartes* (Ithaca, NY: Cornell University Press, 2001).

2. See Kent Bloomer and Charles Moore, *Body, Memory, and Architecture* (New Haven, CT: Yale University Press, 1977).

3. Michel Foucault, *Birth of the Clinic: An Archaeology of Medical Perception* (New York: Vintage, 1994).

4. Juhani Pallasmaa, *The Eyes of the Skin: Architecture and the Senses* (New York: Wiley and Sons, 2012); Sarah Robinson, *Nesting: Body, Dwelling, Mind* (Richmond, CA: William Stout Publishers, 2011).
 5. Vitruvius, *On Architecture: Books 1-V: Loeb Classical Library*, trans. Fred Granger (Cambridge: Harvard University Press, 1931); Vitruvius, *On Architecture: Books VI-X: Loeb Classical Library*, trans. Fred Granger (Cambridge: Harvard University Press, 1934).
 6. Marco Frascari, "A 'Measure' in Architecture: A Medical-Architectural Theory by Simone Stratico, Architetto Veneto," *RES Anthropology and Aesthetics* 9 (1985), 82.
 7. Frascari, "A Measure," 85.
 8. Beatriz Colomina, "X-Ray Architecture: Illness as Metaphor," *Positions* 0 (2008), 34.
 9. Robinson, *Nesting*, 27; Des Chene, *Spirits and Clocks*, 28-29.
 10. See Kent Bloomer and Charles Moore. *Body, Memory, and Architecture*, (New Haven: Yale University Press, 1977).
 11. Juhani Pallasmaa, *The Architecture of the Image: Existential Space in Cinema* (Building Information Limited, 2001), 32.
 12. Diana Agrest, "Architecture from Without: Body, Logic, and Sex," *Assemblage* 7 (1988), 29.
 13. Victoria Rosner, *Modernism and the Architecture of Private Life* (New York: Columbia University Press, 2008), 1- 2.
 14. Henri Lefebvre, *The Production of Space* (Hoboken, NJ: Blackwell, 1992). Quoted in Michael P. Brown, *Closet Space: Geographies of Metaphor from Body to the Globe* (Routledge, 2000), 59. See also Beatriz Preciado, "Architecture as a Practice of Biopolitical Disobedience," *Log* 25 (2012), 124 [121-134].
 15. Colomina, "X-Ray Architecture," 31. On mechanized embodiment, see David B. Morris, "How to Speak Postmodern: Medicine, Illness, and Cultural Change," *Hastings Center Report* 30:6 (2000), 8 [7-16].
 16. Annmarie Adams, *Medicine by Design: The Architect and the Modern Hospital 1893-1945* (Minneapolis: University of Minnesota Press, 2008), xvii, 6.
 17. Adams, *Medicine by Design*, 109.
 18. For an early example, see Nitin K. Ahuja, "Fordism in the Hospital: Albert Kahn and the Design of Old Main, 1917-25," *Journal of the history of Medicine and Allied Sciences* 67:3 (2012), 398-427).
 19. In "The Architecture of the Hospital: A Study of Spatial Organization and Medical Knowledge," *The British Journal of Sociology* 39:1 (1988), 86-113, Lindsay Prior argues that hospital design is influenced by shifts in medical theory and innovation. Adams, however, argues that hospital design is the result of collective input from patients, nurses, doctors, and architects.
 20. Much has been written about and debated regarding EBM. The seminal article is David Sackett, et al., "Evidence Based Medicine: What It Is and What It Isn't: It's About Integrating Individual Clinical Expertise and the Best External Evidence," *BM: British Medical Journal* 312:7023 (1996), 71-2.
 21. Ericka Sue Johnson, "Out of My Viewfinder, Yet in the Picture: Seeing the Hospital in Medical Simulations," *Science, Technology, and Human Values* 33:1 (2008), 53-76. In this study, medical students use surgical simulators to peer into a "patient" while they, themselves, are observed by a preceptor, all while being watched and filmed by the study's author.
 22. Michel Foucault, *Birth of the Clinic: An Archaeology of Medical Perception*. (Vintage, 1994). See also Paul Hirst, "Foucault and Architecture," *AA Files* 26 (1993), 53 [52-60]. On owning the objectified images of patients, see Andrea Zittlau, "Pathologizing Bodies: Medical Portrait Photography in Nineteenth-Century America," *Amerikastudien* 58:4 (2013), 543-58.
 23. Juhani Pallasmaa, *The Eyes of the Skin*.
 24. Colomina compares this exposure to that of an X-ray.
 25. Thomas Fuchs, "The Phenomenology of Body Memory," *Body Memory, Metaphor, and Movement*, 10-12, edited by Sabine C. Koch et. al (Amsterdam, The Netherlands: John Benjamins, 2012).

26. Robinson, *Nesting*, 5.
27. Fuchs, "Phenomenology."
28. See also, Jasmien Herssens and Ann Heylighen, "Blind Photographers: A Quest into the Spatial Experiences of Blind Children," *Children, Youth, Environments* 22:1, 99–124.
29. Sarah Robinson, *Nesting: Body, Dwelling, Mind* (Richmond, California: William Stout Publishers, 2011).
30. Sarah Robinson, "Nested Bodies," *Mind in Architecture*, eds. Juhani Pallasmaa and Sarah Robinson (Cambridge, MA: MIT Press, 2015), 137–160.
31. Colomina, "X-Ray."
32. Gaston Bachelard, *The Poetics of Space* (New York: Beacon Press, 1994).
33. Morris, "Postmodern," 8. On space as memory, see Juhani Pallasmaa, "Matter, Hapticity, and Time: Material Imagination and the Voice of Matter," *Building Material* 20 (2016), 171–89.
34. Digital technologies have shaped every aspect of architecture. See Rabee M. Reffat, "Digital Architecture and Reforming the Built Environment," *Journal of Architecture and Planning Research* 25:2 (2008), 118–29.
35. Juhani Pallasmaa, *The Architecture of Image*, 18.
36. *Ibid*.
37. In ANY Event, "Electrotecture: Architecture and the Electronic Future," *ANY* (1993), 44–53.
38. Joanne Jakovich and Kirsty Beilharz, "Interaction as Medium in Architectural Design," *Leonardo* 40:4 (2007), 368–69.
39. Timothy Morton, "Queer Ecology." *PMLA* 125:2 (2010), 274.
40. Colomina, "X-Ray," 31.
41. Christina Cogdell, "Growing Living Buildings: Tissue and Genetic Engineering in Architecture and Design," *Toward a Living Architecture? Complexism and Biology in Generative Design.* (Minneapolis, MN: University of Minnesota Press, 2018), 160. See also, Reuben M. Rainey, "The Garden in the Machine: Nature Returns to the High-Tech Hospital," *SiteLINES: A Journal of Place* 5:2 (2010), 14–17.

Filmography

Films are listed with their directors; in the case of a series with multiple directors, the publisher is listed.

At First Sight (1999): Irwin Winker.
Awakenings (1990): Penny Marshall.
Blindness (2008): Fernando Meirelles.
Blindsight (2006): Lucy Walker.
Blink (1994): Michael Apted.
The Book of Eli (2010): Albert Hughes and Allen Hughes.
Bride of Frankenstein (1935): James Whale.
Crimes and Misdemeanors (1989): Woody Allen.
Dancer in The Dark (2000): Lars Von Trier.
Daredevil (2003–2018): Mark Steven Johnson.
Daredevil (2015–2018): Marvel.
The Day of the Triffids (1962): Steve Sekely.
The Descent (2006): Neil Marshall.
Don't Breathe (2016): Fede Alverez.
Don't Breathe 2 (2021): Rodo Sayagues Mendes.
Going Blind (2010): Joseph F. Scott.
In Darkness (2018): Anthony Byrne.
Jennifer 8 (1992): Bruce Robinson.
Jessica Jones (2015–2019): Netflix.
Johnny Got His Gun (1971): Dalton Trumbo.
Love and Honor (2006): Yoji Yamada.
The Masseurs and a Woman (1938): Hirochi Shimizu.
The Matrix Trilogy (1999–2003): The Wachowski Sibs.
The Miracle Worker (1962): Arthur Penn.
Night of the Living Dead (1968): George A. Romero.
Night Walk (1967): Aziz Tazi.
A Patch of Blue (1965): Guy Green.
Pride of the Marines (1945): Delmer Daves.
Profumo Di Donna (1974): Dino Risi.
Rogue One: A Star Wars Story (2016): Gareth Edwards.
The Scent of a Woman (1992): Martin Brest.
See (2019-): Francis Lawrence.
See No Evil (1971): Richard Fleischer.
Star Trek: Insurrection (1998): Jonathan Frakes.
Star Wars (1977): George Lucas.
The Trial of the Incredible Hulk (1989): Bill Bixby.
Two for the Road (1967): Stanley Donen.
Wait Until Dark (1967): Terence Young.
The White Countess (2005): James Ivory.
Zatoichi (2003): Takeshi Kitano.

Bibliography

Aldiss, Brian W. *Billion Year Spree: The True History of Science Fiction.* Garden City, NY: Doubleday & Company, Inc., 1973.
Allen, Corey. "Encounter at Farpoint." *Star Trek: The Next Generation.* Paramount Pictures, September 28, 1987.
Andersen, S. Ry. "The Eye and Its Diseases in Ancient Egypt." *Acta Opthalmologica* Scandinavica 75, 2009. 338–344.
Aristotle. *Eudemian Ethics.* Searchable at: http://www.perseus.tufts.edu/hopper/text?doc=Perseus%3Atext%3A1999.01.0050%3Abook%3D8%3Asection%3D1248b#note-link1.
Aristotle. *On Sense and the Sensible.* Searchable at: http://classics.mit.edu/Aristotle/sense.mb.txt.
Baird, Stuart. *Star Trek: Nemesis.* Paramount Pictures, 2002.
Barasch, Moshe. *Blindness: The History of a Mental Image in Western Thought.* London: Routledge, 2001.
Biggs, Robert. "Medicine, Surgery, and Public Health in Ancient Mesopotamia." In *Civilizations of the Ancient Near East,* edited by Jack Sasson. New York: Charles Scribner's Sons, 1995.
Bole, Cliff. "Hide and Q." *Star Trek: The Next Generation.* Paramount Pictures, November 23, 1987.
Bolt, David. "Aesthetic Blindness: Symbolism, Realism, and Reality." *Mosaic: An Interdisciplinary Critical Journal,* Vol. 46, No.3 (September 2014): 96.
Bozal, Valeriano. *Goya y el gusto modern.* Madrid: Alianza, 2002.
Brodman, James. *Charity and Religion in Medieval Europe.* Washington, D.C.: Catholic University of America, 2009.
Burton, LeVar. "Timeless." *Star Trek: Voyager.* Paramount Pictures, November 18, 1998.
Caps, John. *Henry Mancini: Reinventing Film Music.* Champaign: University of Illinois Press, 2012.
Carroll, Noel. *The Philosophy of Horror or Paradox of the Heart.* New York: Routledge, 1990.
Cheu, Johnson. "Seeing Blindness on Screen: The Cinematic Gaze of Blind Female Protagonists." *The Journal of Popular Culture,* Vol. 42, No. 3 (June 2009): 484–485, 493.
Clover, Carol. *Men, Women, and Chainsaws.* Princeton, NJ: Princeton University Press, 2015.
Comic Vine. Charles M McNider. 2017. https://comicvine.gamespot.com/charles-m-mcnider/4005-9301/ (accessed June 13, 2017).
Derry, Charles. *The Suspense Thriller: Films in the Shadow of Alfred Hitchcock.* Jefferson, NC: McFarland, 2010.
Earth-Two. New York: DC Comics, 1985.
Edelstein, Emma, and Ludwig Edelstein. *Asclepius: Collection and Interpretation of the Testimonies.* Baltimore: Johns Hopkins Press, 1998.
Edwards, Gareth. *Rogue One: A Star Wars Story.* Walt Disney Studios, 2016.
Erasmus, Desiderius. *The Adages of Erasmus.* Edited by William Barker. Toronto: University of Toronto Press, 2001.

Espí Forcén, Fernando. *Monsters, Demons and Psychopaths: Psychiatry and Horror Film.* Boca Raton: CRC Press, 2016.
Estes, J. Worth. *The Medical Skills of Ancient Egypt.* Canton, MA: Science History Publications, 1993.
Everson, William K., *Classics of the Horror Film.* New York: Citadel Press, 1974.
Faltz, Christine. "Dear Dr. Asimov, et al." *Isaac Asimov's Science Fiction Magazine*, February 1991.
Farber, Stephen. "Wait Until Dark." *Film Quarterly,* Vol. 21, No.3 (Spring 1968): 63.
Fox, Gardner, and Stan Asch. "Two New Members Win Their Spurs." Vol. 8, *All-Star Comics.* All-American Publications, 1941.
Frakes, Jonathan. *Star Trek: First Contact.* Paramount Pictures, 1996.
Frakes, Jonathan. *Star Trek: Insurrection.* Paramount Pictures, 1998.
Gabbard, Glenn O., and Gabbard, Krin. *Psychiatry and the Cinema.* Arlington, VA: American Psychiatric Publishing, 1999.
Gioia, T. *Healing Songs.* Durham, NC: Duke University Press, 2006.
Gioia, T. *A Subversive History of Music.* New York: Basic Books, 2019.
Goldstein, Joelle. "18-Year-Old Blind Pianist Prodigy Getting Studied by Scientists for his 'Remarkable' Talents." *People Magazine*, February 24, 2020.
Grabar, André. *Les voies de la création en iconographie chrétienne. Antiquité e Moyen Âge.* Paris: Flammarion, 1979.
Grant, Edward. *Planets, Stars, and Orbs: The Medieval Cosmos, 1200–1687.* Washington, D.C.: Catholic University Press, 1996.
Griffen, John. *Black Like Me.* San Antonio, TX: Wings Press, 1964.
Grossman, Christine F. "The Sight Sickness." Accessed August 11, 2020. https://www.goodreads.com/work/best_book/6649133-the-sight-sickness.
Haldeman, Joe. "None So Blind." *Isaac Asimov's Science Fiction Magazine*, November 1994.
Hart, Gerald D. *Asclepius, The God of Medicine.* London: Royal Society of Medicine Press, 2000.
Hartsock, Chad. *Sight and Blindness in Luke-Acts: The Use of Physical Features in Characterization.* Leiden: Brill, 2008.
Heinlein, Robert A. "The Green Hills of Earth." *The Saturday Evening Post,* February 8, 1947.
Higham, George. *Wax Museum Movies: A Comprehensive Filmography.* Jefferson, NC: McFarland, 2020.
Holdstock, Robert P. *Eye Among the Blind.* Garden City, NY: Doubleday & Company, Inc., 1977.
The Hughes Brothers. *The Book of Eli.* Warner Bros., 2010.
Hunter, Sam, John Jacobus, and Daniel Wheeler. *Modern Art.* Upper Saddle River, NJ: Prentice Hall, 2000.
Kern, Laura. "Senseless Violence." *Film Comment* (May/June 2018): 22.
Kilby, Damian. "Travelers." *Isaac Asimov's Science Fiction Magazine*, February 1990.
Kinnard, Roy. *Horror in Silent Films.* Jefferson, NC: McFarland, 1995.
Kleege, Georgina. *More Than Meets the Eye.* New York: Oxford University Press, 2018.
Klein, Jacob. "Enki and Ninmah." *Context of Scripture: Volume One*, edited by William W. Hallo. Leiden: Brill, 1989.
Kolbe, Winrich. "All Good Things...." *Star Trek: The Next Generation.* Paramount Pictures, May 23, 1994.
Kramer, Samuel Noah, and John Maier. *Myths of Enki: The Crafty God.* New York: Oxford University Press, 1989.
Lawrence, Francis. "Godflame." See. Apple TV+, n.d.
Lee, Stan. *Son of Origins of Marvel Comics.* New York: Simon & Schuster, 1975.
Lee, Stan, and Bill Everett. *Daredevil.* New York: Marvel Comics, 1964.
Lee, Stan, and Steve Ditko. *Amazing Fantasy* #15. Edited by Stan Lee. Vol. 1. 1 vols. New York: Marvel Comics, 1962.
Lowachee, Karin. "Bird Box Never Quite Takes Off." *Fantasy and Science Fiction* (May/June 2019): 196.

Margo, Curtis, MD. "Blindness and the Age of Enlightenment: Diderot's Letter on the Blind," *JAMA Ophthalmology* 131:1, 2013. 98–102.
Markstein, Don. *Dr. Mid-Nite.* January 1, 2008. http://www.toonopedia.com/mid-nite.htm (accessed June 10, 2017).
Marriott, James. *The Descent.* Liverpool: Auteur, 2013.
McAllister, Ray W. *Theology of Blindness in the Hebrew Scriptures.* Dissertation, 2010. http://digitalcommons.andrews.edu/cgi/viewcontent.cgi?article=1088&context=dissertations.
McLaughlin, Thomas P., Shean P. Monahan, Norman L. Pruvost, Vladimir V. Frolov, Boris G. Ryazanov, and Victor I. Sviridov. "A Review of Criticality Accidents 2000 Revision." United States, May 1, 2000. https://doi.org/10.2172/758324.
Mellinkoff, Ruth. *The Mark of Cain.* Berkeley: University of California, 1981.
Miller, Frank, and David Mazzucchelli. *Daredevil: Born Again.* New York: Marvel Comics, 1987.
Modenese, Alberto, and Fabriziomaria Gobba. "Cataract Frequency and Subtypes Involved in Workers Assessed for Their Solar Radiation Exposure: A Systematic Review." *Acta Ophthalmologica* (1755375X) 96, no. 8 (December 2018): 779–88.
Moffic H.S., R. Bailey, F. Clark et al. "Dismantling Racism in Psychiatry and Society." *Psychiatric Times.* 37(8): 1, 11–15, August 2020.
Newland, Christina. "See No Evil." *Sight and Sound* (January 1, 2018): 104.
Nunn, John F. *Ancient Egyptian Medicine.* Norman: University of Oklahoma Press, 2002.
O'Toole, Mark P. 2016. "Disability and the Suppression of Historical Identity: Rediscovering the Professional Backgrounds of the Blind Residents of the Hôpital des Quinze-Vingts." In *Disability in the Middle Ages: Reconsiderations and Reverberations*, edited by Joshua R. Eyler. New York: Routledge. 11–24.
Packer, Sharon. *Superheroes and Superegos: Analyzing the Minds behind the Masks.* Santa Barbara, CA: Prager/ABC-Clio, 2010.
Pallasmaa, Juhani. *The Eyes of the Skin: Architecture and the Senses.* New York: Wiley and Sons, 2012.
Park, Tarjei. "Reflecting Christ: The Role of the Flesh in Walter Hilton and Julian of Norwich." In *The Medieval Mystical Tradition in England: Exeter Symposium V*, edited by Marion Glasscoe. Suffolk: Boydell and Brewer, 1992. 17–38.
Paterson, Mark. *Seeing with the Hands: Blindness, Vision and Touch After Descartes.* Edinburgh: Edinburgh University Press, 2016.
Pérez-Sanchez, Alfonso. *Ribera, 1591–1652.* Madrid: Metropolitan Museum of Art, 1992.
Réau, Louis. *Iconografiaì del arte cristiano. Iconografiaì de la Biblia. Antiguo Testamento, vol. 1.* Barcelona: Del Serbal, 1995.
Reizenstein, Charles, and Stan Asch. "Doctor Mid-Nite: How He Began." *All-American Comics*, April 1, 1941: 1–8.
Ritner, Robert K. "Daily Ritual of the Temple of Amun-Re at Karnak." *Context of Scripture: Volume One*, edited by William W. Hallo, 55–57. Leiden: Brill, 1997.
Robinson, Kim Stanley. "The Blind Geometer." *Isaac Asimov's Science Fiction Magazine*, August 1987.
Rosenberg, Jakob. *Rembrandt: Life and Work.* New York: Phaidon, 1968.
Rowden T: *The Songs of Black Folks: African American Musicians and the Cultures of Blindness.* Ann Arbor: University of Michigan, 2009.
Rubin, Miri. *Gentile Tales: The Narrative Assault on Medieval Jews.* Philadelphia: University of Pennsylvania Press, 2004.
Rybin, Steven. *Michael Mann: Crime Auteur.* Lanham, MD: Scarecrow Press, 2013.
Saramago, José. *Blindness.* Translated by Giovanni Pontiero. New York: Harcourt Brace, 1997.
Schama, Simon. *Rembrandt's Eyes.* New York: Knopf, 1999.
Shaw, Bob. *Night Walk.* EBook. London: Gollancz, 2011.
Shaw, Larry. "Loud as a Whisper." *Star Trek: The Next Generation.* Paramount Pictures, January 9, 1989.
Shelley, Mary. *Frankenstein: Annotated for Scientists, Engineers, and Creators of All Kinds.*

Edited by David H. Guston, Ed Finn, and Jason Scott Robert. The MIT Press, 2017. https://doi.org/10.7551/mitpress/10815.001.0001.
Shelley, Mary Wollstonecraft. *The Last Man*. Edited by Anne McWhir. Orchard Park, NY: Broadview Press, 1996.
Stuart, Don A. "Blindness." *Astounding Stories*, March 1935.
Thomas, Roy. *Infinity, Inc*. #19—"Last Crises on Beatty, Scott, and Rags Morales. JSA Classified—Skin Trade" Part One, Spare Parts. Vol. 19. New York: DC Comics, 2007.
Thomas, Roy. *Infinity, Inc*. #20—"Stormy Weather." New York: DC Comics, 1985.
Thomas, Roy, and Dann Thomas. *Infinity, Inc*. #21—"Shadows at Midnight!" New York: DC Comics, 1985.
Tibbetts, John C. "*Don't Breathe* review." *Film & History*. 46.2 (Winter 2016): 104.
Tunstall, Kate E. *Blindness and Enlightenment: An Essay*. London: Bloomsbury, 2011.
Varley, John. "The Persistence of Vision." *The Magazine of Fantasy and Science Fiction*, March 1978.
Varma, Rohit, Thasarat S. Vajaranant, Bruce Burkemper, Shuang Wu, Mina Torres, Chunyi Hsu, Farzana Choudhury, and Roberta McKean-Cowdin. "Visual Impairment and Blindness in Adults in the United States: Demographic and Geographic Variations From 2015 to 2050." *JAMA Ophthalmology* 134, no. 7 (July 1, 2016): 802–9. https://doi.org/10.1001/jamaophthalmol.2016.1284.
Wachowski Twins. *The Matrix*. Warner Bros., 1999.
Wachowski Twins. *The Matrix Revolutions*. Warner Bros., 2003.
Wadman, Meredith. "The Physician Whose 1964 Vaccine Beat Back Rubella Is Working to Defeat the New Coronavirus." *Science | AAAS*, March 21, 2020. https://www.sciencemag.org/news/2020/03/physician-whose-1964-vaccine-beat-back-rubella-working-defeat-new-coronavirus.
Wagner, Matt, and John K. Snyder III. *Doctor Mid-Nite—D.O.A*. Vol. 1. New York: DC Comics, 1999.
Wells, H. G. "The Country of the Blind." *The Strand Magazine*, April 1904.
Weygand, Zina. *The Blind in French Society from the Middle Ages to the Century of Louis Braille*. Stanford: Stanford University Press, 2009.
Wheatley, Edward. *Stumbling Blocks Before the Blind: Medieval Constructions of a Disability*. Ann Arbor: University of Michigan Press, 2010.
Whittington, William. *Sound Design and Science Fiction*. Austin: University of Texas Press, 2007.
Wilson, Bronwen. "Visual Knowledge / Facing Blindness." *Seeing Across Cultures in the Early Modern World*, edited by Dana Leibsohn and Jeanette Favrot Peterson. Farnham, UK: Ashgate Press, 2012.
Winter, Bodo. "Horror Movies and the Cognitive Ecology of Primary Metaphors." *Metaphor and Symbol* 29 (July 2014): 162.
Wyndham, John. *The Day of the Triffids*. New York: Carroll & Graf Publishers, Inc., 1993.

About the Contributors

Jeffrey **Bullins** is an associate professor of communication studies at the State University of New York, Plattsburgh. His research focuses on film sound and genre, particularly horror. Previous essays and presentations have examined sound in the *Saw* film franchise, the soundtrack of the Western, and early talkies. He has also worked as a sound designer and mixer on horror (and other genres) features and short films.

Reja-e **Busailah** was born in Jerusalem, Palestine, in 1929. He earned a BA in English from the University of Cairo; MS in special education from Hunter College; Ph.D. from NYU. He taught English at Indiana University Kokomo for 30 years and won a Fulbright scholarship to teach English in Morocco. His *In the Land of My Birth: A Palestinian Boyhood* (2017) won the 2018 Palestine Book Awards for best memoir.

Jason W. **Ellis** is an assistant professor of English at the New York City College of Technology, CUNY, where he coordinates the City Tech Science Fiction Collection and codirects OpenLab. He coedited *The Postnational Fantasy* (McFarland, 2011) and a special issue on *Star Wars: The Force Awakens* of New American Notes Online (nanocrit.com). He holds a Ph.D. in English from Kent State University an MA in science fiction studies from the University of Liverpool.

Carlos **Espí Forcén** is a professor of ancient and Medieval art in the Department of Art History at the University of Murcia, Spain. He has written one book and several peer-reviewed articles on medieval antisemitism, two books on the illustrations of German alchemical manuscripts, and several peer reviewed articles on mental illness in the Middle Ages, ancient and medieval hunting and other topics of ancient art.

Fernando **Espí Forcén** earned his M.D. from the University of Murcia and his Ph.D. on the history of psychiatry. He completed psychiatry residency, child and adolescent psychiatry and psycho-oncology fellowships in the U.S. His dissertation on mental health in the Late Middle Ages was awarded Best Ph.D. by the health science program for 2015. He founded the Journal of Humanistic Psychiatry and authored *Monsters, Demons and Psychopaths: Psychiatry and Horror Film*.

Howard L. **Forman** is an assistant professor of psychiatry at Albert Einstein College of Medicine and is the director of the Addiction Consultation Service at Montefiore Medical Center. He has coauthored essays in edited collections on psychiatry and popular culture.

About the Contributors

Brenda S. **Gardenour Walter** holds a Ph.D. in medieval history from Boston University, specializing in the history of medieval medicine and hagiography. She was a Fulbright scholar in Madrid and a National Endowment for the Humanities fellow at the Wellcome Institute for the History of Medicine (London). Her books include *Parasites, Worms, and the Human Body in Religion and Culture* (2012) and *Our Old Monsters* (2015).

Jaq **Greenspon** is a professional writer who spent his formative years in Hollywood, where he wrote movies and TV shows as well as numerous books and articles about the entertainment industry. Upon completing his MFA in Creative Writing from UNLV, he began teaching as an associate professor at Vytautas Magnus University in Kaunas. He holds a Ph.D., and his dissertation was about comic book heroes and World War II.

Curtis W. **Hart** is an Episcopal priest who served as Director of Pastoral Care and Education at the New York Presbyterian Hospital, Weill Cornell Center, New York. He is involved regularly in teaching medical students and is Editor-in-Chief of the *Journal of Religion and Health*.

George **Higham** utilized his background in sculpting and special effects along with his degree in film from NYC's School of Visual Arts (and over 25 years experience in forensic radiography) to author *Wax Museum Movies: A Comprehensive Filmography* (2020) for McFarland.

Jerome M. **Karp** is a resident physician in the Department of Radiation Oncology at NYU Grossman School of Medicine. He is an editor of *Sacred Training: A Halakhic Guidebook for Medical Students and Residents* on the intersection of Jewish law and medical care. In addition to his M.D. degree, he also holds a Ph.D. in biochemistry.

Andrew J. **McLean** is a psychiatrist from the Upper Midwest United States, who has written on community resilience, prejudice, as well as mental health disparities in Indian Country. He wrote this from his home, which rests on the ancestral lands of the Dakota Oyate and Dakota/Lakota Peoples. He acknowledges those who have resided here for generations and recognizes that their spirit permeates this land.

H. Steven **Moffic** is an award-winning psychiatrist who specializes in cultural challenges in psychiatry. In college, he became interested in jazz music, earning the nickame the nickname "Dr. Jazz" when he reviewed records. That interest and familiarity with cross-cultural interaction then spread to helping underserved minority groups. He received the one-time Hero of Public Psychiatry designation from the American Psychiatric Association.

Sharon **Packer** is a physician and psychiatrist who has a private practice and also supervises psychiatry residents for the Icahn School of Medicine at Mount Sinai. She has authored and edited many books, including *Dreams in Myth, Medicine and Movies* (2003) and *Arkham Asylum: Essays on Psychiatry and the Gotham City Institution* (2019).

Caleb **Puckett** works at Park University in Parkville, Missouri. He is active in a range of pursuits, including writing, editing, and instructional design. His creative and academic work has appeared in a host of publications, both in the United States and abroad.

Eric **Sandberg** completed his Ph.D. at the University of Edinburgh and is an assistant professor at City University of Hong Kong and a Docent at the University of Oulu. He is the author of *Virginia Woolf: Experiments in Character* (2014); coeditor of *Adaptation, Awards Culture, and the Value of Prestige* (2017), and editor of *100 Greatest Literary Detectives* (2018). He is lead researcher on a NOS-HS project exploring nostalgia in contemporary culture.

Eric J. **Sterling** is the Ida Belle Young Endowed Professor of English at Auburn University at Montgomery, where he has taught for the past 27 years. He earned a Ph.D. in English from Indiana University. He is the son and grandson of Holocaust survivors. His book *Life in the Ghettos During the Holocaust* was published in 2005, and he has also published many refereed articles on the Holocaust.

Index

Abel 67
ableism 37, 144, 149
Aboriginal Peoples 8, 23–4, 119–120
Abraham 112
Abu Al-'Ala' Al-Ma'arri 52
Academy Award 77, 105, 139
Achaeans 162
Acts of the Apostles 70
ADHD (attention deficit hyperactivity disorder) 10–11
Aeschylus 98
African-American 8, 16, 18, 24, 62, 75, 86, 131–143; *see also* Black
Afro-Caribbean 24, 130
aggression 130, 142
Ahijah 111
AK-47 103
Al Schmid, Marine 105, 109n3
Alaska 120–121
Alaskan Natives 120; *see also* Aboriginal Peoples; American Indian; Native American
Alberta First Nations 120; *see also* Aboriginal Peoples; American Indian; Native American
Alexander the Great 66
All the Light We Cannot See 163
All-American Comics 84–86
All-Star Comics 86
Allah 51
Alzheimer's Disease 30, 131
amaurosis 61
"Amazing Grace" 131–132
American Association for Pastoral Counselors 93
American Indian 120–124; *see also* Aboriginal Peoples; Native American
American Indian Myths and Legends 125
American Indian Sight Initiative 121
American Psychiatric Association (APA) 2, 9, 24

American Public Health Association (APHA) 97
Andes Mountains 120
Antigone 154, 158
antipsychotic medication 8, 13; *see also* AAP; FGA; *Mellaril*; SGA; thioridazine
anti-Semitism 22, 27, 99, 168, 171, 205
Antisocial Personality Disorder (ASPD) 175
anti-war 76
Apache 126
apartheid 131
Apollo 156, 164
Appolon 157
archetype 25, 31, 95, 128, 154, 156, 159
architecture 185–197, 189n30
Aristotle 183
Arrowverse 91
artificial intelligence (AI) 10
asceticism 184
Asch, Stan 84
Asclepius 182
Asher, Dr. Michael 2
ASL (American Sign Language) 3, 12, 145, 150
Asperger 10; *see also* ASD; autism spectrum disorder
Association for Clinical Pastoral Education 93
Assyria 69
astigmatism 120
At First Sight 2, 18, 78
Athena 155, 182
atypical antipsychotic medication (AAP) 8; *see also* antipsychotic medication
Auerbach, Rabbi Shlomo Zalman 115
augury 155, 182
Auschwitz 169, 174–176
Autism Spectrum Disorder (ASD) 10; *see also* Asperger
Awakenings 2

210 Index

Babylon 181
Banos, Roque 42
Barasch, Moshe 163, 181
Bates, Deacon L.J. 136
Bates, Norman 42
"The Bathing of Pallas" 155
Batman 84–85
Battle Hymn of the Republic 145, 150
Battle of Tenaru 103–104, 106, 108
Bava Ben Buta 111
Beethoven 137
beggar 16, 31, 72 , 169–172, 174; *see also A Beggar in Jerusalem*
A Beggar in Jerusalem 168–169, 170, 174
Berry, Chuck, 137
bete-machine 188
Beth Chapel 86–88; *see also* Doctor Midnight
Bethune, Tom Wiggins 135
Bible 17, 23, 62, 66, 68–69, 131, 141, 179 , 181; *see also* Old Testament
Bibliotheca 155
Bill and Melinda Gates Foundation 6–7
bipolar affective disorder (manic-depression) 121
black 8, 16, 60, 67, 130, 138–139, 142; *see also* African American
black bile 182
Black Snake Moon 136
Blake, Naomi 160
Blind Blake 134
Blind Boone 135
Blind Boy Fuller 134
Blind Boys of Alabama 8, 24, 137
Blind Boys of Mississippi 8, 24, 137
"The Blind Geometer" 39
"The Blind Guitarist" 71
"Blind Homer" 17, 66, 161
Blind Joe Death 134–135
Blind Joe Taggard 134
Blind Lemon Jefferson 134, 136–137
"The Blind Man's Meal" 72
blind spot 132
Blindness 61
Blink 15, 38
Bloom, Alan 5
blues 131–143; *see also* R&B; Rhythm N' Blues
Bolshevik 23, 99
Borges, Jorge Luis 26, 161, 166
"Born Again" 90
braille 10, 62, 100, 107, 117, 140, 167n1; *see also* Braille, Louis
Braille, Louis 185
brain death 114
Brilliant Corner (BC) 131

Brûlé Sioux 124; *see also* Aboriginal Peoples; American Indian; Native American
Buddhism 30, 123
Busailah, Tanya 2
Butterfield, Roger 104
Butterflies Are Free 76
Byzantine 67, 71

Cage, John, 130
Cain 67–68
Canada 15, 120, 191
Caravaggio 18, 70
Carruthers, James D. 134
Carson, Johnny 139
Cartesian 28, 188, 190; *see also* Descartes
"Castle Garden" 7
cataract 8, 13, 18, 56–57, 78, 120–121, 180, 183
Cauldron Of Blood 15
Cavett, Dick 139
Charles, Ray 8, 24, 139–140, 142
Chasid *see* Hasid
Cheyenne 127; *see also* Aboriginal Peoples; American Indian; Native American
Chlamydia Trachomatis 30, 120
Christianity 16, 18, 22, 31, 52, 54n1, 66–67, 69–71, 123, 132, 179, 183–184
Circe 158
civil rights 18, 75, 131, 133, 145, 150
Civil War 98–100, 133, 145, 150
The Closing of the American Mind 5
Code of Hammurabi 181
Coetzee, J.M. 164
Collins, Billy 139
Colomina 194, 196
colorblind 18, 145, 150
comic book 83–85, 154
Communist 100
contagion 17, 56, 61
Controlled Substances Act (CSA) 122
cornea 23, 114–115, 120–121
Corrothers, James D. 135
country blues 136–137
The Country of the Blind 17, 26, 30, 36, 56, 61, 164–165
Coyote 127
crematorium 174
Crimes and Misdemeanors 22
criminal 22, 34–36, 38–38, 40,42, 82–83, 85, 89–90
Cromwell, Oliver 21, 95
crucifixion 168, 170–171
curse 16–17, 26, 52, 55, 112–113, 163, 180, 183
Cyclops 26, 89, 164

Dagon 69
The Dance of Death & Other Plantation Favorites 134
Dancer in the Dark 79
Daredevil (character) 19–20
Daredevil (media) 19, 21, 31, 80, 83, 85–86, 89–91, 160
"Dark Was the Night" 136
David, Jean Louis 71
The Day of the Triffids 17, 31, 57, 61, 165
DC Comics 84
deaf 2–3, 12, 59–60, 74, 76, 115, 150, 183
deaf-blind 59–60
"The Deceived Blind Men" 126
deconstructionism 146
The Defenders 91
Delilah 23, 26, 68–69
delirium 122
Delphi 132
demon 16, 69
Dene 127
De Niro, Robert 2
Derrida, Jacques 146, 151, 186
de Saussure, Ferdinand 146, 150
Descartes, Rene 179, 185; *see also* Cartesian
The Descent 40–41
detective 20, 25, 38–39, 83, 158, 160
Detroit 140
diabetes mellitus (DM) 7, 12–14, 96–97, 120
diabetic retinopathy 12–13
Diderot 27, 179, 185
dinosaur 10–11
disability 8, 14–15, 16, 18–19, 21, 26, 28–29, 37, 40, 59, 75–76, 78–79, 81, 83, 86, 89–90, 102, 115–116, 118, 180, 186, 193, 195
Disability Studies 186
Disney 21
dissociation 174–175
Dix, Otto 18, 72
Dr. Charles McNider 84–89; *see also* Doctor Mid-Night; Dr. Mid-Night; Dr. Midnight
"Dr. Jazz" 24, 130, 142
Doctor Mid-Night 88
Dr. Mid-Nite 84–90
Dr. Midnight 20, 29, 87–88
Doctorow, E.L. 163
Doerr, Anthony 167n6
Don't Breathe 40–41
Dosa Ben Harkinas 111
double-blind 146, 151
Down Beat 131
dreams 41, 53, 77, 124, 132, 138, 195
Duerr, Heidi Anne 2

Ebers Papyrus 180
Ebert, Roger 78
Ecclesia 22, 184
echolocation 41
Egypt 66, 131, 180–181
Eli 111
Eliot, T.S. 159
Elisha 181
Ellis Island 6–7
Enki 180
Enlightenment 17, 27, 55, 67, 71, 123, 179
Esau 23, 68, 112
Estes, Sleepy John 134
Eudemian Ethics 183
evil eye 16, 30, 51
existential 28, 93, 180
Eye Among the Blind 58, 202
eye for an eye 67, 181
The Eyes of the Skin 185

Fahey, John 134, 139
Fanon, Franz 24, 130, 142
Fantastic Four 83
Feherfalu 174
Feinstein, Rabbi Moshe 115
Feinstein, Sasha 131
field hollers 138
"Finding Light in the Darkness: Treating Patients with Visual Loss" 2, 9
firearms 99–103
Fishburne, Lawrence 61
"The Five Spot 1964" 139
The Flash 84, 86
folk musician 134
folk religion 16
folklore 16, 121, 125; *see also* myth; mythology
The Forgotten 168, 172
Foucault, Michel 186
Foxx, Jamie 139
Frankenstein, or the Modern Prometheus 16, 55
"French Freud" 146, 151; *see also* Lacan, Jacques
Freud 5–6, 30, 130, 146, 161

Gallaudet 3
Garfield, John 14, 22, 103, 105
Genesis 67–68, 181
genetic 9, 12, 120, 176
genocide 168, 170, 177
Geordi La Forge 8, 16, 60, 62
geriatric 14
glaucoma 13, 24, 93–94, 97, 139
Gloucester 162
god 27, 60, 127, 155–156, 180

212   Index

God   34, 48, 51, 58, 60, 67, 69, 93, 95, 111–112, 115–116, 118, 131, 138, 168, 170, 173–174, 181–183
Godwin, M. Leona   14, 32n5
Golding, William   165
Goodman, Benny   134
gospel [music]   133–134, 136–138
Gospel at Colonus   137–138
Gospel of Mark   70
Gospels   69
"Got the Blues"   136
Goya, Francisco   17, 71
Great Patriotic War   101
Great Spirit   123
Greek   5, 16, 25–26, 28, 54n1, 66, 132, 137–138, 154–157, 168, 179, 182, 189, 184
"The Green Hills of Earth"   17, 57–58
Green Lantern   84, 86
grenade   77, 84, 104, 106
Griffin, John   142
Griffin, Merv   139
griot   133
Guadalcanal   103, 105–107
guitar   71–72, 136, 140–141
gun   23, 41, 58, 76, 90, 99–102, 108–109, 174

hallucination   121–122, 165
hallucinogen   122, 124
Hamill, Mark   103
The Handbook of Native American Mythology   125, 129n15
handicapped   86, 90; *see also* disabled
Hangman's Blues   136
haptic   28, 188–189, 193–196
Harris, Corey   133
Harris, Thomas   37
Hasid   27, 168–169, 172–173, 176
Hauy, Valentin   185
heaven   51–52, 155, 128, 164, 169, 173
Hebrew   17, 23, 27, 116, 131, 141, 170, 179, 181
Hebron   48, 51–53
Hector   162
Heinlein, Robert A.   17, 57
Hellenistic   66; *see also* Greek
"Hellhound on My Trail"   133
Hepburn, Audrey   34, 82
Hera   155
Herodotus   158
heterochromia iridis   169, 174–176
heuristics   25, 146, 150
hip-hop   134, 141
Hippocrates   182
Histories   158
Holdstock, Robert   58
Holocaust   26–27, 168–175, 177
Homer   17, 66, 137, 161–162

Homer & Langley   163
Hooty   87
Horowitz, Rabbi Yaakov Yitzchak Halevy   173
Horus   27, 180
Hourman   87
Hugo Award   17
hypnagogic hallucination   122
hypnopompic hallucination   122
hysterical blindness   132

"I Live in Music"   130
iconoclast   67
Iliad   66, 161
illusion   121
"In the Dark"   20, 79
The Incredible Hulk   19, 83
incubation   182
incubus phenomenon   122
"Indian Sore Eyes"   6, 120
Indigenous Peoples   24, 119–125, 128
Industrial Revolution   17, 55
Infinity, Inc.   86–87
"The Inflated Tear"   138
insight   2, 14, 24, 28, 31, 34–37, 83, 93, 94, 111, 113, 124, 130, 132, 141–142, 145, 148–149, 153, 156–160, 183
Institute for Palestine Studies   44
Inuit   121, 127; *see also* Aboriginal Peoples; American Indian; Native American
Isaac   23, 68, 111–112
Isaiah   170
Islam   16, 54n1, 66; *see also* Muslim
Israeli   169
Israelite   27, 112, 170

Jacob   23, 68, 111–112
James Bay Cree   120; *see also* Aboriginal Peoples; American Indian; Native American
Japan   18, 74, 80–81, 103–104, 106, 108
jazz   24, 130–134, 138–139, 141–142
Jazz Digest   130
Jazz Times   131
Jennifer 8   15, 38
Jerusalem   16, 25–26, 47–49, 52, 70, 114, 122, 168–170, 172, 174
Jerusalem Syndrome   122
Jessica Jones   20
Jesus   18, 69–70, 137–138, 168, 170–171
Jewish   18, 68–69, 99, 112, 118, 131, 134, 168–175
John [the Apostle]   70
Johnny Got His Gun   76
Johns Hopkins, Bayview, Medical Center   97

Index

Johnson, Blind Willie 134, 136
Johnson, Mark Steven 80
Johnson, Robert 133–134, 137
Joyce, James 166
JSA (Justice Society of America) 86–87, 89
Judaism 22, 66, 114, 184; *see also* Jewish
Justice Society of America 86–7, 89

kaleidoscope 163
kalkus (malevolent witch) 124
Kareya 127
Karloff, Boris 15
Karo, Rabbi Joseph 114
Karuk (Karok) 127
Keller, Helen 74, 141
Kiev 98–99, 104
Kilby, Damien 61
King, the Reverend Dr. Martin Luther, Jr. 145, 150
King, Stephen 159
King Lear 162
King Louis IX 179, 184
"King of the Blues" 137
"King of Swing" 134
"The King of the Delta Blues Singers" 133
"King" Oliver 130
Kingpin 90–91
Kirk, Rahsaan Roland, 138–139, 142
Kitano, Takeshi 19, 80
Kreon 164
Kwakiutl 127

Lacan, Jacques 146–147, 150; *see also* French Freud
Lailatulqadr 51
Lamech 67–68
The Langoliers 159
The Last Man 55
Lay Health Educators Program 96
Lee, Stan 20–21, 83, 89–91
The LEGO Movie 159
leper 112
Leviticus 117, 141, 182
lex talionis 181
Lifton, Robert, Jay 174–175
"Living for the City" 140
Locke, John 185
Long Lonesome Blues 136
Longstreet 160
loon 127
Lord of the Flies 165
Lot 181
Love and Honor 81
Luke Skywalker 103
lynching 133

Machi (benevolent shaman) 124
machine gun 99, 106, 108
Maclain, Duncan 83, 160
macular degeneration 13–14, 93
"Magical Negro" 142
Magoo, Mr. 21
Mahler, Margaret 76
Maker (Great Spirit) 95 123, 126–127
Maltz, Albert 105
manic-depression (bipolar disorder) 121
Māori 125
Mapuche 124
Margolin, Mikhail 22, 98–104, 109
Marines 14, 22, 114, 104, 108–109
Martin, Laurie 2
martyr 168, 171
Marvel 20–21, 83
The Masseurs and a Woman 74
"The Match Seller" 18, 72
The Matrix Trilogy 17, 61, 159
Matthew 70
McDowell, Malcolm 62
McGee, Brownie 136
MCM 102–103
McTell, Blind Willie 134
medicine man 124, 127
medieval 16, 22, 54n1, 67, 82, 118, 179, 183–184
Mellaril (thioridazine) 8
Mengele, Josef 168, 174–177
Menominee 126
mental institution 172
mescaline 122
Mesopotamia 179–181
mesquite tree 120
Messiah 18, 70, 170–172
meta-human 86
*Metamorphos*es 155–156
metaphor 168–174, 179
Metropolitan Museum of Art (MMA) 72
Michelangelo 189
Michigan State School for the Blind 140
Middle Ages 67, 70
Midon, Raul 141
Midrash 111–112
Miller, Frank 89–91
Milton, John 21, 76, 94–95, 166
mindfulness 123
miracle 18, 21–22, 70, 74, 125, 137–138, 179, 184
The Miracle Worker 74
Miriam (sister of Moses) 131
Mishnah 115; *see also* Talmud
"Mississippi to Mali" 133
monster 33–34, 39, 41, 48, 55, 89
Mopsus 183

214 Index

Morpheus 61
Morris, Stevland 140; see also Wonder, Stevie [Little Stevie Wonder]
Moscow 100–102
Moses 112, 131
Mosquito Blues 136
Moss, Carrie-Anne 62
Motl 7
Motown 140
Mr. Magoo 21
murder 5, 15, 37–39, 80, 168, 171, 174–175
Murdock, Matt 20, 83, 89–91; see also Daredevil
music therapy 131
Muslim 31; see also Islam
Musicophilia: Tales of Music and the Brain 2
mutant 89
mute 56, 76, 115
mystic 25, 27, 90, 158, 168–170, 172–173, 176, 179, 184
myth 5–6, 17, 23, 25–27, 30, 55, 119, 123, 125, 132, 154, 156, 159, 176, 180–181; and American Indian 125, 129n15; and Egypt 27, 184n6, and Greek 154; Oedipus 5, 25, 159; and Tiresias 25, 154

NAACP 133
Nahum of Gizmo 111
National Association of Catholic Chaplains 93
National Institute of Health (NIH) 131
Native American 6, 23–24, 119–129; see also Aboriginal Peoples; American Indian; Indigenous Peoples
Native American Church 122
Native Languages of the Americas 125
Natural History 183
Navy Cross 105
Nazi 101, 168–169, 172–175
Nelson, Willie 139
"New Age" 123
"New Negro" 133
The New Objectivity 18, 72
New Orleans 134
New Testament 17, 67, 69, 77, 183
night blindness 9
Night of Power 51
Night Walk 58
Nimnah 27, 180
Nixon, Pres. Richard 122, 139
Nobel Prize 17, 60
nuclear fusion reactor 56

Oceania 120
oculocentrism 28, 144–145, 147, 149, 152, 18

Odysseus 26, 158, 164, 166
Odyssey 17, 25, 66, 154–155, 157–160, 166
Odyssey, O Brother, Where Art Thou? 25, 159
Oedipus 5, 25, 30, 132, 137–138, 154–155, 158–160, 164, 166, 179, 182
Ohio State School for the Blind 138
Ojibwa 124
Old Testament 68; see also Bible; Hebrew Bible; Torah
Oliver, Joe "King" 130
Olympics 100, 102
On Sense and the Sensible 183
Onchocerciasis 6; see also river blindness
Operation: Barbarossa 101
ophthalmia 50, 180
optic nerve 58
oracle 132, 137–138, 183
Orbison, Roy 139
organ donation 114–115
Ovid 156
Owl 21, 85, 87

Pacino, Al 77
Pagan 112
pagan 16, 54n1, 67, 112
Pallasmaa, Juhani 185–186, 189, 194–195
Paradise Lost 95
pastoral counseling 21–22, 93–95
A Patch of Blue 18, 75
patriarch 23, 111, 189–191, 194, 196
Paul of Tarsus (St. Paul) 70
Pearl Harbor 103, 106
Pentecostal 138
"The Persistence of Vision" 59, 61
Peter, Paul and Mary 136
peyote 122
Philistines 26, 68–9, 163, 181–182
Philosopher King 183
photokeratitis (snow blindness) 121
Picasso, Pablo 17, 71–72
Pieter Cross 88; see also Doctor Mid-Nite; Dr. Mid-Nite
pilgrimage 116–117, 122, 184
Pima 126
plague 55–6, 158
Plato 183
Pliny 183
poet 15–17, 21, 25, 52, 66, 94–95, 139, 161
Poitier, Sydney 75
Poseidon 164
possession 124, 171, 193
post-apocalyptic 57, 62, 165
postmodern 27–28, 180, 186, 189, 193, 195–196

post-traumatic stress disorder (PTSD) 21, 75
Prado (Museo Del Prado) 66, 71
Presley, Elvis 135
Pride of the Marines 14, 22, 103, 105–106, 108
priest 23, 111, 115, 170, 180–181, 184
Princess Leia 103
Professor Xavier 89
prophet 154, 156–158, 166
protest music 131
Pseudo-Dionysius 184
psilocybin 122
psychedelics 24, 122–123
Psychiatric Times 2
psychoanalysis 5, 20, 25, 28, 132, 144–146, 149–150
psychosis 8, 121–122
psychotropic medication 6–7, 11; *see also* antipsychotic medication; atypical antipsychotic; SGA
PTSD (Post-Traumatic Stress Disorder) 75
Pueblo 126
Puritan 21, 95

Quaker 96
Qur'an (Koran) 51

rabbinic texts 111
"Race Records" 136
racism 75, 110n5, 131–132, 135, 137–138, 141–142
radar 3, 90
radioactive 20, 33, 57, 90, 193
ragtime 135
Ramadan 51
Ramleh 48, 52
rap 134, 141–142
Rashi 112–113
Rav Joseph 111
Rav Sheshet 111
Raven 126–127
Ray 139
reconstruction 132–133, 143
Red Dragon/Manhunter 15, 37–38
Red Sea 131
Reeves, Keanu 61
Reizenstein, Chuck 84–85
Rembrandt 18, 69
Renaissance 163, 189
retinitis pigmentosa 9
retinopathy 12–14, 120
retrolental fibroplasia (RLF) 14, 140
rhythm n' blues (R&B) 133–134, 141
Ribera, Jose De 17, 70–71

river blindness 6; *see also* onchocerciasis
Robinson, Sarah 189, 194
rock 'n' roll 134
Rogue One: A Star Wars Story 62
Roman Empire 18, 66–67, 70–71
rubella 59–60
Russia 22–23, 98–102
Russian Revolution 39, 99

Sabbath 113–114, 116
Sacks, Oliver 2, 18, 78
sacrifice 63, 80, 98, 107, 112–113, 126, 170, 181
sage 20, 111–112, 114–116, 121, 169
saint 68, 70, 184
Saint Foy 184
Samson 18, 23, 26, 68–69, 111, 163–4, 181–182
samurai 18, 31, 80–81; *see also* Zatoichi
Saramago, Jose 26, 31, 60–61, 164–6
savant 135
Scent of a Woman 77
schizoaffective disorder 121; *see also* psychosis
schizophrenia 121; *see also* psychosis
Schmid, Al 22, 98, 103–106, 108–109, 110n6, 110n7
Scientific Revolution 17, 55
second generation antipsychotic medication (SGA) 8, 13; *see also* atypical antipsychotic medication
secondsight 60, 154
See 56
See No Evil 15, 36–38
See That My Grave Is Kept Clean 136
seeing-eye dog 13
Seeing Voices: A Journey into the World of the Deaf 2
seer 25, 27, 126–127, 154–155, 157–160, 168–174, 182–183
The Seer Who Could Not See 126
seizure 122
Sennacherib 69
sensory deprivation 121
separation-individuation 76; *see also* Mahler, Margaret
Seth 180
Seva 121
Shaarei Zedek (Hospital) 114
Shakespeare 162
shaman 123, 131
Shanke, Ntozak 130
Shaw, Bob 58
Shehina (Shechina; Shekhina) 169
Shelley, Mary 16, 55
Sherlock Holmes 160

Sherman, General William T. 98
Shimizu, Hiroshi 74
Sholem Aleichem 6
Shulchan Arukh 113
Siberia 23, 102, 124
sign language 3, 12, 145, 150; *see also* American Sign Language; ASL
Silver Age 86
Sioux *see* Brûlé Sioux
Six-Day War 168–170, 172
Skywalker, Luke 103
slavery 133–135, 138
sleep deprivation 122, 124
sleep paralysis 122
smallpox 120
snake 136, 155–156, 182
snow blindness 8, 121
Snyder, John K. 88
social media 195
Sodomite 180
soldier 29, 71, 76, 86, 98–99, 103, 105–106, 108, 174
Sons of Origins of Marvel Comics 83
Sophocles 1, 137, 164, 166, 179, 182
Soviet Union 101–102
Spider 126–127
Spider-Man 20, 83
Stalin 101
Staple Singers 136
Star-Spangled Banner 145, 150
Star Trek 8, 16, 60, 62
Star Wars 23, 62, 103
Starman 86
The Story of My Life 74
Strand 160
suicide 5, 39, 76–78, 80–81, 162, 172
Sullivan, Ann 74–75
Sullivan, Ed 139
Sumerian 27, 180
superhero 19–21, 29, 80–81, 83–84, 85–89, 98
Superman 84
supernatural 21, 25, 119, 123, 154, 168, 172–173, 183
superstition 16, 31, 54n1
surgeon 84, 86, 107, 192
survivor 39–40, 53, 56–57, 62, 133, 172, 174
survival guilt (guilt of the survivor) 172
Synagoga 22, 184
synesthesia 163

"Talking Book" 140
Talladego School for the Negro Deaf and Blind 137
Talmud 23, 111–113, 115–118
Tawhaki 125–126

Terry, Sonny 134, 136
Tewa 127
Thebes 16, 25, 154, 156, 158, 166
thioridazine (Mellaril) 8
Thoth 180
Tibetan Plateau 120
Tiresias 16, 25–26, 154–160, 166, 168; *see also* myth
Tobias 69
Tobit 69
Torah (Old Testament; Hebrew Bible) 114–116, 130–131, 141; *see also* Hebrew Bible; Old Testament
Torres Strait Islander 120
Tosefta 118
trachoma 6, 120
"Travelers" 61
The Trial of the Incredible Hulk 19
trickster 126–127
Trojans 162
Trumbo, Dalton 76
"Two Blind Old Women" 126

ultraviolet light (UV) 56–57, 142
Ulysses 167
USSR 102–103; *see also* Soviet Russia; Soviet Union

VA (hospital) 10, 12, 14
Veeho 127
Vesalius, Anton 189
veteran 12, 14, 18, 72, 77, 99, 104–105, 107, 109
Vickers, Salley 25 159
vigilante 19–20
vision quest 8, 123–124
visionary 148, 153, 157, 169–173
"Visions" 141
VISOR (Visual Instrument and Sensory Organ Replacement) 16, 60
Vita Contemplativa 185
Vitruvius 28, 189
vivisectionist 175
"Volunteered Slavery" 138
Voyager 136

Wagner, Matt 88
Wait Until Dark 15, 35–35, 37, 42, 82
Waiting for the Barbarians 164
Waldenberg, Rabbi Eliezer 114
A Warrior's Honor 81
Washington, Denzel 62
The Waste Land 26, 159, 166
"Watergate Blues" 139
Wax Museum Movies: A Comprehensive Filmography 15

Index 217

Wells, H.G. 17, 26, 31, 56, 61, 165
Western (Wailing) Wall 169
"What I'd Say" 139
Where Three Roads Meet 159
"White Sickness" 26, 165
WHO *see* World Health Organization
Wiesel, Elie 27, 168–170, 172, 176–177
Wiggins, Blind Tom 134, 135
Williams, Robin 2
Wineberg, Rabbi Yehiel Yaakov 115
Winnebago 126
Wisakatchekwan 126
Wonder, Steve 8, 14, 24, 137, 140–142
Woolf, Virginia 161
Wordsworth, William 161

World Health Organization (WHO) 6
World War I (First World War; Great War) 72, 76, 99
World War II (Second World War) 19, 72, 102, 110n7
Wyndham, John 57

X-Men 89

Yiddish 6
Yupik 121

Zatoichi 19, 80; *see also* samuri
Zeus 155
Zyklon B, 174